D0189324

Change-**ABLE**

Organization

MORE ADVANCE PRAISE FOR

CHANGE-ABLE ORGANIZATION

"The book contains many valuable tools for managers to improve the performance of their organizations. I found the watercraft analogies insightful, informative, and educational. I highly recommend it for managers at all levels."

— Youssef El-Mansy, Director
Portland Technology Development, Intel

"This book is experience-based, straightforward, and is an excellent source for those needing to change an organization."

— J. B. Woods, Senior Vice President
Bank of America NT&SA Advisory Services

"*Change-ABLE Organization* is a valuable addition to the scarcity of high quality books on management of change and the characteristics of high performing organizations that come with it. It is a pleasure to see how well cultural elements have been integrated in the larger train of thought."

— Fons Trompenaars, International Consultant and Author
RIDING THE WAVES OF CULTURE

"*Change-ABLE Organization* helps lead your efforts for the most significant competitive advantage — SPEED. It provides an organization with a framework for the fastest way of getting from where you are to your chosen destination. I am impressed with the clear description of this proven methodology."

— Dave Toole, President
GaSonics International

"Within hours of reading this book, we
tion to assess client situations, to defin
and to begin implementing decisions f
toward a more Change-ABLE culture.'

Team

"Finally, someone has accurately comi
business operations today, and the pra
mented to overcome them. Companie
will be using these techniques, wheth
ally learned."

— Ke
US Media Ope

"Organizations need to periodically
well as constantly flex and change in
needs and remain competitive. Dani
help leaders and managers develop

— Tommy Geor
Motorola Ser

"The authors have discovered an in
practices that are common to succes
us through some difficult times at F

— I

"The prescription is simple and cle
are stunning."

Change-ABLE Organization

Key Management Practices for Speed and Flexibility

William R. Daniels
John G. Mathers

This publication may not be reproduced, stored in a retrieval system, or transmitted in whole or in part, in any form or by any means, electronic, mechanical, photocopying, recording, or otherwise, without the prior written permission of the authors.

Change-ABLE™ is owned by American Consulting & Training, Inc. (ACT). No use is permitted without prior written permission from ACT.

Library of Congress Catalog Card Number: 96-78804

Copyright © 1997 by American Consulting & Training, Inc.

ACT Publishing
655 Redwood Highway, Suite 395
Mill Valley, California 94941
(415) 388-6651; (800) 995-6651; FAX (415) 388-6672
E-mail: Lila@ACTcanoe.com

All rights reserved.

Printed in the United States of America

ISBN: 1-882939-02-6, soft cover
ISBN: 1-882939-03-4, hard cover

Acknowledgments

♦ ♦ ♦ ♦

We cannot acknowledge all the people who have influenced this book, though we are truly grateful for the circle of professional associates and clients who have nurtured our learning with their experience and infectious curiosity throughout our careers. One of the great joys of writing a book is that it provokes the memories of all these relationships. We will list here only a few of those who have been very directly involved in making the book a reality.

First, we must thank Maribeth Riggs, the project leader for this book. She prepared the manuscript for printing and has been our internal editor. She has kept the authors and the rest of the Book Task Force moving together by playing the role she calls "Border Collie."

Other members of the Task Force have contributed directly to the quality of this work. Patricia Wiggenhorn, our external editor, focused on the project not just through her editing but also as a friend and teacher. Gary Selick was the lead consultant for our work with Etec Systems and the person who gathered the data for Chapter Fifteen. Lila Sparks-Daniels has planned and implemented the marketing and distribution of the book with assistance from our business manager, Billie Riboli. Erica Riggs brought our sketches together as the book's graphics. Peter Ivory of Magus Design enriched our understanding while translating our work into the software tool called *ACT Canoe, Team Performance Manager.* We have faced many "tough situations" on the way to delivering this book, and we have learned much about the necessity of teamwork from this Task Force.

We are especially grateful to Steve Cooper, Trish Dohren, Keri Daniels, and Roy Earle of the management team at Etec Systems, Inc. for their cooperation on Chapter Fifteen.

Special thanks to Carol Tisson at Intel, whose suggestions several years ago were the seeds from which our concept of the Key Management Practices grew. We are also especially thankful to Naomi Chavez (formerly with Intel, now with Cisco Systems), John Bash and Timm Esque (both at Intel), who have been longtime contributors to our refinement of the Breakthrough Systems practices.

Fons Trompenaars was our primary inspiration for the discussion of Basic Assumptions, and his attention to our manuscript has been very helpful.

We also wish to thank the following people who took the time to read and comment on early drafts of the manuscript: Marilyn Barker, Roy Earle, Diane McGraw, Georgia Ireland, Tom Justice, Jan Kaufman, Pat McCormack, Perviz Randeria, Aileen Selick, Steve Thompson, Stuart Vexler, Sandi Wong, Mike Tinker, and Vance Frame. They know how much they have improved the book, but we swore them to secrecy to diminish our embarrassment about the awkwardness of earlier drafts.

Distinguished among these early readers is Rick Dehmel, whose hawk-eyed precision and hard work helped shape and sharpen the book's content.

Each quarter, for two years, the following group of internal and external consultants working to implement and maintain the Key Management Practices of the Change-ABLE organization have gathered to advise each other and the authors about what was important and effective. Their advice has been an important resource for this book: Independent — Pat Patterson, Natalie Chambliss, Cynthia Kneen, Joan Cavalli, Rick Dehmel; Amdahl — Lou Carson, Mark Zubek; Applied Materials — Elizabeth Munn; Bank of America — J. B. Woods; Caplette & Associates — Michelle Caplette; Cisco Systems — Naomi Chavez; City of Oakland — Jan Kaufman, Perviz Randeria; Etec Systems — Keri Daniels, Trish Dohren, Stephanie Fujii; Genesco — Angela Dunn; Gold Leaf Consulting — Capri Keogh; Industrial Design Corporation & Technology Development Corporation — Jeannine Yancey; Intel — Marilyn Barker, Nellie Calame, James Koch, Jr., Carol Tisson; Johnson, Raughley & Associates — Andrew Johnson; Levi Strauss & Co. — Pat McCoy; Lucasfilm Ltd. — Tom Forster; Magus Design — Peter Ivory; Motorola - Semiconductor Products Sector — Mike Perna, Katherine Wilt; Seagate Recording Media — Phyllis M. Pineda; Space Systems/Loral — Angela Dodson, Georgia Ireland; State of California Dept. of Consumer Affairs — Sue Durst, Bob Triboli.

As always, our spouses, Lila Sparks-Daniels and Peggy Mathers, have been indispensable sources of support in our quest to develop *community* in business.

Heartfelt thanks to you all!!

William R. Daniels
John G. Mathers

Mill Valley, California

Contents

Section

I

*Concepts & Terminology,
Recommendation, and
Watercraft Analogies*

Concepts & Terminology

Overview

This chapter emphasizes this book's unique orientation to organizational change —defining the term "Change-ABLE™," and these related key concepts:

1. There are five functions of management making up an organization's system of governance, within which are specific Key Management Practices. When these practices are performed in an integrated way, they make an organization Change-ABLE.
2. All over the world, external, social, and economic environments are becoming so complex and dynamic, most organizations cannot adapt. Inadequate management practices keep them "stuck."
3. Underlying the management practices of all organizations are certain unconscious Basic Assumptions. Organizations use these Basic Assumptions as ready-made strategies for resolving some of life's fundamental Survival Dilemmas. We define seven of these Survival Dilemmas:

   - Dilemma #1: Internal or External control of the environment?
   - Dilemma #2: Past, Present, or Future orientation?
   - Dilemma #3: Universal or Particular rules?
   - Dilemma #4: Ascribed or Achieved status and power?
   - Dilemma #5: Affective or Neutral expression of emotions?
   - Dilemma #6: Individualism or Communitarianism?
   - Dilemma #7: Diffuse or Specific commitments?

4. In stuck organizations, inadequate management practices express Extreme Assumptions — habits the organization develops by choosing only one of the alternatives presented by the dilemmas — thus exposing itself to all the negative consequences of not choosing other alternatives. Change-ABLE organizations, by contrast, operate from Reconciled Assumptions — not a middle position or compromise, but an assumption that finds synergy between the opposed alternatives.

We provide a glossary of terms used frequently throughout the book and preview the structure of the book.

The Uniqueness of Change-ABLE Organizations

Most managers and consultants approach organizational change as a Special Event. One form of this is the "Turnaround." A strident leader is brought in to put the organization on a crash diet so that it can fit into that fancy new dress for a brief party with investors. A second form of this approach is called "Restructuring." The Board of Directors tries to alter the course of the ship by shuffling the chairs on the deck — making a brief splash with "new blood" and "new vision." A third form of the Special Event is the "Change Program" — the "Total Quality Program," the "Customer Service Program," the "Employee Empowerment Program," the "Reengineering Program," etc. In about two years, these programs must fight for their lives (and usually lose) as line managers move from passive resistance to outright attack, declaiming the programs as expensive distractions from the essentials of the business.

We have been a part of all these Special Events during the cumulative 50 years of our consulting experience. We have experienced the initial enthusiasm that became frustration and disappointment as we watched organizations reject these efforts. Like desperately sick bodies rejecting a heart transplant, few organizations are ABLE to accept these well-intentioned solutions to their recognized problems.

Several years ago, we started looking at how our most successful clients dealt with change. These organizations have sustained rapid growth for years while achieving ever higher levels of efficiency and quality and renewing themselves with radical redesign of their operational processes and structures. Thousands of decisions to change are made and implemented every day. Change is woven into the very fabric of these organizations. They are like a school of fish — thousands of individuals flowing gracefully around obstacles, or suddenly accelerating to capture a food supply, or turning as one to scare off predators by flashing the school's enormous size. Like a school of fish, these organizations are constantly moving — they are fast, focused, and extremely flexible!

We have come to call such organizations Change-ABLE. Why can these organizations make continuous and radical change while others fail? We see a pattern. For one thing, these organizations do not approach change as a Special Event but engage instead in a set of Key Practices supported by certain Basic Assumptions. These practices and assumptions make organizations Change-ABLE. The purpose of this book is to define and recommend them.

Identifying the Key Management Practices of Change-ABLE Organizations

It is not easy to isolate common patterns of management practices as there are so many unique and important factors in understanding each organization. It helps to recognize that organizations consist of two major sets of sub-systems. The first set is for matter and energy processing — production processes. The second set of subsystems is for organizational governance — management practices.

The first, most obvious set is the one for processing materials and energy. It consists of the loading docks where trains or trucks deliver materials and supplies, and the entry gates through which employees enter the work areas. It is the arrangement of work spaces and equipment where people perform the organization's work and the delivery areas that send products to warehouses or perform services for customers. This multifaceted set of sub-systems comprises one large system through which materials and energy move in four stages: Inputs, Process, Outputs, Customers.

If there were nothing more than these four stages, there would only be a mechanical system — like a coffee maker. If it runs at all, a mechanical system runs in completely predetermined and precisely coordinated ways without ever changing. When change does occur (break down or damage from some outside force) the whole system stops working. The system has no ability to adapt to changes in any of its parts. And it, of course, can't change the function for which it was originally designed. A coffee machine can't turn itself into an orange juicer. Human organizations are not mechanical systems.

It is the addition of the second set of sub-systems — those devoted to self-governance — that distinguishes mechanical systems from human organizations. The purpose of these governance sub-systems is to protect the organization from that which threatens its ability to achieve its purposes and to increase the organization's ability to take advantage of its opportunities to succeed. These sub-systems make the organization able to reposition itself when its external environment changes, and they give the organization the capacity to take corrective action in response to internal breakdowns. It is within this second set of sub-systems that the key practices of the Change-ABLE organizations can be found.

These sub-systems are essentially information processing activities. They include collecting information, analyzing it for threats or opportunities, and storing it as memory, goals, and plans. These practices also trigger habitual responses to familiar needs for change, or make decisions regarding what to do in unusual situations. In the human body, these functions are performed primarily by the nervous system, including the sensory system and brain. In organizations, people structure their relationships to apply these abilities to gover-nance. These management practices constantly adapt and control the organization's use of its resources to process materials and energy.

Especially important to the effectiveness of this governance are five interdependent functions:

1. Organizational structure — the arrangement of channels and protocols for communication between individuals and groups;
2. Planning — the determination of purpose, strategy, goals, priori-ties and the allocation of resources;
3. Performance feedback — the assessment of how well the organiza-tion is actualizing its plans;
4. Decision-making — how the organization achieves resolution to its issues and secures commitment for its resolutions; and
5. Managing Individual Contributors — the effectiveness and effi-ciency with which people manage themselves as they perform the organization's work. If these functions are performed well, the organization constantly adapts the allocation of its resources to assure both short-term and long-term success.

Within each of these five functions, we have identified a Key
Management Practice. When practiced together systematically, these
Key Practices cause organizations to become and remain Change-
ABLE. The chart below shows each function and the related Key
Management Practice used by Change-ABLE organizations:

Being Change-ABLE in Response to the External Environment, or Being Stuck

In the authors' experience, all healthy organizations have some
form of Key Management Practices. But even healthy organizations
may perform them at very different levels of sophistication. Critical
factors influencing the level of sophistication are the organization's
external, social, and economic environments.

In simple and relatively stable environments, less disciplined
forms of management practices can achieve high levels of organizational efficiency. This is possible because the amount of uncertainty is
small. The organization doesn't have to engage in much learning and
can respond effectively to its environment with relatively few familiar
processes and outputs. Coordinating the organization's processes and

Function	Key Management Practices in Change-ABLE Organizations
Structure	A Hierarchy of Linked Teams
Planning	Performance Plans
Performance Feedback	Work Reviews
Decision-Making	Group Decision-Making
Managing Individual Contributors	Breakthrough Systems

human competencies is easier, and less information processing is
required for the governance of the organization. So, simple forms of
the five management practices are sufficient to keep an organization
healthy in such environments.

In complex and dynamic environments, organizational efficiency
is more difficult to achieve because uncertainty is much greater. A

wider range of outputs and human competencies is required to adapt to a more varied market and the surprises created by new forms of competition. Much more information processing is required to keep the organization integrated as it learns and adapts. More sophisticated forms of the Key Management Practices are found in the healthy organizations operating in these environments, and we describe these more sophisticated forms in this book. Sophistication does not necessarily mean complexity — on the contrary, sophistication is usually found in the elegant simplicity and rigorous persistence of Key Management Practices.

When an organization is capable of only the less sophisticated Key Management Practices and has the bad fortune of being exposed to a more complex and dynamic environment, its health deteriorates. It becomes stuck — no longer fully capable of responding to its threats and opportunities.

If organizations attempt to fulfill the functions of governance without using all of the Key Management Practices, or if they fail to use them in an integrated way, they face their world as cripples. The entrenched inefficiency of these organizations is so great, they inevitably fail. We refer to them as stuck cultures — organizations with little ability to change.

There are three types of stuck organizations, which we refer to analogously as water craft: Rafts (Bureaucracies), Dory Regattas (Professional Associations), and Galleys (Representative Management).

The best organizations in the market today perform all five of the Key Management Practices in an integrated fashion. These are what we call the Change-ABLE organizations. Using the same watercraft analogy, Change-ABLE organizations are like Sea-Going Canoes — very swift, efficient, and flexible.

The Role of Basic Assumptions in Sustaining Management Practices

The external environment is not the only factor affecting the ways in which organizations perform the functions of governance. Management practices are also an expression of what members of the organization assume is required to promote its survival. These assumptions were probably formed at a time when the practices were sufficient to keep the organization healthy. Because the practices worked and were so frequently required, their effectiveness stopped being questioned. Their appropriateness and necessity then became assumed. The unconscious quality of these assumptions permits the organization to respond to its familiar survival problems with swift and effective habitual behavior. These Basic Assumptions combine with the practices to operate as the organization's culture.

Unfortunately, the Basic Assumptions often continue generating the same management responses long after the environment changes and the particular practices are no longer appropriate. In such cases, these Basic Assumptions become a source for organizational resistance to change. They cause the organization to deny its failures, or to respond to its crises by performing the same practices more stringently, hoping that additional effort expended in familiar ways will work once again. In either case, the Basic Assumptions have become dysfunctional, and are a significant factor in keeping people in the organization from learning new, more appropriate practices. The assumptions thus contribute to keeping the organization stuck.

Fons Trompenaars, a scholar and researcher specializing in organizational culture, highlights seven Survival Dilemmas with which the Basic Assumptions of any culture must deal. A dilemma is a situation in which one is confronted with a choice between two equally undesirable alternatives — to choose either alternative will mean accepting the negative consequences of not having chosen the other. Trompenaars suggests that cultures are an expression of the Basic Assumptions they made about how these seven Survival Dilemmas should be resolved. We will use these same seven dilemmas in our effort to describe and compare Change-ABLE and stuck organizations. Here is a brief definition of the seven dilemmas:

Dilemma #1: *Internal* or *external* **control of the environment?**
This dilemma is based upon whether the organization assumes its survival depends upon submission to the forces in its external environment or upon control of these forces. (To appreciate the significance of this dilemma, imagine the

difference each assumption will make on an organization's planning practices, its definition of individual competence, and its methods of Work Review.)

Dilemma #2: *Past, present*, or *future* orientation?
The second dilemma deals with the organization's assumptions regarding time. Is survival best served by attention to the past, the future, or the present? How much time does the organization think it has? Is time seen as a repetitious cycle in which change is essentially an illusion, or is it a linear sequence of unique moments evolving toward some new status of existence? (Imagine how the assumptions behind the various answers to these questions affect the organization's attitude regarding tradition and other types of databases, or the effect they will have upon the organization's sense of urgency in all of its management practices.)

Dilemma #3: *Universal* or *particular* rules?
Does the organization assume all organizations are obligated to play by the same rules in what is assumed to be the same game, on a universally level playing field? Or is the organization's survival best served by making up its own rules, defending its sovereignty, and exploiting outsiders? (Consider the effect these different assumptions will have upon the organization's strategic planning.)

Dilemma #4: *Ascribed* or *achieved* status and power?
Is organizational survival dependent upon recognizing and honoring people for who they are, or is it dependent upon honoring them for what they do? Are the ascribed characteristics, such as race, sex, age, and social class the reliable criteria for status and power, or should status and power be given only to achievers—those who perform well on behalf of the organization regardless of their ascribed characteristics? (Consider how these different assumptions will affect the organization's leadership, the way it assigns responsibility and roles, and the intensity of its Work Review.)

Dilemma #5: *Affective* **or** *neutral* **expression of emotions?**
Is the organization best served by allowing people to freely express their emotions, or should everyone control emotional expression? (Consider how different assumptions will influence the processes by which organizations develop trust and confidence, define teamwork, and engage in decision-making.)

Dilemma #6: *Individualism* **or** *communitarianism?*
Does the organization make an extremely individualistic assumption operating from the belief that if every individual does what will promote his or her own well-being the organization's survival will be automatically assured? Or does the organization make a communitarian assumption, believing that the survival of all is best served when individuals subordinate their personal needs in service to the needs of the organization? (Consider how these different assumptions affect an organization's structural design and the extent to which it relies upon group work.)

Dilemma #7: *Diffuse* **or** *specific* **commitments?**
Is the organization's survival best served by building groups in which the members make such deep and nearly total commitment to each other that their individual concerns become diffuse, or is it better for each person to make and honor more limited and specific commitments with many different people? (Consider how different assumptions affect the organization's structural design and decision-making practices.)

Extreme vs. Reconciled Basic Assumptions

Trompenaars further suggests that when a culture resolves these dilemmas by assuming that at all times, only one of the alternatives is appropriate — what we will refer to as an Extreme Assumption — the culture becomes simpler and better defined, but it also becomes more rigid. His suggestion is consistent with our observations. We usually find that stuck organizations operate from Extreme Assumptions.

The alternative to Extreme Assumptions is not finding a middle position between the alternatives, but making Reconciled Assumptions. While the middle position might lead to a compromise in which both sides lose, a Reconciled Assumption achieves synergy between the seemingly opposed alternatives. By preserving both alternatives, choosing one in any specific situation stimulates its opposite to a higher level. For instance, in a Reconciled Assumption for Dilemma #6, individualism drives groups to a more mature level of teamwork — beyond dependence or independence to genuine interdependence in which individual identity and diversity are preserved and utilized.

Trompenaars suggests that the vitality of a culture depends upon the extent to which it finds resolution for Survival Dilemmas with Reconciled Assumptions, thereby availing itself of a wider range of survival strategies. This, too, matches our experience. Change-ABLE organizations operate from Reconciled Assumptions, and this contributes to their continuous inquiry, creativity, and change. They are more flexible in response to their threats and opportunities, and, incidentally, more difficult to understand.

In our description of each of the stuck cultures, we will highlight only what we consider to be their two or three most extreme and problematic assumptions — the biggest contributors to their stuck position. A special chapter is devoted to describing all seven of the Reconciled Assumptions we see operating in Change-ABLE organizations — its processing of matter and energy to deliver products and services.

A Glossary of Key Terms

Throughout the book, the following terms will be capitalized. Refer to this glossary for their definitions.

Agenda Type: A type of issue that will require a group's decision-making process. In Regular Meetings, there are four of these: Pass Downs, Work Review, Recommendations Review, and News.

Basic Assumptions: These are ready-made strategies for survival that have worked in the past and have been used so often, they operate unconsciously. The organization's Basic

Assumptions are expressed in its patterns of behavior, especially its management practices. A Basic Assumption is the way the organization resolves a Survival Dilemma. The authors refer to two forms of these Basic Assumptions: Extreme Assumptions and Reconciled Assumptions.

Breakthrough Systems: One of the five Key Management Practices. Breakthrough Systems distinguish how Change-ABLE organizations manage the workforce. In Change-ABLE organizations, management makes sure Individual Contributors manage their own work under the following conditions: 1) clarity about expected results; 2) self-monitored, informal feedback systems permitting continuous assessment of current performance compared to expected performance; and 3) control of the resources necessary to meet the expectations.

Consensus Decision-Making: A Group Decision-Making process in which the procedural ground rule states that the *status quo* will prevail as the group's decision unless all members can agree that at least one alternative is better. If any one member continues to believe that the status quo is better than all alternatives presented by the group, confirmation of the status quo is the group's resolution.

Consultative Decision-Making: A Group Decision-Making process in which the procedural ground rule states that one of the group's members will be the group's decider (usually the group's leader). At the end of the group's discussion, the decider (who also participates in the discussion) sums up his or her learning on the basis of the discussion and states what he or she believes is the appropriate resolution. The decider's preference becomes the group's resolution.

Dory: A small, one-passenger row boat with a deep enough hull to be stable in still and rough waters. The authors use this watercraft as an analogy for professionals.

Dory Regatta: A special event involving many Dories brought together to display the craftsmanship of their owners and to share stories about travel adventures. The authors use this event as an analogy for professional associations.

Extreme Assumption: A Basic Assumption in which a strong preference is shown for only one of the alternatives presented in a Survival Dilemma. Extreme Assumptions make an organization simpler, but also more rigid — the organization denies itself access to the survival strategies that are suggested by the rejected alternative. Reconciled Assumptions are preferable to Extreme Assumptions.

Functional/Technology Team: A group comprised mostly of Individual Contributors. Members share common technical expertise and are usually led by a manager. The manager "brokers" the members' talents to various organizational projects and other tasks. The members meet occasionally to review each other's work and promote each other's development toward higher levels of expertise.

Galley: A large boat propelled by many rowers, all of whom sit backward in the boat. The rowers are governed by a captain who determines the seating of the rowers, the pace of the rowing, and the boat's direction. The authors use this watercraft as an analogy for Representative organization — the style of management in which the members of a management team come together to represent the interests of their separate domains of authority.

Group Decision-Making: One of the five Key Management Practices. Group Decision-Making distinguishes how Change-ABLE organizations perform the management function of decision-making. The process consists of procedures that bring the group to resolution while encouraging and preserving disagreement among the members. It requires all members to engage in the process expecting to understand, disagree, and commit. There are only two well-tested forms of Group Decision-Making: Consensus and Consultative processes.

Individual Contributor: Someone who directly performs the organization's work — the processing of matter and energy to deliver products and services. Some operate machinery on manufacturing lines, others are professionals such as engineers, scientists, or market analysts.

Key Management Practice: A specific management practice distinguishing Change-ABLE organizations from stuck organizations. There are five such practices: Linked Teams, Performance Plans, Work Review, Group Decision-Making, and Breakthrough Systems.

Leader: Someone who is able to cause organizational change. This term is usually used to distinguish Managers, who focus on organizational maintenance, and those who are agents of change. In Change-ABLE organizations — because of its system of management practices — both of these maintenance and change roles are performed by Managers throughout its structure. Leadership is widely dispersed. We refer to those with governance roles in the Change-ABLE organizations as both Managers and Leaders — often we will refer to them as Team Leaders.

Linked Teams: One of the five Key Management Practices. Linked Teams distinguish how Change-ABLE organizations perform the management function of organizational structure. In Change-ABLE organizations, the structure operates as a system of integrated management teams and a variety of other team structures made up of Individual Contributors.

Manager: Someone with a full-time role in an organization's governance. This person exercises the organization's formal authority to control the use of its resources.

Negotiable Task: A task low in predictability, but high in delay tolerance. These tasks are initiated by an unexpected request and usually take the form of a short-term project. When the request for the task is made, the performer is expected to negotiate a definition of deliverables, schedule, and budget that is appropriate for the priority of the request.

Network Team: A Regular Meeting in which the membership and resources are drawn from a cross-section of the organization's divisions. It exercises authority to integrate cross-functional work. A Network Team can also be a Nominal Group and, therefore, ineffective.

News: Announcements of changes taking place within the group's domain of authority that will probably affect how at least three members of the group will employ their resources. These announcements are reminders or notice of emergencies, not Pass Downs. News is one of four Agenda Types for Regular Meetings.

Nominal Group: A dysfunctional group — a group in name only. Group dynamics prevent the gathered individuals from exchanging necessary information with each other. Because of these dynamics, the group's function could be performed as well or better by one of its individuals.

Pass Downs: A decision made at a higher level of authority that comes down to the group for its understanding and commitment. The group is expected to make whatever decisions are necessary to assure that its resources are allocated in compliance with the higher level decision. Pass Downs are one of four Agenda Types for Regular Meetings.

Performance Plan: One of the five Key Management Practices. Performance Plans distinguish how Change-ABLE organizations perform the management function of planning. Every Manager operates with a brief statement of less than 7 results that he or she is attempting to deliver within the next 12 months. Though brief, the statement is comprehensive — the few results represent how at least 80 per cent of the Manager's resources will be employed.

Professional: An Individual Contributor who engages in case-by-case problem solving. Each case is at least potentially unique and usually requires skilled analysis and a unique, custom-fitted solution.

Project Task: A task high in predictability (made so through planning) and high in delay tolerance (slack time being deliberately allocated as appropriate during planning). These tasks always aim at achieving a unique and at least partially innovative result (the project goal) and are non-repetitive.

Raft: A large platform made of buoyant materials on which cargo can be floated from place to place over relatively calm and predictable waters. The authors use this watercraft as an analogy for bureaucracy.

Recommendations Review: A group evaluation of a recommendation brought to it by a Task Force or some other expert source. The group decides whether or not to invest the recommendation with the resources required to make it an operational reality. Recommendations Review is one of four Agenda Types for Regular Meetings.

Reconciled Assumption: A Basic Assumption that preserves both alternatives in a Survival Dilemma and finds synergy between them — application of either alternative stimulating a deeper understanding of the possibilities in both. Organizations that operate from Reconciled Assumptions avail themselves of a broader range of survival strategies and exhibit greater creativity and adaptability than organizations operating from Extreme Assumptions.

Regular Meeting: Sometimes referred to as a Management Team Meeting, a group of people, usually Managers, who come together at a regularly scheduled time to decide how the group's resources should be utilized, and to evaluate whether or not these resources are being used according to their decisions. A Regular Meeting can also be a Nominal Group and, therefore, ineffective.

Routine Task: A task high in predictability and delay tolerance. These tasks are often, though not always, done repetitively, in high volume, and at high-speed precision.

Sea-Going Canoe: A large boat propelled by many paddlers, all of whom face forward. The Leader works from a raised platform in the middle of the canoe to point out the landmarks by which the paddlers guide their own work and chatter together to assure that everyone is paddling appropriately. The authors use this watercraft (we have in mind the Sea-Going Canoes of Polynesia) as an analogy for the Change-ABLE organization.

Self Managing Team: A group comprised mostly of Individual Contributors. In addition to control over the resources necessary to perform its tasks, the group also performs most of its own personnel functions. It may be responsible for any or all of the following: member selection, orientation, work assignment, performance evaluation, discipline, and termination.

Self Sufficient/Integrated Production Team: A group, comprised mostly of Individual Contributors. Within its membership, the team has all the expertise and control of resources necessary to perform a specific cross-functional process. Self Sufficient teams are a form of Regular Meeting — the group controls the use of some part of the organization's resources.

Survival Dilemmas: All communities of human beings, including organizations, must choose patterns of behavior promoting their survival. In many cases, such choices must be made from alternatives that are apparently opposed to each other. To choose one of the patterns of behavior exposes the organization to the negative consequences of not having chosen the other one. The organization is thus confronted with "Survival Dilemmas." Seven of these dilemmas are defined earlier in this chapter. Once the organization shows its preference, the choice becomes a Basic Assumption and starts operating continuously at an unconscious level.

Task Force: A group of subject matter experts, which is chartered to explore one specific issue — a complex problem, decision, or plan — and to provide a recommendation to the chartering body. The group is temporary, and is dissolved when its recommendation has been delivered. A Task Force can also be a Nominal Group and, therefore, ineffective.

Task Types: By looking at two variables inherent in any task, Predictability and Delay Tolerance, the task can be categorized as one of four types: Routine, Project, Troubleshooting, or Negotiable.

Team: The authors use this term as a synonym for group.

Troubleshooting Task: A task low in predictability and also low in delay tolerance. These tasks are always an emergency requiring immediate attention — when they occur, they take priority over other tasks the performer may also be responsible for doing.

Work Review: One of the five Key Management Practices. Work Reviews distinguish how Change-ABLE organizations perform the management function of performance feedback. Work Review is the most important agenda item in Regular Meetings. The members of the Regular Meeting evaluate whether or not the resources controlled by the Team are being efficiently utilized to accomplish the management Team's (the Leader's) Performance Plan. It acknowledges success and takes corrective action on issues that could lead to failure. Work Review is one of four Agenda Types for Regular Meetings.

The Book's Four Sections

Section One: Concepts & Terminology, Recommendation, and Watercraft Analogies

Section One begins with the introduction to key concepts and frequently used terminology. Chapter Two contains our recommendation, a concise statement of why it is necessary to be Change-ABLE, and the specific forms of managerial practice and assumption making Change-ABLE organizations so effective. We conclude the section with Chapter Three, which provides watercraft analogies for understanding the three most prevalent stuck organizational cultures and for further appreciating the uniqueness of the Change-ABLE culture. These three chapters empower the reader to determine how to use the rest of the book.

Section Two: The "Stuck" Cultures

Section Two contains Chapters Four-Six, each devoted to one of the stuck cultures. These chapters describe the ineffectiveness of each culture's managerial practices and the Key Basic Assumptions contributing to keeping the culture stuck. The purpose of this section is to provide the reader with a diagnostic tool for understanding what has gone wrong in these organizations.

Section Three: Practices of Change-ABLE Organizations

Section Three, Chapters Eight-Thirteen, contains an introductory chapter and a chapter on each of the five Key Management Practices as they operate in Change-ABLE organizations. Chapter Thirteen describes the seven Basic Assumptions underlying this unique organizational culture. This section elaborates our recommendation in specific detail and provides readers with checklists allowing them to monitor their progress toward becoming Change-ABLE.

Section Four: Becoming Change-ABLE

This final section focuses on the actions Managers can take to move toward being Change-ABLE, no matter what culture they operate in currently. Chapter Fourteen describes our methodology for assisting organizations to transition into being Change-ABLE. Chapter Fifteen offers a case study of Etec Systems, an organization currently making this transition. Finally, Chapter Sixteen in this section offers a list of warnings that can help Managers and Leaders avoid making the mistakes that have become familiar to us.

Summary

This chapter defined the Change-ABLE organization's unique approach to change. Change-ABLE organizations don't see organizational change as a Special Event. Instead, they weave change into the very fabric of their day-to-day operations. Because of the system of five Key Management Practices, these organizations are engaged in continuous improvement and radical change. They show an unusual ability to respond to the threats and opportunities in their social and economic environments and, therefore, are growing very rapidly while maintaining high levels of quality and efficiency.

These additional concepts were defined and briefly previewed:

1. There are five management functions, each containing a Key Management Practice distinctive in Change-ABLE organizations.
2. Stuck organizations are those unable to adjust to the socioeconomic environment that is growing more complex and dynamic all over the world. These stuck organizations are not using the Key Managerial Practices to make them Change-ABLE.

Function	Key Management Practices in Change-ABLE Organizations
Structure	A Hierarchy of Linked Teams
Planning	Performance Plans
Performance Feedback	Work Reviews
Decision-Making	Group Decision-Making
Managing Individual Contributors	Breakthrough Systems

3. Basic Assumptions are the ready-made, unconscious strategies by which organizations attempt to promote their survival. The organization uses Basic Assumptions as it attempts to resolve certain Survival Dilemmas confronting all communities. Seven of these Survival Dilemmas were defined.

4. The inadequate management practices of stuck organizations are expressions of Extreme Assumptions — assumptions that only one of the alternatives in a Survival Dilemma is appropriate, thus losing access to the survival strategies suggested by the rejected one. This makes the stuck organizations too simple and rigid for adaptation to complex and dynamic business environments. Change-ABLE organizations, by contrast, operate from Reconciled Assumptions — not a middle position or compromise, but an assumption preserving both alternatives in a Survival Dilemma and finding synergy between them. In these organizations, every application of one alternative's strategy stimulates a deeper understanding of the possibilities in the other alternative. These Reconciled Assumptions give Change-ABLE organizations access to a larger range of survival strategies, thereby keeping the organizations flexible and creative.

5. A glossary of commonly used terms was provided as a reference for readers.

6. The four Sections of this book were previewed.

2

The Recommendation

Overview

Chapter Two presents this book's message in the form of a brief recommendation, which has four parts:

1. The social and economic environments favoring Change-ABLE organizations are briefly scanned.
2. The five Key Management Practices are defined.
3. Seven Basic Assumptions that support these practices are also defined and recommended.
4. A method for becoming Change-ABLE is described.

Why Become a Change-ABLE Organization?

In early 1995, *Newsweek* magazine featured a photograph of a Samburu tribesman in Africa. Wearing a red plaid robe, he stood barefoot in front of his cattle corral with a spear in his left hand. In his right hand, pressed to his ear, was a cellular phone!

The picture was a fitting announcement for a future in which the year 1995 may be heralded as a critical juncture. In 1995, the hardware and software of information technology converged to make even a laptop a multimedia tool that was fully integrated with all its component parts — printer, CD ROM, fax, telephone, television, and computer networks. Computers and peripheral technologies are entering the second stage of their lives. The days when information technology was limited to engineers and big business are rapidly passing. We now have the power to combine sound and graphics — the fastest and most familiar forms of communication — and we are learning to make the technology useful to all, even those who are illiterate.

At the intersection of information technology and global market readiness, a crisis brews. The global marketplace favors organizations capable of sustaining consistent and dramatic growth, while simultaneously producing major improvements in products and services every 18 to 24 months. Those serving the Chinese market today, for instance, are required to increase their capacity more than 100 per cent a year, while simultaneously pushing the leading edge of their technology. If they don't get bigger and better immediately, they will leave broad segments of the market unattended, creating an irresistible vacuum for competitors. The crisis is this: until quite recently, very few companies have successfully sustained a growth rate of 20 per cent a year for more than three to five years.

Most companies simply disintegrate under the pressures created by a 20 per cent growth rate. Leadership wavers and becomes diluted, and too many new faces create competency and trust problems. Communications break down and the companies come apart with all the noise and chaos of a sinking ship. How will our organizations survive the pressures caused by responding to these new markets? Can human beings bear the stress of such long-term continuous change?

Yes! As consultants for over two decades, we have worked with organizations demonstrating a remarkable ability to respond to change. We've worked with Technology Design and Construction (TDC) as it learned to build some of the world's largest microprocessor factories, racing from groundbreaking to first silicon in 20 months. We've coached Cisco Systems, an exploding Internet company that experiences more change in nine months than most companies experience in 20 years in a market that reinvents itself every 18 to 24 months. And we have worked with Genesco, a former Fortune 100 company, as its management team initiated a strong comeback in the footwear industry.

We have been exhilarated and disturbed when working with continuously changing organizations. They don't seem to follow the familiar MBA rules. So much of what they do looks spontaneous — sheer opportunism, or simply, whatever works. The complexity of structure (is there one?); the density of meetings (do they do anything else?); the lack of privacy (micro management?); and the sharing of resources (who's in control?); cause many a newcomer to despair of ever making sense of what's happening. But the benefit of being exposed to this sort of organization in different global markets over a period of years has given us the opportunity to uncover a pattern — actually a culture. Like all cultures, these organizations are comprised of a very complex system of assumptions and practices. We call such organizations Change-ABLE.

Do you have to start right to be Change-ABLE? Most of the Change-ABLE organizations we know did. These organizations began with bold ideas and simple principles and reinvented themselves as they wrestled with day-to-day challenges. Our goal is to help other organizations convert to this culture. This is a different challenge. Starting right is hazardous, but getting right after the organization has a long history is even harder. Successful organizations are in trouble because their now useless practices are more deeply reinforced. However, our experience, thus far, makes us believe that all organizations can heal themselves and recover their ability to be responsive to the new opportunities and threats.

The first requirement is a clear concept of what healthy, Change-ABLE organizations look like. The model we offer consists of a set of Key Management Practices expressing a unique set of Basic Assumptions, and is a standard against which any organization can evaluate itself. Keeping this model in mind instills the creative tension an organization needs to persist in the journey toward renewal. We present this model now as a recommendation.

The Recommendation

Adopt these five Key Management Practices:

Linked Teams: Make your current management structure operate as a system of Linked Teams, capable of reliably closing the organization's performance feedback loop between Individual Contributors and executives every week.

Performance Plans: Make every Manager in your organization operate from a memorable list of key results achievable this year, with the ability to tell you what will be done about them by Friday afternoon of the current week.

Work Reviews: Make everyone in your organization participate in Regular Meetings focusing on the evaluation of the team's work performance, with your executives holding such meetings at least once a month and all other levels holding Work Reviews at least once a week.

Group Decision-Making: Make every item on the agenda of every Regular Meeting, including Work Reviews, require and receive a rational Group Decision.

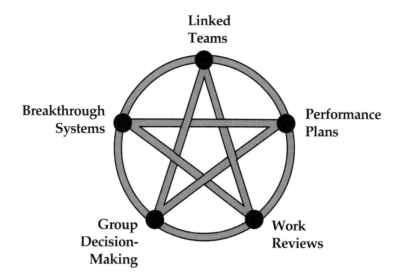

Breakthrough Systems: Make sure those who do the organization's work are clear about the results expected from their performance; monitor their own performance with simple, informal feedback systems; and control the resources necessary to meet their performance expectations.

These are the key practices of Change-ABLE organizations. Taken one at a time, they are not new. Practiced together, they become a unique and powerful system of human cooperation unknown in most organizations.

Assumptions Sustaining the Practices

To sustain these practices, Change-ABLE organizations operate from the following Basic Assumptions:

- Everything — including nature itself — is constantly changing. We participate in making the change creative.
- There is no time but the present, which is full of our past and contains our future.

- We play by the rules as long as we participate in making the rules.
- We must respect and reward those whose good works serve our ability to learn. There are no entitlements to status and authority — only reputations based on performance.
- We should freely express our joy and approval, yet carefully express negative feelings through problem solving.
- Survival depends not only upon skilled individuals but, even more so, upon their cooperation.
- We must commit to the organization's purpose, then be explicit about the immediate contributions we will make.

Begin Immediately, Whatever Your Domain of Authority

It is always logical and practical to start this organizational renewal within the executive teams of an organization. We believe this leads to the most rapid results. But, we have seen variations that also work. We have seen relatively autonomous divisions renew themselves in the body of an organization that was, for the most part, stuck. In these cases, the organization benefited from the division's new effectiveness and its profitability. (We regret to say, however, that not all of their organization adopted the model.) We have also seen a few cases where many of the Managers in the middle of a stuck organization created small "base camps" of renewal and eventually linked up their camps to renew the organization as a whole. In these cases, the process was very slow, but with great commitment and persistence from the middle Managers, it worked.

In practice, we find it nearly impossible to "talk people into a new set of Basic Assumptions." We know the assumptions and practices are interdependent, and we believe the most direct path to changing both is to start with the practices. To become Change-ABLE, an organization starts acting that way and discovers what happens. As the organization's new practices provoke the environment's rewards, the constraints of the old assumptions are challenged. New assumptions then emerge, make peace with the organization's environment, and sustain the new practices as habits.

The path is neither easy nor certain. Our experience is that any organization on the Change-ABLE path will see significant results in six to nine months, but the complete transformation usually takes at least two or three years. Nothing about this sort of organizational development smacks of a quick turnaround, a pilot project, a change program, or a restructuring. Becoming Change-ABLE is more difficult and real than any of these phrases suggests. But all organizations should get on the path and persist. The Change-ABLE are already among us, and they are awesome competitors.

Summary

Chapter Two made a recommendation in four parts:

1. Social and economic environments, all over the world, are becoming more complex and dynamic, presenting opportunities and threats that only very flexible and fast-changing organizations are able to convert to success. It is time to become Change-ABLE.
2. Five Key Management Practices make organizations Change-ABLE:

    *   A hierarchy that operates as a system of Linked Teams;
    *   Performance Plans for all Managers;
    *   Work Reviews as the central focus of Regular Meeting;
    *   Group Decision-Making for all significant management decisions; and
    *   Breakthrough Systems for the self-management of Individual Contributors;

3. Seven Basic Assumptions support the Key Management Practices.
4. The process can begin immediately, whatever your domain of authority. Focus on the Key Management Practices will stimulate change in Basic Assumptions.

Using Watercraft Analogies To Describe Four Organizational Cultures

Overview

Chapter Three describes the culture of the Change-ABLE organization by using watercraft analogies to compare it with other prominent organizational cultures. It provides four analogies:

1. The Raft is an analogy for Bureaucracies.
2. The Dory Regatta is an analogy for Professional associations.
3. The Galley is an analogy for Autocratic/Representative organizations.
4. The Sea-Going Canoe is an analogy for Change-ABLE organizations.

A Watercraft Analogy for Organizational Cultures: Raft, Dory Regatta, Galley, and Sea-Going Canoe

Many of the components of complex organizational cultures operate at the unconscious level. Their foundation is made up of the Basic Assumptions regarding what it takes to survive. These assumptions have worked so often and for so long, they have become unconscious. The language, behavior, architecture, tools, clothing, food, and artwork of organizations are expressions of these unconscious Basic Assumptions.

Cultural components may appear to be simple and obvious, but they are often quite complex and not very easy to talk about. When we approach such complex subjects, we have found the use of analogies to be very helpful.

We will attempt to define the culture of the Change-ABLE organization with watercraft analogies. By describing and comparing these watercraft, you will get a feel for the unique culture of the Change-ABLE organizations.

The Raft — An Analogy for Bureaucracy

Made of naturally buoyant materials like wood and reeds, the Raft is an ancient form of watercraft. The Raft's flat structure and buoyancy enable it to lift and move cargo. Rafts come in all sizes. The ideal environment for a Raft is calm, still water. If there is a current at all, it needs to flow steadily, without rapids or other obstructions. A calm environment is important because Rafts don't have much control over their mobility—they are moved by the currents or the use of poles. The larger the Raft, the less control its crew has over its movements.

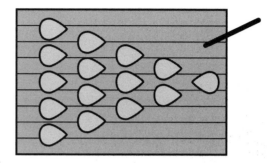

The Raft

Raft crews realize that survival and the successful transportation of cargo depend upon the condition of the water and its currents. Crews know they can't control the water; they simply go with the current and occasionally pole themselves away from shoreline snags, debris, or other Rafts.

Progress is usually slow. There is time to spare on deck, so the crew is kept busy checking and protecting the cargo. A really good Raft is character- ized by the way its cargo has been organized, stacked, covered with tarps, and tied down with perfect knots. The deck is clean and divided into areas of responsibility for each crew member. The Leader inspires the crew to do its work with vigilance and pride.

Things don't change much on a Raft, and over time, rules and proce- dures evolve. Each day tasks are done according to regular cycles. Good crew members know that there is a place for everything and everything in its place; a time for everything and everything done on time. Rules, procedures, and schedules are the "practices" of planning on the Raft. Anything more is pretentious. A strategic plan is not needed. Each trip is about the same as the last one. Changes are uncontrollable — caused by unexpected volumes of water or changes in the current. The crew must go along with change, but the range of uncertainty is limited since they have been over the same waters many times and have discussed their experiences on these same waters with former generations of crewmen. In this case, history is important. It provides the guidelines of tradition and validates rules, procedures, and schedules.

Discipline aboard the Raft is maintained by regular and surprise inspections to examine the orderliness of each section of cargo and the record

of each crewmember's scheduled tasks. The reward for passing many inspec-
tions is promotion to control a larger portion of the deck or control of more
precious cargo. A relationship always exists between longevity in the crew and
status. It is not possible to be in control of a large part of the deck without
having been aboard a long time. Longevity preserves the traditions of the Raft
and protects it from the environmental variances in which it operates. Aboard
the Raft, all issues of governance are deferred upward to the older, more
responsible members of the crew, and perhaps all the way up to the Leader. It
is a well-defined hierarchy of authority, and, for those who are interested, it is
a very well-defined career path.

Crewmembers learn their jobs in a few weeks. There isn't much room
for making mistakes — everything is done according to specific regulations.
The problem is staying interested in the work, which doesn't require much
attention and often allows the mind to wander. Crewmembers often enjoy the
ride — passing familiar countryside along the banks and dreaming up
entertaining stories and songs. If one crewmember gets cranky and decides to
pick fights with others, such behavior is not acceptable to leadership and will
be punished if discovered. But Raft behavior usually leaves room for some
snarling, nipping, and sharp-tongued teasing. For the most part, life on the
Raft is considered to be pretty good — steady work and an orderly routine.
Those who stay on the Raft for a while usually take great pride in their way of
life, often becoming suspicious of anyone who lives differently. These rafters
actually feel sorry for anyone uneducated about how the waters flow. Raft
crewmembers sometimes label people who don't like the Raft as those who
don't like the "natural" or traditional order of things. And rafters believe that
eventually nonrafters will become troublemakers.

The Raft is analogous to classic bureaucracy, which emerged as
hierarchy (the Holy Order) thousands of years before Christ. It was
understood as part of nature — a gift of the gods. Bureaucracy
changed very little, and when it did change, it was usually due to the
intervention of powers beyond the comprehension of most of the
organization's members — by revelation to the Leaders.

Only in the last two centuries has the hierarchy been secularized
as bureaucracy. Even in secular form, however, this culture continues
to expect little change, to see itself as a victim of change when it does
occur, and to practice the norms of Leader/tradition dependency, in
full compliance with rules and procedures.

Private industry gave up on bureaucracy early in the twentieth century, but many governments and public services are still bureaucratically run. Bureaucracy still rules the majority of the world's population, but it does not do well in an environment characterized by intense competition and rapid change.

The Dory Regatta — An Analogy for Professional Association

The security of the Raft — with its rules, procedures, and schedules — is too confining for some — those who long for autonomy and mobility. These restless individualists get off the Raft and into an altogether different kind of watercraft — the Dory.

A Dory is a small rowboat with a stable, watertight hull that makes flotation possible. A Dory can be made to go into rapid currents, choppy waters, or even rough seas. Dories provide autonomy and mobility. A Dory can go where Rafts cannot or would not dare to go: upstream, downstream, back and forth, from shore to shore. A Dory goes faster than the Raft and is suited to exploring the unknown.

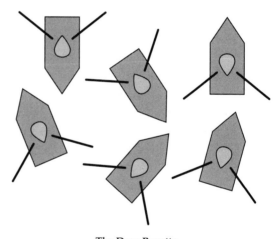

The Dory Regatta

The Dory's small size does pose some constraints. Its range is limited, and it cannot carry large cargo. A single rower must maximize energy for mobility, and the Dory uses the principle of leverage inherent in rowing.

Rowing is an efficient use of physical energy, but it presents a navigation problem. The rower sits backward in the boat, feet braced, while the big muscles of the back, arms, and legs pull the oars. The rower must pick a landmark in the rear to steer a course. The rower tries to keep a straight wake and must constantly check to see if, in fact, the Dory is moving efficiently to its destination. Inevitably, there are significant readjustments to be made—the boat is always zigzagging on its course.

Since the Dory carries little cargo, the rower must earn a living creatively. Usually Dory people find a way to associate with Rafts — to barter the knowledge and mobility the Dory provides. Dories serve the Raft by racing downstream to scout the waters, or upstream to collect forgotten cargo. Sometimes the Dory serves as a courier for any food or medication needed on the Raft. It also carries mail from other Rafts and villages along the shore.

Raft people recognize the usefulness of Dory people. But Dory people, who live outside the procedures and routines of the Raft, seem strange to them. Raft people use the services of Dory people, but they are always relieved to see the Dory push off.

Dory people are better planners than Raft people; they have to be. With their limited cargo space, Dory people must plan their supplies shrewdly. Dory people know that each trip is likely to be a bit different from any other, and they must be prepared for as many contingencies as their small boats will permit. But Dory people's most important skill is their opportunism—their ability to seize a chance to provide a valuable service for a paying customer. On any journey, survival is dependent upon these reactive skills as much as on any planning. Every day presents new possibilities, and surviving into tomorrow depends upon how well today's possibilities are converted into profitable realities. Most opportunities will be unique — different personalities to contend with, different needs to serve, different available resources, different abilities to pay.

Dory people live by their wits. The more they move about, the more they learn. And the more they learn, the more they have with which to bargain. Knowledge, autonomy, and mobility are their competencies and the source of their livelihood.

Dory people seem to enjoy solitude in most of their work. Sometimes, however, they hold regattas. This gives Dory people a chance to look at each others' boats and watch each others' rowing and navigation techniques. Dory people want to get close enough to get a good look at the other Dories, but not so close that anyone can fully explore the condition or contents of their own boats. Since everyone is facing backward, there is also a real danger of running into each other. A certain distance must be maintained for everyone's good. So while moving about during the regatta, everyone whistles or sings a little song — a friendly way to warn each other to stay away.

At Dory Regattas the boats are brought near enough to allow the rowers to sit and talk. They learn of new and different places or hear new perceptions about familiar waters. A special sort of barter takes place — the barter of knowledge. Since exaggeration can be used to get attention, the validity of each story is assessed carefully. Dory people exchange information cautiously, building their own traditions and enlarging their base of knowledge. The point of a Dory Regatta is to acquire as much information as possible while remaining autonomous and mobile.

No decisions are made at Dory Regattas. No one is inherently better than anyone else — no one has the right to direct another's behavior. Differences are simply a matter of the unique situations each Dory rower has encountered and the inventiveness or cleverness with which the situations were handled. Respect is optional. Everyone is free to look, listen, and evaluate. There is no obligation to adopt anyone's ideas or skills.

The Dory is a good analogy for the Professionals. Originally, the Professionals were shamans, magicians, and seers. They have become physicians, lawyers, scientists, engineers, and consultants. Their mode of operation is still case-by-case problem solving dependent upon their highly developed diagnostic and prescriptive abilities. Each case is unique. Nobody can tell them how to handle the case ahead of time; no one will know what should be done until the professionals themselves have performed the diagnostic phase of the task. Professionals go to their tasks alone. They gain skill from experience and the sharing of that experience with fellow professionals.

The Professional's curiosity and ambition have been driving forces in history. Their creativity is leading the current information technology revolution — a revolution that is changing these knowledge workers themselves. The depth of specialization to which they can and must go to remain on the front edge of discovery tends to isolate and minimize the value of the discoveries. The Professionals' work must be integrated with that of other specialists to make their discoveries of practical value. This forces them into greater interdependence with other knowledge workers and into membership in large academic and commercial organizations. Attendance at the Regatta has become mandatory — the regattas are now called "project teams." These project teams still cooperate like a Dory Regatta—the professionals come together in the same work area and try to keep from bumping into each other.

The Galley — An Analogy for Representative Organization

The Galley, a long, low ship propelled by oars, combines some of the advantages of the Raft and the Dory. The Galley is a big boat capable of long-range travel in all kinds of waters. It carries its own provisions and has plenty of room for cargo. Its full mobility allows it to challenge its environment. The Galley has the same leverage advantage as the Dory, but it fills its benches with rowers. Some Galleys have one man to an oar, some have two or three pulling the same oar. Rowers still sit backward in the boat and still have no way of knowing where the boat is going or how the journey progresses. Galley rowers are

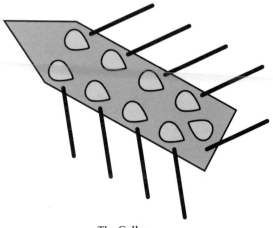

The Galley

unable to row with the autonomy of the Dory — teamwork is essential on this boat. Every rower must pull on the beat determined by the Leader. To be a good member of the team, rowers must continuously pull hard in time with the beat.

But teamwork does not extend to having responsibility beyond one's own oar. If in the process of pulling hard a rower causes the boat to go in circles, that is not the rower's problem — it is the Leader's problem. After all, the rower doesn't even know where the boat is supposed to be going.

No one can pull as hard as possible all the time. Exhaustion and damage to the body set in very quickly. Survival depends upon taking advantage of food, water, and fresh air rations. It also depends upon learning to look like the oar is being pulled as hard as possible, even when "laying on the oar." Laying on the oar is an acting skill that allows rowers a little rest when needed. Skillful actors have the ability to notice when other actors are laying on the oar. They know, however, that it would be unwise to call attention to another's acting — which could provoke retaliation. Part of teamwork, then, is to "politely" ignore others who are taking unscheduled rests. The norm is: pull your own oar, let the Leader worry about how others are pulling theirs.

The Leader stands on a raised area at the back of the boat with one hand on the tiller. The Leader is the only person who knows where the boat is going and the only person capable of judging whether or not the boat is making appropriate progress.

The Leader tries to balance the rowers, so that when they pull as hard as possible they will keep the boat going in a straight line. However, the balance is never perfect, and the Leader must make corrections with the use of the tiller.

The Galley is especially dependent upon its Leader for effectiveness. Navigational skills, organization, and discipline of the crew are all in the Leader's hands. All crew members pull their oars as the Leader determines. If everyone plays their part, the boat goes with a minimum of zigzagging to its far-flung destination.

Everyone in the Galley gets to see a lot more of the world than those on the Raft or in the Dories. Galley rowers share in a large database about the world. Leaders congregate in their own clubs and hangouts to share with each other their methods for maintaining order aboard their Galleys. Rowers get together to brag about their boats and Leaders. They cannot help looking down on the simple folk in Rafts and Dories.

The Galley, which has been thriving since World War II, is the most dominant form of organization in the industrialized world today. Big, powerful, wealthy, and effective compared to all other prior forms of organization, the Galley is now the prevalent form of industrialization—harnessing the energies of many people and specialties. It seems to have an unlimited ability to grow, eventually organizing under an Admiral as a fleet of Galleys.

The Galley culture, however, has never been quite right. Leader-dependence crushes the individuals who accept this role of leadership.

No individual is capable of that much autonomous responsibility, given the amount of uncertainty and complexity contained in the new global market environment. Also, dependence upon single individuals for leadership of such huge enterprises subjects large parts of society to considerable risk.

The Galley is also threatened from within. Galley concepts of hierarchy and teamwork are repulsive to the professional/knowledge workers — almost as abhorrent as Rafts. But thoughtful problem solving is becoming more and more the nature of the Galley's work. That which is predictable and routine is passing rapidly into the domain of robotics; the work that remains must be performed by knowledge workers. The Galley's culture is challenged today, both by complexity and uncertainty without and by the restlessness of thoughtful members within.

The Sea-Going Canoe — An Analogy for the Change-ABLE Organization

The limits of the Galley are especially apparent when compared with our final example, the Sea-Going Canoe. These boats are also very large and capable of carrying provisions and cargo. They are long, narrow, close to the water, and propelled with amazing swiftness by their paddlers.

Paddlers sit on both sides of the Canoe, just as rowers do in the Galley. The striking difference is that paddlers are facing forward in their seats. Their eyes are on the landmarks and stars that guide the Canoe to its ultimate destination. The Leader stands among the paddlers on a raised platform, able

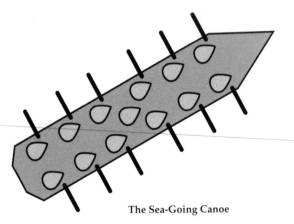

The Sea-Going Canoe

to see what comes over the horizon a little before the other crew members. The Leader then instructs the crew members about where to look for the next navigational guide.

Each paddler knows the boat's ultimate destination and the specific landmarks determining the immediate direction of the Canoe. Thus informed, paddlers continually adjust their own paddling to ensure that the Canoe goes as it should. Though the Canoe uses less leverage than the Galley, the subtle adjustments independently made by each paddler, combined with the shape of the Canoe, allow it to move with greater efficiency and speed than would be possible with the same number of rowers in a Galley.

In the Sea-Going Canoe, the paddlers constantly chatter as they paddle. They tell each other and the Leader what they see that might affect the course of the Canoe. They encourage and advise each other about how to paddle. Experienced paddlers know how to pace themselves and help others learn to do the same. They know when in the journey everyone will be required to paddle very hard and help prepare the other paddlers for these periods of special effort by making sure they are properly nourished and rested.

The Sea-Going Canoe requires teamwork. But, in this boat, teamwork goes beyond being a good paddler. Each paddler is expected to know the condition of the whole Canoe and to be responsible for sharing information that keeps the whole Canoe right. Paddlers respect the unique perspective of their Leaders, but they are not as Leader-dependent as the Galley rowers. Concern for the Canoe's discipline and navigation is widely dispersed among the paddlers.

The abilities, preferences, and knowledge of each paddler are well-known to everyone else in the Canoe. People are appreciated as unique and are permitted room to be themselves. They are expected to take care of themselves. They are also expected to consider the needs of others and to make adjustments to ensure an appropriate distribution of the Canoe's supplies and work. In the Sea-Going Canoe, people rarely appeal to a Leader for reconciliation of differences or for the settlement of grievances. Most of the time they handle these things among themselves. If one or two individuals cannot reach resolution, other paddlers are invited into the conversation until a satisfactory resolution is achieved.

The Sea-Going Canoe has long been an option as a form of organizational culture and is often chronicled in organizational literature. Indigenous to the United States, this form of culture was well documented by Rensis Likert and his colleagues in the late 1960's at the University of Michigan's Institute of Social Research (ISR). The culture we call the Change-ABLE organization is, we are convinced, the current flowering of what ISR called "System Four."

ISR's field discovery (not mere theory) was popularized and thoroughly misrepresented as "participative management." This popular misrepresentation became a human relations movement, envisioning an authority-free community in which people sought authenticity and spontaneity in their relationships. The intended result was for the organization to become an instrument of self-actualization for its members. It also was assumed that such respect for the uniqueness of individuals would lead to job satisfaction, morale, and eventually, high levels of productivity. Though ISR and many others continued to prove that no such romantic illusion had ever worked for more than a year or two, the vision persists today. The Change-ABLE organization — the Sea-Going Canoe — is not a friend of this fantasy.

The Sea-Going Canoe is a highly disciplined, systematically deliberate organization. It makes better use of its human resources than the Galley, respecting and utilizing everyone's minds in the process of its governance. The Change-ABLE organization holds everyone accountable to its overall purpose and focuses the diversity of its people to maximize the organization's opportunities. The Change-ABLE organization has more current and reliable information, analyzes it more intelligently for decision-making, and is able to implement its decisions more efficiently because of its members' involvement and commitment. These elements combine to make it smarter and faster than the other cultures.

Summary

Chapter Three presented four watercraft analogies to describe and distinguish the culture of Change-ABLE organizations:

1. The Raft was offered as an analogy for bureaucracy, the ancient organizational culture still prevalent in public administration and highly regulated industries everywhere in the world.

2. The Dory Regatta was offered as an analogy for professional associations, another ancient culture which is growing in its prevalence along with the growth of knowledge power. The Dory Regatta is often a subculture within larger organizational cultures.
3. The Galley was offered as an analogy for Autocratic/Representative organization, a culture that is currently dominant in the domain of private enterprise wherever it is allowed in the world.
4. The Sea-Going Canoe was offered as an analogy for Change-ABLE organizations, the participative culture that is rapidly growing and winning in the competitive environment of private enterprise.

This chapter expresses the authors' belief that the future belongs to the Sea-Going Canoes. These fast, flexible, highly focused organizations are the form of human cooperation that will eventually characterize all aspects of society — public administration, professionalism, and private enterprise.

Section

II

The Stuck Cultures

4

The Raft — Going With the Flow

Overview

Chapter Four describes the culture of bureaucracy (Rafts). Bureaucracy does not use the Key Management Practices or Basic Assumptions of Change-ABLE organizations:

1. The social and economic environment of bureaucracy has to be stable and free of competition.
2. Bureaucracy's structure incorporates elaborate levels and divisions and sprawls out in a rational but impractical symmetry.
3. Bureaucracy's planning is also elaborate but largely pretentious.
4. Bureaucracy's performance feedback is primarily a ceremony of self-congratulation.
5. Bureaucracy's decision-making is a process of one-on-one communication between superiors and subordinates that is tightly constrained by the information, opinions, and the initiative of the superior.
6. Bureaucracy's management of the work force is essentially a system of negative feedback.
7. Certain Extreme Assumptions of bureaucracy keep it inflexible:

   - Bureaucracy's Extreme Externalism (Dilemma #1)
   - Bureaucracy's Extreme Universalism (Dilemma #3):
   - Bureaucracy's Extreme Individualism (Dilemma #6):

The Shrinking Environment of Bureaucracy

In this chapter, we explore the practices and assumptions of bureaucracy. This organizational form is rarely found in the open marketplaces of the world, as the Raft quickly succumbs when competing with Galleys or Sea-Going Canoes. However, wherever competition is forbidden, as in government administration, government-owned or protected industries, or in industries so heavily regulated that entry is nearly impossible and competition among the enfranchised is minimal, bureaucracy reigns. These competition-free zones still exist everywhere in the world, because most of the suppliers and customers in the global economy are under the control of bureaucratic cultures. They are therefore, important to understand.

It must also be said that these bureaucratic organizations are under pressure they are not likely to withstand for much longer. Human aspirations for greater freedom and a higher quality of life grow restless and revolutionary within the constraints of bureaucracy. With every passing day, it becomes more obvious that there are more efficient and effective ways of cooperating. The still waters in which these Rafts once glided are now becoming turbulent.

Structure: The "Holy Order" of Bureaucracy

The organizational structure of a bureaucracy is usually a large, tall, and somewhat symmetrical hierarchy. Bureaucracy has a long history of organizational design reflecting still the ancient belief that the organization was an imitation of heavenly order and a gift of the gods to human society. In its current forms, bureaucracy reflects the more secular rationalism of the nineteenth century and that era's belief in a perfect and right way to organize. All of these assumptions are still reflected in the shape of bureaucratic structure.

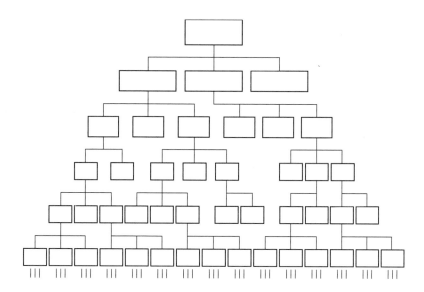

Bureaucracy

The hierarchy of the Raft is large. It assigns a special element of its functional structure to every conceivable task the organization will ever perform. It attempts to predict every part of the organization's work and to anticipate it with a position of accountability.

A good organizational design for the Raft makes certain that no particular position outweighs individual performance. It is generally assumed that individuals have limited capacity, and there is little belief in the possibility of enlarging that capacity through learning or information technology. Structures are elaborate because they attempt to cover every task with a functional position of limited authority, appropriate for what is assumed to be a very limited individual.

The Raft has many layers of management. Even in small organizations of only a few hundred people, there will be as many as 7 to 12 layers. These layers arise from the fairly small spans of managerial control, which are based upon the assumption that individuals can only adequately coordinate and control the work of a few direct reports.

Finally, the hierarchy of the Raft is symmetrical. This is partially a reflection of the rational minds designing it, but it also reflects the political dynamic going on within the bureaucracy. In this culture, status is strictly tied to position in the hierarchy. Managers want to be sure they have a domain of authority similar to their peers.

The hierarchy is graphically represented as a series of boxes connected together with lines. The implication of the artwork is reflected in the behavior. Managers exercise their formal authority through a series of one-on-one communications, delegating downward to Individual Contributors who, in turn, report upward to their Managers. This process creates a slow and imprecise organization. Human beings, even with the best of intentions, are inherently poor communicators, neither broadcasting nor receiving messages clearly. Even in the best of cases, as we pass messages through this one-on-one network, they become distorted. Add to that the motivation to look good and avoid accountability for serious mistakes, and the network becomes a seriously dysfunctional system of communication and governance. Typically, the bureaucracy is slow and a bit stupid.

Additionally, the hierarchy of the Raft is clumsy. Policy and procedures dictate the flow of information until it reaches the proper position of authority. There, it is logically assumed the combinations of information empower the position holder to make a fully informed decision. The task of integration among peer positions, therefore, is always the responsibility of the individual to whom the subordinates report. Subordinates attempting to facilitate coordination among themselves are "out of line" — functioning outside their domain of authority. Integration is always the boss's function, but the one-on-one pattern of communication inevitably leads to unsynchronized subordinate performance. In the Raft, the left hand really doesn't know what the right hand is doing.

This system has little ability to adjust to complexity. If there is pressure to increase the variety of outputs, or to utilize a greater variety of technical specialties, or to increase productivity, the network of managerial communication quickly overloads. Individuals at all levels in the network are confronted with new volumes of information, plus the task of creating and learning all the new policies and procedures the change requires. The task of integration requires more information processing than most individuals can push through their nervous systems. The network then gets even slower and less coordinated in its performance.

The most common response to overload in the Raft culture is the acquisition of more staff. Deputies, administrative assistants, and special assistants are very common throughout the ranks of the hierarchy. The accumulation of a cadre of staff assistants becomes, in fact, a symbol of status.

When the Raft culture attempts to speed up the functioning of the hierarchy with meetings and cross-functional structures, it usually makes a mess of it. Group work and cross-functional operations fly in the face of the Raft's Basic Assumptions regarding good organization. The Raft assumes every significant task should have its own permanent structure and dedicated resources. If the task is important, it must have its own direct chain of command or it will surely suffer the consequences of ambiguous authority and accountability.

Cross-functional groups are always seen as stopgap measures for dealing with temporary and relatively unimportant issues. The assigned individuals are called departmental representatives — but are seen by their bosses as "on loan" only to audit the meeting on behalf of the department. These representatives usually are lower level authorities and, in some cases, are actually departmental castaways. Departmental honor and suspicion, however, require every department to be represented in nearly every cross-functional meeting. So, although the issues may not be especially important, the groups dealing with them tend to be quite large. Size alone is enough to cause these groups to fail as rational information processors.

Groups are further blocked from taking decisive action by the inability of members to act on behalf of their departments. If such a group makes a decision at all, it requires at least one round of "shuttle diplomacy" between members and their respective departmental authorities. To act without such diplomacy sets off alarm bells in the Raft; it is seen by higher level Managers as a form of insubordination and often provokes punishment. Needless to say, under such conditions, cross-functional groups barely work, and when they do, they work very slowly. They make little contribution to solving the organization's problems of integration and information overload.

This abusive use of groups and their consequent failure reinforces the bureaucracy's principles of organization: reasonable information processing can only be done by individuals; and authority and accountability can only be assured if there is a well-defined chain of command made up of subordinates who report to only one boss.

Planning: Pretentious Documentation

The practice of planning in the bureaucracy involves some fascinating ceremonies. Planning is usually an elaborate process, a seasonal activity typically taking anywhere from three to six months. The process includes documenting the vision, mission, goals, and objectives of the organization and the determination of a budget sufficient to achieve the plan. It is not unusual to see the planning process driven right to the bottom of the organization. All targets, milestones, and sub-objectives are linked and nested within each other, often codified by number, so the whole thing can be put together as one splendid document. A glance through the document gives the impression that all of the intentions and resources of the organization are thoroughly defined, integrated, and aligned.

The plan is presented and officially authorized in a ceremony conducted by upper level Managers. In public administration, for instance, this ceremony is an act of the elected officials. It looks and feels like a serious effort at governing the organization. Certainly the intensity and fervor people bring to the process would cause one to believe it is of great significance.

A second look, however, indicates the planning process is essentially a pretense. These plans do not guide the actual behavior or performance of the organization. A sure sign of this is how the organization can continue to operate for long periods of time without such a plan or budget while it waits for the plan's final approval. Furthermore, within 90 days the plan is shelved and forgotten, or has been transformed to a mere symbol — like a beautiful art book decorating a coffee table. This second look reveals that if the plan and the actual performance of the organization happen to coincide, it is because the current flows just as it did in the previous year.

The plan delivers a simple message: the coming year is going to be the same as last year, give or take 5 per cent. The organization's Leader often initiates the planning ceremony by announcing what this percentage of variance must be. "Cut by 3 per cent," she announces. Then everyone goes back to last year's plan/budget, does the mandated calculation and adjusts the objectives to fit. The final act is to include contingency clauses, much like the "Act of God" disclaimers in insurance contracts: "if anything but this happens during the year, then all commitments are canceled contracts." The bureaucracy builds into its plan an escape from belief in or commitment to it. In summary, the plan says, "We don't expect things to change very much, and if they do, nobody knows what will happen."

The planning process has little effect on most of the organization's performance. Requests for additional funds and positions may be denied, in which case peoples' plans for raises and promotions are postponed. But the planning ceremony rarely affects anyone's performance anyway. Performance is guided by memory of job descriptions. So, in an attempt to affect performance, the bureaucracy changes its policy and procedures and redesigns and redefines the organization's positions. This endless "refinement of the system" is the organization's best effort at change. Like the crew on the Raft, they always tinker with the rigging and shuffle the cargo into different stacks, without affecting their fundamental direction — the Raft goes with the current.

The inability to affect performance is especially poignant when the planning process is translated into a performance appraisal system to determine pay and promotions. Motivational theory suggests this makes the plans so personal that they must significantly affect an individual's performance. But bureaucracy depersonalizes the system of appraisal by creating formulas and forced statistical distributions among pay grades and appraisal ratings. The range of awards is so small, typically between 3 and 5 per cent, that after taxes the amount is psychologically insignificant. In the culture of the Raft, no one wins through performance appraisal and very few ever experience unusual punishment. The message is "same as last year," although it is delivered with all the secrecy and agony one would expect of significant deliberation.

The last evidence of the pretense of planning in the bureaucracy is its annual report. At the bottom line, the report is two messages in a variety of mixtures. First, the good news: some things happened as we had anticipated. The news is good, regardless of the organization's performance, as long as there were no surprises. Second, the bad news: catastrophes occurred and we did the best we could — we hope nothing like this ever happens again. The report is descriptive. It contains no organizational evaluation. Since the plan raised no expectation other than to struggle through another year, a mere description of its struggles is the only report it can make. The only judgment possible is that, since it survived, it must have done something right.

Performance Feedback: for Your Information Only

Without serious planning, performance feedback is bound to be very limited in its contribution to the governance of the organization, and this is surely the case in bureaucracy. Performance feedback takes place, but only as information sharing events. Department heads give activity descriptions—usually highlights. No standards, trend lines, goals, or external comparisons are offered, so no one in the audience is informed enough to question whether what is being presented is good or bad.

Reports are made in this mode because no one expects anyone else in the audience to take responsibility for what has happened. Presenters don't expect problem solving, so they don't report their problems except as a preface to their description of a wonderful solution. They report what is good and strong. So the ceremony, if it has any value at all, is a celebration of successes. The dark side is that such reports encourage denial of organizational failures and the need for change.

Decision-Making: One-on-One

In the culture of the Raft, decisions are not usually made in meetings. Decision-making is done in one-on-one channels of communication. A boss and a subordinate make decisions about the part of the organization the subordinate is managing. The subordinate rarely consults with a peer or direct reports. Decision-making in the organization, therefore, appears to happen in secret. People do not know how the decisions are being made or exactly who makes them. They hear about them only as Pass Downs — mandates from above.

Because the decision-making environment is always a communication between one person of superior formal authority and another person of subordinate formal authority, information, ideas, and decisions tend to flow downward in the organization. The bureaucracy is, therefore, usually characterized by significant amounts of autocratic decision-making.

Group intelligence isn't seen as necessary in the Raft. Things are not expected to change that much. Most of what people need to know is covered by the traditional interpretation of policy and procedure. Critical decisions are prescribed. As long as everyone fulfills the responsibilities of their positions, there will be no need to enrich the decision-making process with group deliberation. Such meetings can only cloud the issues of individual accountability for doing what is already known to be appropriate.

Managing Individual Contributors: Guessing in an Environment of Negative Feedback

Individuals working in Breakthrough Systems are rarely found in bureaucracies. The expectations for their work may have been explained during orientation — years before — but they do not remember. They guess what they are supposed to be doing and, as long as nobody gets on their case, assume they have guessed correctly. The feedback system is almost purely negative. When Individual Contributors make mistakes, management gives them disapproving attention. When they are doing the right thing, management ignores them. Under these conditions, jobs define themselves as "activities one can do that nobody tells you to stop doing."

Managing by negative feedback (sometimes called Management by Exception) leads to an enormous loss of productivity. People fill their time doing the things that don't matter enough for someone to tell them to stop. Large amounts of work emerge that are irrelevant to the organization's purpose and burden it with useless expense.

The negative feedback system, furthermore, discourages all forms of initiative. Once a pattern of behavior that goes unpunished has been discovered, it is wise not to vary from it. For instance, any unusual case or circumstance not immediately understood is interpreted as "outside my domain of authority," and referred to someone else, usually up the organization's hierarchy. The upper channels of the bureaucracy are typically clogged with the paperwork of decisions and actions that should be made at lower levels of management and by Individual Contributors. The overworked executive with a large staff of administrative assistants is typical of bureaucracy; it is the system's way of compensating for its lack of Breakthrough Systems.

Extreme Assumptions of Bureaucracy

In all organizations, the seven Survival Dilemmas described in Chapter One are resolved by some Basic Assumption. All Basic Assumptions are expressed in the way each organizational culture governs itself. In our analysis of stuck cultures, we will only explore the few Basic Assumptions so extreme in their position that they make a significant contribution to keeping the organization inflexible. In the case of bureaucracy, there are three such Extreme Assumptions.

Bureaucracy's Extreme Externalism (Dilemma #1)

The first of the Extreme Assumptions regards the bureaucracy's orientation to its social and economic environment. It assumes its external environment is fixed, well-known, and in full control of the organization. The organization is not capable of changing the environment; it is only capable of going along with it.

The extremity of the bureaucracy's assumption of helplessness is reflected in its practices. Since the external environment is fixed, it should be possible to fix the purpose of the organization and design a perfectly rational structure of positions, policy, and procedure to serve that purpose. In this way, the bureaucracy is seen as an extension of natural order and sometimes goes so far as to claim the authority of nature for its operations. In such extreme cases, to resist or attempt to change the bureaucracy is interpreted as unnatural, dangerous, and criminal — perhaps even evil. When the external environment presents the bureaucracy with catastrophic change, the cause is attributed to mysterious and angry forces to which the bureaucracy can only submit as a humble victim.

This Basic Assumption leads to passivity and hopelessness. In public administration, it often manifests itself in the sense of helplessness when confronting the political forces making up the external environment. "Everything depends upon the whim of the elected officials, and they are not in control of their own whims — they are waving like flags in the swirling winds of public opinion," complains the public administrator. In fact, the executive function gets elected every two to four years regardless of competence or prior experience, and this executive turmoil keeps the bureaucracy confused. Elected officials give up belief in their plans and hunker down around a few simple policies, procedures, and services — hoping the political storms will pass over them without causing too much destruction. In their hearts is the righteous vision of a day when government will be allowed to work properly — stabilized and protected from the corrupting influence of politics. In the meantime, these officials suffer.

When organizations are required to change, the assumption that everything is externally controlled is a primary source of resistance. Many of the Leaders and Individual Contributors make the unconscious assumption that they do not have the power to change the system. They expect those who try to be discovered, punished, or just worn down. They withhold their commitment to the change effort and wait for the "foolishness" to pass.

Bureaucracy's Extreme Universalism (Dilemma # 3)

The next significant assumption defining the uniqueness of bureaucracy is its extreme universalism. The bureaucracy believes there is one set of policies and procedures predicting and prescribing everything needing to be done, and it sees disobedience of these rules as the cause of all its problems. This assumption is closely related and complementary to the assumption of external control. The natural world is an orderly system, operating according to a discoverable set of natural laws. Human organizations should operate by similar and compatible rules. This gives the bureaucracy its impersonal nature. Who you are or how you are feeling is quite irrelevant. What matters is — do you know your position, are you aware of its constraints, and are you performing the responsibility of that position without violating the constraints? If you operate within the universal rules and procedures, everything will be fine.

This extreme universalism poses another significant source of resistance to becoming Change-ABLE. Every suggestion of change is seen as a challenge to the entire rationally integrated design of the organization. If the bureaucracy contemplates change at all, it thinks of it in terms of enlarging the scope of the organization's purpose and expressing that enlargement in a new organizational structure and procedure. Instead of embracing new practices, it only defines the practices as a new set of policies and procedures. The bureaucracy sometimes goes so far as to consign these policies and procedures to a new department to further refine and audit the implementation. It is as if the bureaucracy is saying, "Yes let's change — but in the usual, slow, methodical way. After all, any change that must be made should be made the right way — as we have done it in the past."

The bureaucracy's extreme universalism also keeps it from noticing the huge number of exceptions to its procedural solutions. It explains away the exceptions using the familiar language of its policies and procedures. The fundamental conclusion is always, "This exceptional case is not very important, it will soon pass away and it is not, therefore, a legitimate subject of our concern or action." If the world isn't actually operating in conformity with the bureaucracy's policies and procedures, the bureaucracy believes it soon will be and waits in faithful denial for the coincidence.

Bureaucracy's Extreme Individualism (Dilemma # 6)

The third assumption of bureaucracy distinguishing it from the Change-ABLE organization is its extreme adherence to individualism. This individualism is expressed by dividing up work into tiny pieces for autonomous performance. Every position is defined in such a way that whoever fills the position is guaranteed to meet the position's requirements! The individual is expected to get into the position, perform all its specified tasks, and remain within the prescribed constraints of its responsibilities and authority. The whole process of rational analysis —dividing work into its specific subparts — also divides the workforce. Within the bureaucracy, individuals are expected to work alone rather than as members of an interdependent group.

The assimilation process makes individualists of Managers and employees within the bureaucracy. When it is suggested the organization depend upon group work for speed and flexibility, individualists seem puzzled and suspicious.

The puzzlement results from the existing perception that bureaucracy *is* a form of group work. It is a collection of carefully designed parts that interact in well-defined ways to achieve a common purpose. What else could group work be? As soon as these individualists are collected in a room, they try to define the meeting's purpose, divide it up into parts, and assign a part to each member. Of course, before a member can accept such an assignment, it must fit within the domain of the member's current organizational position and will have to be approved by the member's boss! If there is any difficulty in achieving the group's purpose in this way, the group tends to elect one of two options: redefine the purpose so it can be divided into independent units of effort and distributed within the constraints of the organization's current design — i.e., adapt the group to the status quo—or, claim the meeting was not well-planned in the first place and disband.

Group work, when suggested to bureaucrats, sounds like a way of confusing the issues of accountability — a participant might get punished for someone else's mistake! This shouldn't happen in a world properly designed and following the right set of policies and procedures; such injustice is too high a price to pay for flexibility and speed. Group work, therefore, like any other violation of the constraints of one's position, is a mistake — a temptation that should be rejected.

It is extremely difficult to instill creative tension in the culture of bureaucracy. The bureaucracy usually has to be in the late stages of disintegration before members awaken from their habitual passivity. Such awakenings come about only after a large monopoly is torn asunder by its government, when the institutions of banking or transportation are deregulated, or when an enterprise such as the military-industrial complex is forced to commercialize its services. We are beginning to see it in the privatization of much of what has been historically considered the services of public administration. The remnants of the great bureaucracies that are able to transform themselves into viable commercial enterprises do so because they are finally able to adopt the practices and assumptions of the Change-ABLE organization.

Summary

This chapter explored one of the world's most common organizational forms — bureaucracy. Within its five functions of management, we found none of the Key Management Practices that would make bureaucracy Change-ABLE, and we discovered its management practices are the habitual expression of certain Extreme Assumptions.

1. Bureaucracy is so slow and inflexible, it functions only where the social and economic environments remain stable and free of competition.

2. The structure of bureaucracy is a large, tall, symmetrical hierarchy, operating as a system of one-on-one channels of communication between each subordinate and his or her one boss. The design of the structure is believed to be perfectly matched to the organization's tasks, and its operation is believed to be rationally directed by a comprehensive set of policies and procedures. The channels are overloaded and the system tends to work slowly, with highly distorted information and a serious lack of integration.

3. Planning in bureaucracy is essentially pretentious — the actual direction of the organization is a function of policy and procedure. The organization doesn't expect much change, and has little confidence in its ability to deal with change if it occurs.

4. Performance feedback in bureaucracy is also minimal. Performance is described merely for purposes of information sharing, and Managers tend to report only recent highlights — the communication events become ceremonies of self-congratulation.

5. Decision-making is accomplished in one-on-one communications between a boss and a subordinate. Inevitably, the boss dominates making the process autocratic and limiting decision-making to the information and opinions of the boss. Little initiative is taken by anyone to exceed the prescriptions of the organization's policy and procedure.

6. Individual Contributors are managed through negative feedback, i.e., punishment or threats of punishment for failure to follow

policy and procedures. Their objective is to find the pattern of behavior provoking the least attention from management, and to refer all exceptions to the pattern to someone else.

7. The three Extreme Assumptions supporting Bureaucracy's management practices are:

- Bureaucracy's Extreme Externalism (Dilemma #1) — a belief that its own existence is an expression of the order inherent in the natural, social, and economic environments, and that it is completely subservient to these external forces.
- Bureaucracy's Extreme Universalism (Dilemma #3) — the belief that there is a natural set of rules applying to all, and that those rules are expressed in the design, policy, and procedures of bureaucracy.
- Bureaucracy's Extreme Individualism (Dilemma #6) — the belief that each person should have a well-defined job perfectly integrated with all other tasks through the organization's design, policy, and procedure. The system expects each person to work in perfect isolation, using channels of communication only to confirm that all is being done as expected.

Because of its inflexibility, bureaucracy is under attack everywhere in the world. As it crumbles, its functions must be picked up by a more intelligent organizational form. There is a huge amount of work to be done, and it should be done by Change-ABLE organizations.

The Dory Regatta:
Working Alone ...Together

Overview

Chapter Five describes the culture of professional associations (Dory Regattas). Professionals overlook the Key Management Practices and operate from certain Extreme Assumptions that make their efforts to cooperate less effective than Change-ABLE organizations.

1. Professional work, or case-by-case problem solving, has certain inherent characteristics that have traditionally isolated Professionals from managerial control and from each other.
2. The structure of professional associations is usually a two-level hierarchy dominated by a council of Professional practitioners. These practitioners tend to disrupt the efforts of the lower support personnel to get organized.
3. Planning is minimized by the Professionals' inability to predict the volume and specific nature of the work they must do — they simply respond to as many opportunities as possible.
4. Performance feedback in professional associations is not frequent or comprehensive; once certified, Professionals are usually left to evaluate themselves.
5. Decision-making is a process of voting, which is vulnerable to political power-play and fundamentally irrational.
6. The ambiguity of goals and responsibilities makes self-management very weak among Professionals and their support staffs.
7. The weak management practices of Professionals are habitual expressions of two Extreme Assumptions:

   - Professionalism's Extreme Internalism (Dilemma #1)
   - Professionalism's Extreme Individualism (Dilemma #6)

The Inherent Individualism of Professional Work

Chapter Three introduced the Dory Regatta as a symbol for professional cooperation and professional organizations. The Dory Regatta culture is most common among medical Professionals, scientists, engineers, lawyers, and consultants. It is also found as a subculture of corporate staff Professionals, such as planners, accountants, and Human Resource specialists.

Professional work, by definition, is case-by-case problem solving. Each problem is potentially unique, and slight differences between problems may be very significant. The quality of Professional work depends upon being well-trained for both diagnostic and prescriptive work.

The fact that every problem is potentially different prohibits Professionals from using most of the disciplines familiar to bureaucracy. No one can completely predict the procedures a Professional must follow. Even Professionals will not know what is appropriate until they have been introduced to the specific problem. For Managers who earnestly want to control and systematize human performance, the Professional is, therefore, a mystery and a frustration. If the Manager intrudes with traditional methods of standardization appropriate to routine work, the quality of the Professional's performance is destroyed.

Professionals have always been a problem for management hierarchy and something of a threat to its system of authority. They come from a different kind of power base: knowledge power. Their power is growing because they have invented tools to automate routine work. The work remaining for humans to do is increasingly made up of the unique cases requiring their skilled analysis and inventive solutions. The formal authority of management (its traditional control over access to the organization's resources), is increasingly challenged to demonstrate its ability to add value to the inventiveness of its Professional Individual Contributors — to find ways to make large-scale cooperation an advantage for those whose work always produces a unique solution for a unique customer.

The traditional answer to the problem of Professional governance is to replace the specificity of standards and procedures with more generalized goals. The Professional oaths and codes of ethics are examples of this approach. They operate as guidelines within which Professionals are expected to manage their work. Accordingly, doctors must do whatever they can to maintain patient health and to prolong life. The rest of governance, to the extent that it exists at all, is to establish standards by which individuals can be certified as members of the profession. The training processes are certified, and the trainees are examined and tested.

Once Professionals are certified, they are the equal of any other such Professional. The profession is an association of peers — a group of colleagues. This peer status is very precious and important to Professionals. Peer status acknowledges Professional autonomy — the fact that no one has the authority to tell any other Professional what to do. No association of Professionals must ever assume the right to interfere in the self-management of its individual practitioners.

Structure: Two Levels in Conflict

Professional organization, then, is a very loose sort of large-scale cooperation. When we look at its first management function, structure, we notice how flat it is. In a clinic, law office, or consulting organization, the Professional partners form a governing committee, comprising the upper level of the structure. Everyone else makes up the lower level, which is there to serve and support the Professional performance of the level above. The Professionals have both formal and knowledge power superiority.

These two layers represent the organizational chart. From each circle representing a Professional in the upper level, draw a line to every other circle in the level below. The message here is that any support person can be called upon for service by any of the Professionals at any time.

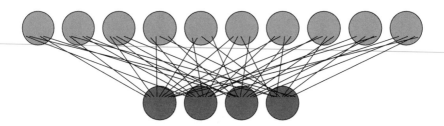

The Professional Organization

For economic reasons, the lower level of support is quite lean, since support staff is seen as overhead. Only by sharing these resources can Professionals achieve economy of scale from their association.

Professionals expect to be served at any moment by whomever is available. This, of course, creates considerable tension within the organization. Professionals compete for support services and especially for the attention of the most talented. Those serving in support roles are constantly whipsawed by the demands of the Professionals — with the most talented under the most stress. Since Professionals assume they are peers to each other, there is no one empowered to make resource decisions. As a consequence, the competition among Professionals takes covert form and the ambiguity in the roles of the support people never gets cleared up.

Planning: Sheer Opportunism

When one analyzes planning practices in Professional organizations, the absence of formal planning is immediately obvious. The mode of operation is to allot a certain amount of time to do as much work as possible. Professionals literally "hang out their shingles" and see how many clients come. It is usually slow at the start, and as business picks up, Professionals try to catch up and overload themselves. Many exhaust themselves in the process.

In response to the suggestion of Performance Planning, Professionals say their work is too unpredictable. Neither the volume of work nor its specific nature is foreseeable. Doctors can't predict how many patients they will see or by what method they will attempt to heal those patients. Engineers can't tell how they are going to design a product; they don't know until they've started the project. So how can a Professional make a Performance Plan except to say "I'll do as much of my work as well as I can, and of what use is such a plan?"

The budgeting process is an attempt at planning. However, this process often involves looking at how much money is left over from the prior period of work and deciding how much of it to spend on capital improvements as opposed to taking it out in salaries or bonuses. Using the budget as a tool — a simple guideline for revenue generation, operational efficiency, capital improvements, and profit — is beyond the scope of the planning efforts of many professional organizations.

Performance Feedback: Maintaining Appearances

Performance feedback is nearly nonexistent in the professional organization. The closest this culture gets to performance feedback is its determination of bonuses for Professional partners. This is usually done according to a formula that considers little else beyond revenue generation and the acquisition of new clients. An argument can be made that these criteria are ultimately reliable as measures of Professional work. In fact, much malpractice and fraud go undiscovered for years before the effects show up in these bottom line metrics.

Another practice called performance feedback is the professional convention or meeting. Here, certain members of the profession make presentations regarding their work. The only cases usually examined are the ones in which leading edge issues or techniques are explored and in which some degree of success has been achieved. Occasionally, there may be some tough questions or challenges mounted from the audience. But the event is expected to inform and educate the audience, not evaluate the presenter, and the discussion is usually polite and devoid of substantial or critical thinking. The event generally promotes a little professional development and bolsters the status of those who chose to make presentations.

The only other form of performance feedback in the Dory Regatta is the rare occasion when a member is censured. A member must repeatedly and flagrantly violate the guidelines of the profession to merit such attention. Serious charges either from clients or other Professionals must be brought against the defendant. Then, typically, a panel of fellow Professionals convenes to examine the situation. Again, the Professionals assume they are the only people able to understand the situation well enough to make a judgment about the quality of their work. The event is rare, the findings often inconclusive, and the sanctions usually mild. Clients are supposed to trust this process of self-evaluation. The suspicion, of course, is that Professionals are as much interested in preserving their profession's reputation as they are in exposing incompetent practitioners within their ranks.

Once Professionals are certified, it is unlikely their work will ever be carefully reviewed again. The lack of genuine performance feedback among Professionals accounts for the abuse of knowledge power. The growing number of spectacular cases of fraud and malpractice is diminishing the professions' credibility in the minds of the public. It is doubtful the absence of this management practice will be tolerated much longer.

Decision-Making: Irrational Voting

In the Dory Regatta, voting is the usual decision-making process. All important decisions are reserved for the Professionals, and, once again, their devotion to peer status provides everyone with equal influence. The procedure honors the principle of equality by giving each Professional one vote for all issues of significance, i.e., all issues affecting a Professional's ability to work. The governing body of Professionals gets together, discusses the issues, and reaches resolution by majority vote.

This procedure, in spite of appearing to be fair, polite, and reasonable, is actually a highly irrational form of power play. The evidence is in two parts. First, prior to the meetings, the Professionals form and confirm their alliances on the critical issues. Forms of irrational persuasion — bargaining, lying, manipulation, and intimidation — are often involved in the process of power block formation. Second, if you take a secret vote prior to the meeting, you will find very few votes changed after discussion. People come to the meeting with their minds made up and their alliances already formed. At the end of the discussion, the vote is influenced by those predetermined commitments. The discussion is an opportunity to publicly justify one's position — having nothing to do with inquiry or learning. If the discussion goes on for very long, members get restless and call for the motion; they know the discussion is superfluous to the resolution.

These relatively poor decisions often fail in implementation because the disagreeing members have no feeling of obligation to honor them. The idea of disagreeing and committing to perform lacks intellectual and moral integrity for many Professionals. Their position is, "Unless I agree, I am certainly not going to commit. I owe it to myself and to the profession to stand firm by what I know is right." With this justification, the decision is more or less overtly ignored and the power play is continued after the meeting as though the decision had not been made. The majority then tries to placate its rebel minority, reinforcing the refusal to commit and weakening every decision. As a result, the Professional organization remains loose and impotent as an association, or it breaks apart, acknowledging the fact that it is not a very effective form of cooperation.

Managing Individual Contributors: Ambiguity and a Contest for Resources

At the individual level of Professional performance, nothing resembles a Breakthrough System. The only operating expectation is to do one's best on every case that comes along. The individual's ability to evaluate performance for pace and quality is impossible with such ambiguous expectations and results in a completely irrational struggle for resource control. Since there is no way to demonstrate what is actually required to be effective, the struggle for control of resources becomes a matter of pure desire and the power to acquire. The behavior expresses the principle: get as much of the most precious supplies, equipment, and talent as possible.

A Professional's support staff sometimes tries to plan, create job descriptions, and set some work standards. This is very difficult to do, however, given the frequency of interruption by the Professionals they serve. Any semblance of hierarchy or priority attempted by support people is soon circumvented by the mandates of the Professionals who insist on being served by whomever they choose, whenever they choose. Professionals usually undermine every effort to support them in a systematic way, as anything requiring such cooperation is at odds with those who have power in the professional organization.

Extreme Assumptions of Professionalism

All seven of the Basic Assumptions identified in Chapter One are at work in professional organizations. But we will only examine those which, by virtue of their extremity, contribute to the inflexibility of professional organizations. There are two such Extreme Assumptions that act as sources of resistance when Professionals first start using the practices of Change-ABLE organizations.

Professionalism's Extreme Internalism (Dilemma #1)

Professionals genuinely believe in their ability to exert control over the external environment. They see themselves as masters, not victims. They master their own bodies and spirits through years of disciplined study and practice. They master vast amounts of information. They acquire, control, and release the most enormous energies of the universe. They learn to teach and inspire others, moving through life as sources of influence and forces the environment must contend with. The professional organization represents an extreme form of internal orientation to the environment.

Professionals are proactive. They are impatient with those who are passive, feeling that it is better to make things happen than to wait and see what happens. They condescend to those who do not acquire and exercise the power of knowledge. Professionals are critical thinkers, always tempering respect with a learned skepticism. Too much belief in anything will eventually block progress toward greater knowledge and the perpetuation of life and well-being.

From this extreme internal orientation to nature comes a rebel spirit. Historically, the professions emerge from a period of social persecution, and the memory still seems fresh in the minds of their practitioners. Professionals question all current systems and instinctively defy all forms of governance.

Professionalism's Extreme Individualism (Dilemma #6)

The second Basic Assumption unique to professional organizations is their extreme belief in individualistic strategy for survival.

Many Professionals would go beyond saying, "By taking care of themselves, each individual makes his or her best contribution to the survival of the group." They also might say, "By taking care of myself, I enhance my ability to take care of others." These benevolent caretakers are individuals who see themselves as uniquely precious.

Most Professionals are unsympathetic to group work. They see it as a means of seeking and enforcing agreement —social pressure to adopt ideas that appear to be intellectually compromised or downright stupid. To the Professional, the word "meeting" connotes time wasted that could be spent in useful pursuit of more information.

The individualistic mindset of Professionals may come from their long sojourns in academic institutions. The academic community's abhorrence of plagiarism and advocacy of intellectual freedom combines to make the long hours of study a lonely hike beyond the end of the trail. This profound respect for originality is deeply embedded in the character of most Professionals by the time they achieve their certification, causing many of them to become secretive — afraid of being "ripped off" by other members of the group. It also causes many of them to think of themselves as insufficiently "brilliant" and "creative"— and, therefore, defensive about the disclosure required in group work. The academic community's pursuit of originality is often achieved by sacrificing Professional cooperation.

Without the inclination to respect group work, Professionals can never develop the skills required for teamwork. Their own awkwardness dooms every meeting they attend to the very failure they find so distasteful. Without an understanding of group inquiry and problem-solving, their conviction that they would do better working alone is reinforced. Professionals believe poor thinking is inherent in the nature of groups, and group work is not often seen by them as a set of skills to be mastered.

The combination of these two Extreme Assumptions — the internal orientation to nature and individualism — expresses itself in the practices of Professional organizations. When the practices are replaced with those of the Change-ABLE organization, the assumptions are challenged, often accompanied by misunderstanding, resistance, and distress. However, the inherent needs of Professionals are better served by Change-ABLE practices. As they continue their quest for expertise, Professionals find themselves knowing more and more about less and less. Remaining alone in their individual isolation renders their discoveries and inventions impractical. The practices of the Change-ABLE organization integrate Professionals' gifts through genuine teamwork, bringing their work to full social and economic significance. In this way, the Professionals' old assumptions are modified in their extremity to support their participation in a more flexible and powerful form of organization.

Professionals are now discovering that information technology makes possible the exploration of such complex new knowledge, the old knowledge compartments are no longer worth habituating. Great breakthroughs are coming from the interaction of Professionals across the lines of their traditional specialties. They are discovering that the process of interdependence — teaching each other and learning from each other — is essential to new levels of knowledge power. This territory of knowledge is large enough to provide plenty of glory for everyone and there is little chance for any individual to claim a truly significant piece of it. The full use of information technology necessitates intellectual interdependence and cooperation. At the vanguard of knowledge power, therefore, we find the professions attempting to dismantle their Dories and fashion instead sleek-hulled, Sea-Going Canoes.

Summary

Chapter Five described the culture of professional associations. Its management practices and Basic Assumptions are not those of Change-ABLE organizations.

1. The inherent uniqueness of the problems Professionals solve has created a tradition of separation, both from the direct-and-control practices of hierarchy and from governance by each other.
2. Their organizational structure is relatively flat, consisting of peerage of Professionals over a second layer made up of support personnel. Roles and relationships are ambiguous, and the exercise of authority is weak and confusing.

3. Planning is minimal in professional associations. In fact, Professionals are opportunistic, taking on as much work as they can given the limits on their personal energy and time.

4. Performance feedback comes from voluntary submission of Professionals' work as case studies for their colleagues — a process biased in attention to new and successful work. Any form of criticism or censure within the professional association is rare, and clients suspect that the disciplinary procedures that are used are distorted to protect the reputation of the profession.

5. Decision-making is a process of voting, subject to irrational pressures like political power-play. The resolutions of the decisions are often ignored by the outvoted minority.

6. The management of both the Professionals and the support staff is characterized by ambiguous expectations, minimal feedback, and an irrational struggle for resources.

7. Management practices are habitual expressions of two Extreme Assumptions:

    - Professionalism's Extreme Internalism (Dilemma #1): Internal orientation to the natural, social and economic environments — a belief that, as Professionals, they can and should master the natural world, including all aspects of human nature.
    - Professionalism's Extreme Individualism (Dilemma #6): Individualism — a rebel-like adherence to the autonomy of each Professional.

The complexity and scale of the problems Professionals now confront at the cutting edge of their work necessitates a more sophisticated form of cooperation. To deliver greater social and economic benefits while upholding the quality of their work, Professionals must integrate their talents and adopt the Key Management Practices of Change-ABLE organizations.

The Galley — Under
Autocratic Control

Overview

This chapter describes Representative organizational cultures (Galleys). These organizations dominate private enterprise and often see themselves as focused, fast, and flexible. But in fact, they lack the Key Management Practices and Basic Assumptions that could make them a match for Change-ABLE organizations.

1. We call this culture Representative organization because it encourages Managers to represent the interests of their various departments at all times. Managers are urged to devote themselves to the success of their various departments and are promoted on the basis of departmental performances. Galley culture has dominated private enterprise since the end of World War II, and its management practices are heavily reinforced by its past successes.

2. The structure of the Representative organization is a large, fragmented hierarchy in which interdepartmental cooperation is very weak.

3. Planning in Representative organizations is important, not as a means to organizational guidance, but as a weapon in the contest for organizational resources.

4. Performance feedback in Representative organizations is essentially a one-on-one communication as in bureaucracy, though it is sometimes performed in a group setting. Meetings are Nominal Groups in which all agenda types are used by the departmental representatives to confirm that the autonomy and resources of their own departments are not threatened by any other department's claims.

5. Decision-making is often misnamed as "consensus" or "consultative" in Representative organizations. Beneath the group discussion is an actual process of voting accompanied by intense and irrational power-play.

6. Individual Contributors also form informal groups for self-management, often in competition with other such groups and in opposition to management.

7. Management practices in Representative organizations are a
    habitual expression of three Extreme Assumptions:

    - Representative Organization's Extreme Internalism (Dilemma #1)
    - Representative Organization's Extreme Particularism (Dilemma #3)
    - Representative Organization's Extreme Individualism (Dilemma #6)

The Prevalence of Representative Organization

In management literature, "Representative" organization connotes a culture where Managers act as representatives of their
department's concerns. In our watercraft analogy, we refer to this
culture as a Galley, a large boat full of rowers facing backward and
dependent upon the Leader to get the boat to its destination. The oars
are analogous to the organization's departments, and the rowers, like
the department heads, are only responsible for pulling their oars —
taking care of their own departments.

Representative organizations rose to dominance during the
twentieth century and are now the most prevalent form of private
enterprise. We will take some time exploring and illustrating this stuck
culture because, in our opinion, its inflexibility poses not only a
problem for the private sector, but a potential problem for global
politics as well. When these large enterprises get into competitive
trouble, as they now are, they tend to look to their government's
military power both for protection and for additional competitive
leverage. It is especially important to understand Representative
organizations to assure their peaceful passage to renewal as Change-
ABLE organizations.

Structure: Departmental Turf Wars

The Galley's structure has many layers and many vertical
divisions. There are serious efforts everywhere to flatten these structures, but it never seems possible without cutting the organization up
into many more semiautonomous business groups. The organization is
then exposed to certain strategic risks: it has divided itself up so that
better integrated competitors can conquer it piece by piece. Further-

more, it is often only a matter of months before new business units are replicating the tall hierarchy of the parent from which it was spawned. Galley culture loves many layers of structure!

The Galley's hierarchy appears to operate as a system of one-on-one communications and management staff meetings. Closer observation reveals the meetings do not operate as a system of Linked Teams. Team members do not come to share accountability for the results in the Leader's plan or to participate in the exercise of the Leader's domain of authority. Instead, they come to represent their departments (hence the name, Representative organization). The meetings are usually described as information sharing, but even a cursory evaluation of the meetings against this stated purpose will find them unjustified in terms of effectiveness and cost.

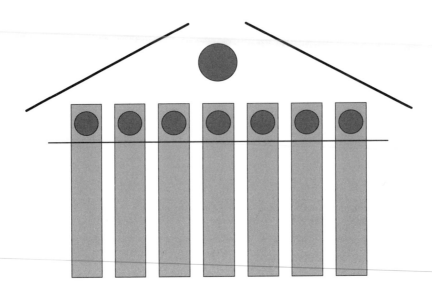

The Representative Organization

Instead, these meetings serve two other purposes more or less consciously. First, each meeting allows representatives to confirm that their delegated realm of authority and allocation of resources have not been diminished, nor their autonomy threatened. Representatives come to the meeting to be sure they are staying out of each others' way. They don't meet to link the organization together, they meet to assure themselves that working together can still be avoided. The meetings are a clear case of Nominal Group work — the "group" exists in name only. This regular assurance of autonomy is, without a doubt, the most important political accomplishment of every Regular Meeting in the Galley culture.

The second purpose of the meeting is to provide an arena for the seasonal contests (usually annual) among representatives for the resources available in the Leader's domain of authority. These contests emerge around three issues: personnel policy, procedure, compensation, and benefits; budget allocation; and cost cutting. The only linkage occurring in these meetings involves temporary alliances assuring competitive advantage over other representatives. Victory in these contests is usually signaled by movement to a higher level in the hierarchy.

Representatives attend the meeting to guard possession of their current oars (the ones awarded in the last contest) and to seek opportunities for larger ones. The ultimate objective is to win the right to pull the largest oar in the boat. By acquiring larger oars, each representative secures the loyalty of the subordinates in their departments. This is the behavior the culture calls "Leadership." Yet the representatives aren't responsible for where the boat is going – that's the Leader's role.

These practices don't create successful cross-functional work. The Galley has committees reaching horizontally across portions of its hierarchy, but these meetings are even less effective than the Regular Meetings described above. The groups have so little influence on the organization's use of resources, they usually die for lack of interest within a few months. As in the bureaucracy, the functions insist on being represented, but representatives with no authority are sent to engage in decision-making. As a result, the meetings are large in size, weak in influence, and intolerably slow to act.

The Galley culture tries to compensate for its weak integration with matrix management. However, the functional Leaders see such cross-functional structures only in terms of raiding their resources, violating their autonomy, and competing for status and promotion. Matrixed project Leaders must run across the traditional functional structure as though they were running a gauntlet. They see the organizational functions as sluggish fortresses to be infiltrated and charmed into productivity for their projects, and they see other project Leaders as competitors for the functional group's resources. Authority and priority issues turn matrix management into a pack of snarling dogs, in which many are mortally wounded. This creates unbearable ambiguity about authority — a power vacuum that threatens to implode the whole structure. Only a firm hand from high in the Galley's hierarchy holds the melee under control. Matrix management in Representative culture, therefore, tends to invite autocracy and to reinforce the culture's Leader dependency.

Integration and linkage are relatively weak in the Galley culture. The hierarchy depends heavily on one-on-one communication between boss and subordinate, thus retaining many of the operational characteristics of the Raft — autocratic, with clogged channels of communication making it slow and inefficient.

Finally, hierarchy in the Galley is a symbol of status. A person's elevation and departmental size are reliable indicators of status. It is systematically correlated to compensation, benefits, and other privileges, such as special parking places, corner suites with windows, and quality furnishings. These symbols of position are appropriate in the Galley and are taken quite seriously.

Planning: A Contest for Resources

Unlike the Raft, the Galley culture takes planning seriously. However, its weak integration defines its articulation of strategy — the organization doesn't have *a* strategy, it has a *set* of strategies — a different one for each major department. Yet, strategic thinking does happen. Strategies are accompanied by goals, objectives, and tactics that are distributed throughout the structure as a set of annual and quarterly Performance Plans. These plans stake out domains of authority and autonomy and are one of the weapons used in the contest for resources — the rationale behind budgets. They also attempt to establish the metrics by which compensation and promotion will be determined. Planning is obviously not an empty process.

A closer look at plans in the Galley reveals a common form. It is an outline — categories of concern with lists of specifics. Each item in the list is preceded with the graphic dot called a bullet, so we call this form a "bandolier"— a belt that holds a lot of bullets. When the bullets are counted, there are often 30 or more!

This long list robs the plan of its most important function — to create a focus of attention. If you turn bandoliers face down and ask their authors to tell you what's in them, most cannot remember more than 20 per cent —they usually can't even remember the major categories. If you go even further and ask authors what they expect their departments to accomplish during the next 90 days, much of what they describe is unrelated to anything in the plan. Clearly, the bandolier does not cause clarity and energy focus in the organization; it isn't even operational in the mind of its author.

Although the bandolier does not function as a plan, it serves another psychological function. The list is long because of the significance attached to the volume of items one is theoretically managing — the volume expresses the Galley's respect for big oars. Long lists connote large domains of authority and status.

Further exploration of the items in the plan reveals the Galley's lack of integration. The categories represent a Manager's domain of responsibility, so they don't come together in a coherent, higher level of accomplishment. This same lack of coherence is noticeable among the bullets within each category. Each item is an isolated activity — expressing the Galley's concern for autonomy. The plan is not memorable because it lacks logical design. Without the document, the author would not be able to keep track of what subordinates have been permitted or urged to do.

Another feature of Galley planning practices is the large number of managerial activities appearing in the plan's list — activities intended to clarify expectations, provide performance feedback, and ensure appropriate utilization of resources. The presence of these activities in the plan is a further expression of the Galley's confusion regarding autonomy, delegation, and accountability.

The Galley's drive for autonomy is so strong, it corrupts the understanding of delegation. In the Galley, subordinates don't see themselves as participants in the Leader's authority; they see themselves as "taking away" a piece of it. They believe authority delegated to them belongs to them exclusively — the Leader isn't supposed to be involved any more. If the Leader continues to monitor the use of delegated authority, the Leader is expressing distrust and this shames the subordinate. The subordinate reciprocates by calling the boss a "micro-Manager," a supreme form of slander in the Galley. Now, even the vertical chain of command begins to break up.

When a Leader buys into this misunderstanding of delegation, it is logical to assume that one cannot be held accountable for authority that was "given away." Managers start looking around for something they can claim with autonomous control. They list the activities of their own managerial processes instead of the results these processes are supposed to support. They will list responsibilities for delivering plans, budgets, and operational reports, their implementation of new software and hardware for management information systems, their recruitment and training of the work force, and their programs for building teamwork and morale. The presence of these managerial processes in a plan is an announcement of the author's expectation of rewards for going through the motions of management — whether or not they yield results. Management accountability is severely damaged in this way.

Another thing to notice about plans in the Galley is the lack of attention to issues of priority. Priorities are either totally ignored or they are addressed in ordinal terms (number one in importance, number two, etc.). Both cases lead to operational confusion.

The plans ignore issues of priority, because Managers don't want to offend and demotivate subordinates working on lower level priorities, or inflate the status and political power of those on higher ones. When the planning process avoids confronting the priority issues, an ambiguous environment is initiated, in which endless covert and distracting power struggles take place. Intelligent cooperation requires the recognition of individual competencies and goals at the core of the organization's performance and the determination of how the rest are to provide support. Teamwork is not promoted by a false expression of equality among Individual Contributors.

When the plan is a long list without mention of priorities, Managers roam around from week to week emphasizing some part of the list. They pull out the lists now and then to remind themselves to whip up some action around a few nearly forgotten items. Lists are great tools for endless intimidation of subordinates. No matter how well subordinates are doing, there will always be list items Managers can use to prove the need for improvement. This powerful but inconsistent attention from management further diminishes organizational focus and integration of action.

When ordinal priority is used, people serve the number one priority too much. Saying, "This is the most important thing," is easily interpreted as, "Do this now and forget everything else." Getting the organization to perform in a coordinated fashion requires a shared perception of relative priorities. Some things are more important than others, but there are always many things that need continuous attention. Expressing priorities in ordinal form tends to obscure this reality.

Planning is an intensely meaningful activity in the Galley. Members of this culture believe in their ability to control their own destiny. Everyone appreciates the enlarged pool of resources the organization's cooperation makes available, but few appreciate the interdependence cooperation requires. Planning becomes a contest for those resources and for the right to use them autonomously.

Performance Feedback: Special Information Sharing Events

The first thing to notice about performance feedback in the Galley culture is that it doesn't happen as part of a regular weekly meeting. It is a special event held on a monthly or quarterly basis. This infrequent schedule is largely due to avoidance; the meetings are not very effective, and the time spent on them is minimized.

The regular members of the management team can't see much purpose in these meetings and wonder why they are required to attend. Observation makes this attitude understandable. Chart the pattern of verbal interaction — who talks to whom — and it becomes obvious that the meeting is a series of one-on-one dialogues between the team Leader and the subordinate members whose work is being reviewed. Very little group discussion ever takes place. So what are the other members of the meeting doing there?

Other members are supposed to be getting information regarding the work of their peers. Performance feedback in a meeting is seen as informational. Significant effort goes into making the presentations interesting and exciting. But members usually leave meetings with almost no memory of what was said by any of their peers. The most they recall is a generalization of the Leader's attitude toward the peer's report. If these meetings had to justify themselves as information dissemination meetings, they would be abolished.

Information regarding a peer's work is not remembered because the information is operationally useless. Reports are not comprehensive; they don't attempt to tell the whole story. In some cases, the validity of what is being reported is questionable. There are motives at work distorting the presentations — the opportunity to look good and avoid punishment. Even if this were not the case, peers fail to get the message because it is actually "none of their business." In the Galley culture, commenting on a peer's performance is literally "out of line" — a violation of one's authority limits. If this behavior is not formally discouraged by the Leader, it is usually covertly disciplined by peer retaliation. In this kind of performance feedback, problems or successes concern only the reporting peer and the Team Leader. They are the only people in the meeting with authority to operate in the peer's domain — and the Leader may be reluctant to exercise authority during the meeting for fear of shaming associates before their peers and gaining a reputation for being a "micro-Manager."

If, in fact, a peer's performance is damaging someone's ability to perform, the usual solution is to seek approval and resources to do that part of the peer's performance oneself. This quest for resources will not take place in the Work Review but in private discussions with the Leader (lobbying). The decision will eventually be confirmed in the next cycle of planning and budgeting. The solution expresses the assumptions of autonomy and the necessity to control all the resources necessary to meet one's commitments. This solution, however, is only a successful raid on a peer's function and resources. It always has two negative side effects: inefficiency due to the duplication of resources and the increase of rancor among Team members.

The fundamental problem with Work Reviews in the Galley culture is a lack of understanding or acceptance of the concept of shared authority and resources. Meetings are boring because there are no decisions to be made by the group. There is nothing to be done with the information being "dumped" in the meeting, so there is little, if any, discussion. Once again, a Nominal Group process evolves — people getting together physically, but not engaging in rational group process or the synergy of group intelligence. The Work Review in the Galley is dead, because it does not authorize group members to share accountability and resources for the team's goals. In these meetings, members take turns talking about how they pull their oars. How the pulling affects other rowers and the progress of the Galley can be discussed only by that rower and the Leader. There is no real group work to do in this setting. The uselessness of the meeting shows in all the common symptoms: poor planning and preparation, poor atten-dance, tardiness, side discussions during presentations, individuals doing routine paperwork or using laptops to answer E-mail, note passing, drowsiness (even snoring), forgetfulness, and poor follow-up. These meetings are dead because they do not authorize group mem-bers to share accountability and resources for the Team's goals.

Decision-Making: Covert Power Play

Most of the operational decisions of the Galley are made in the bureaucratic tradition: one-on-one discussions between Managers and their direct reports. The weekly written report discussed in private is very common to this culture. As a result, the Galley suffers from overloaded management communication channels, bottlenecked and slow decision-making, autocratic and misinformed governance, confusion, and distrust. The Galley is no longer known for being nimble, creative, or especially intelligent. If it achieves its objectives, it happens through a zigzag pattern of long, shallow curves.

In spite of the one-on-one dominance of operational decision-making, there are a lot of Regular Meetings. The actual function or hidden agenda of these meetings was described earlier: the reinforcement of autonomy and competition for resources. For the most part, these meetings are rather plodding, perfunctory events, but they actually achieve important, formal resolutions with serious consequences for the governance of the Galley. We must observe closely the process by which these important decisions are made. Group members go to great lengths to make their processes look like rational group work, but this, in fact, is not so.

A Case Study in Galley Decision-Making

It was our first opportunity to observe the executive staff meeting of a large California organization. In the pre-conference with the organization's CEO, we were told we would have a great opportunity to see how his executive staff had grown into a participative team, making its crucial decisions through rational group consensus.

The CEO explained that the two-hour meeting would be devoted to one issue: reviewing a Task Force's recommendation brought to the staff by the Team's Leader, the Executive Director of Human Resources. The recommendation was for the organization to reduce healthcare benefits for its retirement plan because the current healthcare benefits could no longer be afforded. Part of the recommendation was to provide a two-year grandfather clause — anyone qualifying for retirement and taking it during the next two years could retain the benefits of the old plan, but all other current or new employees would be required to come under the reduced coverage of the new plan.

The CEO warned us the issue had already been discussed in two other meetings during the last month. The whole organization was well-informed about the proposal and generally unhappy about it. To quiet the organization, the executive team thought it necessary to reach final resolution on the issue in the meeting we were about to witness and had effectively promised that to their employees. "So, " the CEO said, "you're going to have a chance to see my Team make a really tough and important decision — and I think you'll be impressed."

There were seven members on this CEO's team. The first to speak briefly summarized his point of view: he was in agreement with the recommendation and believed the adoption of the new plan was the only fiscally right thing to do. The second speaker was even briefer, essentially seconding the opinion of the first speaker.

The third speaker pointed out that some of his employees had formed their own Task Force. They had discovered that under at least one scenario of catastrophic health failure, the new plan would deprive a retiree of up to $1.5 million of coverage. This discovery excited a considerable amount of discussion in the CEO's team. Eventually, the Human Resources executive informed the group that the *ad hoc* Task Force had brought the discovery to his attention a couple of days earlier, and he had confirmed it. The discussion served to warn the executive team that there was real potential for serious labor relations problems. But the team member who had brought the discovery to the meeting concluded by saying his Task Force had not been able to find a better resolution to the fiscal problem than the one already proposed. Unhappily, he had to support approval of the recommendation.

As the discussion reached the end of the first hour, we began to notice that so far, only the CEO and five of the members had spoken. The CEO was overtly undecided, while the five verbal members agreed the recommendation had to be accepted. We also noticed that during their discussion, the vocal five continuously made eye-contact with the silent members of the team, Mac and Norm. These two sat attentively, without any body language indicating how they were feeling about the recommendation. They wore poker faces. A silence fell, with everyone looking at Norm. The signal was clear — the group thought it was time for Norm to speak.

Norm sat up, briefly and accurately summarized the discussion he had heard, and stated that he, too, felt the group should accept the recommendation of the Task Force. His remarks were received by the other verbal members of the team with a nearly audible sigh as they turned their eyes expectantly to the last member, Mac.

Mac's poker face transformed into a deep scowl. Then, with a shake of his head, Mac began to speak. "I've been sitting here in silence trying to figure out what to say. I'm very impressed by the quality of the Human Resource Task Force's work. I can find no fault with its logic or conclusions. I sincerely wish I could support it. But I've got a problem — one that makes me feel very embarrassed and angry."

Mac proceeded to explain that 30 minutes before the meeting all four of his direct reports had come to him as a group. They informed him that they were deeply offended by the organization's threat to take from them the retirement benefits they had worked so long to earn. They all qualified for retirement, and as a matter of principle would do so immediately — within the next 30 days — if the new retirement plan were adopted.

"The SOBs have me cornered," Mac hissed through clenched teeth. "I don't have any way of replacing all that managerial experience. My department's performance is going to take a nose dive for at least a year if this happens. The only thing I can think of to forestall the crisis is to make an exception for my four subordinates. Perhaps if we extend a five-year period for retirement rather than the recommended two, we can mollify them and give me time to implement a succession plan. Without such an exception, I must oppose this recommendation. I think its effect on my department will be a disaster for the whole organization."

After a brief silence, the other members of the team turned their eyes toward the CEO and initiated another hour's worth of discussion. It was basically a plea to adopt the plan as recommended without any exceptions. Toward the end of the hour, the pleading included only thinly disguised charges that Mac had pulled this kind of blackmail on the team before — always to the benefit of his department at the expense of everyone else. It was getting a bit personal and nasty when the CEO finally stopped the discussion.

The CEO then said, "I think the issue has been explored as thoroughly as possible. We promised our people we would make a decision today, so here's the decision: We will adopt the new plan recommended by the Human Resource Task Force, but we will make an exception for the four subordinates reporting to Mac. This is the only exception to be made; no others will even be considered."

The members filed out of the meeting in silent rage. We returned to the CEO's office for our post-conference.

We said, "Your people certainly participate in the discussion with impressive vigor! But what about the consensus decision-making process you promised — where was that?"

The CEO said, "I was expecting to see consensus, but the team just couldn't do it. So I stepped in with the other rational group process — consultative decision-making."

We had our suspicions. One month later, after observing only two other meetings, we were able to predict the outcome of every issue on the agenda of the next meeting. We could also predict how much time would be spent in discussion of each item. The CEO was amused and a little offended. He believed the meetings were a necessary part of the learning required before these decisions could be made. He asked, "How were you able to do that?" We said: "It only took us five minutes. We had a cup of coffee with Mac and reviewed the meeting's agenda with him. We asked how he felt about each item and whether or not he knew someone else on the Team who agreed with him. If anyone else agreed with Mac, we knew the item would be approved. And if Norm happened to be in agreement, the item would barely be discussed — it would be accepted as a *fait accompli*."

We explained to the CEO that, beneath the appearance of consensus decision-making, his executive team was really voting — a classic, Nominal Group Decision-Making process. When group participants know voting is the decision-making process, the discussion changes from education to power play; it becomes a process for building and testing alliances.

In this particular case, voting doesn't seem obvious if it is assumed everyone has one vote — it was six to one, and the CEO called it a victory for the one. But the fact was, the voting was weighted. Mac had seven votes, Norm had three, the first two speakers had only one-half a vote each, and the CEO and other three members had only one vote each. In the case of the retirement plan, there was a deadlock. Mac put his seven votes up against the alliance of all the other members. The CEO broke the tie with his vote, because he could not stand the threat of Mac's failure.

Once this weighted voting was understood, the dynamics of the group became transparent. To get a budget approved, the one-half voters had to win Mac's support prior to the meeting. To buck his resistance, they would, at least, have to know they had Norm's support and then try to line up the others, including the CEO. If they couldn't do that, they had to keep on revising their budget request until one or the other of these strategic alliances could be formed.

When the need for budget reductions hit the organization, the executive team preferred to "cut across the board" — every department reduced by the same percentage. This hit Mac and Norm the

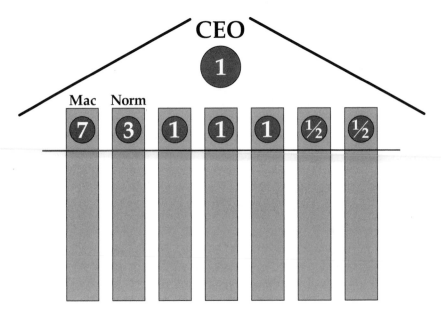

Weighted Voting

hardest, since they had the largest departments. (Mac had about 45 per cent of the organization's total assets under his control, and Norm controlled another 25 per cent). But the real beauty of this irrational resolution is the way in which it leaves the power balance untouched — the weight on everyone's vote goes unchanged.

The only other option this Team could find to cutting across the board was to cut off the weaker departments, especially the 1/2 voters, by selling off their smaller enterprises or absorbing their reduced assets into Mac's or Norm's departments. This option was more likely if the one-half voters, at some time in the past, had somehow offended or threatened Mac or Norm. (Mac and Norm would explain in private that the one-half voters were not really "team players.") The Leaders of these smaller departments usually left the organization, knowing their businesses would never again emerge from the dominance of Mac and Norm.

While this worked politically, the organization, as a result, became more conservative over time. The one-half voters were always the organization's innovative, leading edge. They were small because they were new. They had great profit margins compared to Mac's and Norm's departments but, in absolute terms, they were always comparatively small in gross revenue and organizational reputation. The argument was that in hard times an organization has to "stick to the knitting," preserve its "core competencies," and protect the "cash cow." So, the oldest part of the business always survived the cut.

The scenario ends with intelligent competitors buying up the one-half voters — discarded technologies and enterprising Leaders using them as footholds or expansions of their presence in emerging markets. These competitors grew at the expense of the more conservative, shrinking Galley.

This case is a nearly perfect representation of the Galley's decision-making process. It is irrational power play. Meetings are not opportunities for learning or investing intelligence in decisions. They are a three-ring circus of pure advocacy, persuasion, sales, and intimidation. Disagreement with the dominant alliance can only be expressed covertly, for fear of reprisal. As a result, discussions are full of polite probing, suggestions, and innuendoes — subtle methods for helping the members discover which alliance is dominant with regard to the issue under discussion. Commitment is ensured by removing resources from the control of opponents, and then by threatening future punishment of the non-compliant by the dominant.

The people with the big oars run the ship, without much concern for where the boat is actually going. Even the captain of the Galley must be careful about crossing their authority. If the crew stops rowing, the captain will be fired — the boat won't be going anywhere.

Managing Individual Contributors: Ambiguity, Dissension, and Waste

When management is preoccupied with power play, Individual Contributors are ignored. There isn't much time for providing the basic requirements of high level Individual Contributor performance: clear expectations regarding performance results, a method for self-monitored performance feedback, and control of the resources required to meet the expectations.

Left on their own, Individual Contributors in the Galley culture isolate themselves into a subculture similar to the Dory Regatta, or they form alliances to establish informal standards and work procedures. The first line of management — lead operators, foremen, and supervisors — are usually included in these informal alliances, gaining their primary direction from the dynamics of these small groups. This can lead to efforts to protect Individual Contributors from the demands for hard or unpleasant work, but more often, these informal alliances promote what are believed to be high standards of quality and pace. Most Individual Contributors are actually working hard.

Unfortunately, the failure to integrate Individual Contributor expectations with upper levels of strategy and other organizational function produces results unacceptable to their internal or external customers. Arguments regarding commitments and accountabilities are endless. Small groups use these issues to satisfy their inherent need for identity and to stereotype other groups as inferior. Entrenched distrust and animosity among informal groups of employees are not uncommon. And the Individual Contributors rightfully blame higher level Managers for allowing such unpleasant working conditions to exist. The ambiguity caused by inappropriate and/or poorly defined performance expectation creates a perfect environment for dissension.

The Galley culture is full of information, but performance feedback is scarce. The Galley believes its daily, weekly, monthly, quarterly, and annual cycles of reporting — including performance appraisal — are sufficient. But none of these feedback loops meets the requirement for immediacy (at least every two hours) that would make them effective for Individual Contributors. The larger feedback loops, especially the monthly ones, are useful only to Managers, who will not take the feedback very seriously until its message is replicated by one or two additional months. By the time upper management confirms organizational performance problems, the problems have had time to generate catastrophic consequences. Strangely, the only people knowing the organization is in trouble are the upper level Managers. Their long tolerance of the problem leads people at lower levels to discount its importance.

The feedback loops guiding Individual Contributors are almost entirely informal, and most of them come from fellow workers. Much of the feedback is nonverbal. By watching each other, Individual Contributors constantly reinforce their methods and regulate their rate of work. When they discuss work — what to do or how to do it — they talk with each other far more frequently than they talk with anyone in management. In the stuck cultures, unfortunately, whether the feedback is verbal or nonverbal, it is almost always negative. The message is usually, "Don't do that, stupid!" When approval is expressed, it is used to maintain group membership rather than to reinforce good work. Also unfortunate is the fact that Individual Contributors have a different perception of desirable performance and accomplishment than that held by management. The Galley's work is done in a world separate from upper level management, under a shower of informal and punitive performance feedback.

In the Galley, Individual Contributors almost always underutilize available resources — often by as much as 50 per cent. Much of this inefficiency is due to poor direction, but significant waste is due to a lack of control of the necessary resources. Jobs of Individual Contributors are defined with so little authority or discretion, they must endlessly refer problems to upper management — the same behavior found in bureaucracy. Individual Contributors' access to materials, tools, equipment, and information is restricted by policy and procedure, and much of their valuable time is spent navigating a bureaucratic maze. And, due to the power play behavior of upper level Managers, officiousness and pomposity often accompany the control of access to these necessary resources. As a result, acquisition of the resources necessary to do one's work well becomes a punishing experience. Consequently, Individual Contributors get along with what they've got and delay corrective action when things go wrong. Broken equipment, defective materials, exceptional tasks of all kinds tend to be left lying around for someone else to fix.

The ambiguity, dissension, and waste characterizing the working conditions of Individual Contributors in the Galley are not unknown to upper level management. Their response, however, is rarely creative. They react to problems with hard-nosed mandates and intimidation until workers are forced to formalize their alliances as unions. Or, upper management tries to penetrate the log-jammed confusion with morale improvement programs, assuming that better Individual Contributor morale translates into more productivity. This renders management vulnerable to large-scale emotional blackmail. Individual Contributors can easily excuse poor productivity as management's failure to keep them happy, and they can continually escalate the demands for what happiness requires.

Morale and the will to work are *not* real issues affecting productivity in the Galley; Individual Contributors are simply working without proper focus. They can never be fully productive unless they manage themselves and each other more effectively — with the clear performance expectations, feedback, and resource control provided by Breakthrough Systems. Under such conditions, Individual Contributors work more effectively, not harder, and morale inevitably rises when Individual Contributors know they are being productive in the context of a winning strategy. The issue is whether or not Individual Contributors are able to manage themselves in Breakthrough Systems. In the Galley, there isn't enough organizational integration to provide such a work environment.

Individual Contributors are the sensory system of any organization. When they are confused, the organization's sight is blurred, its hearing is distorted with self-generated noise, and its sense of touch is numbed. Without reliable Individual Contributor participation, an organization's management information lacks the validity necessary for swift and intelligent governance.

Extreme Assumptions of Representative Organizations

As we've said before, all seven of the Basic Assumptions mentioned in the Introduction are at work in all of the organizational cultures. Our attention, in this case, is reserved for three assumptions that contribute to Representative organizations' change resistance.

Representative Organization's Extreme Internalism (Dilemma #1)

The Galley culture assumes its rightful relationship to its environment is one of dominance. To exert such control is seen, at least, as a survival necessity. Often, the exertion of control is seen as a moral obligation. The Galley imagines its rowing as mastery of the sea.

The Galley culture's confidence in its ability to dominate and control its environment makes it fundamentally aggressive rather than responsive. This is displayed in the culture's strategies — the frequency with which it talks of dominating its markets and bashing its competitors. Some of this talk is "hype"; most of it is a serious effort to discover the underlying laws and magic formulas by which markets can be created and manipulated. The failure to dominate is sincerely explained as a failure to understand the right relationship between organizational competencies and the seemingly whimsical needs of customers. The necessary stratagems are close to mystical — the curves and intersections of product life cycles and the tides of international currencies as they are influenced by the moon of economic growth. The Renaissance discovery of the "laws of nature" tantalizes the Galley culture with the prospect of discovering similar "laws of business" that will ultimately lead to control and economic success. The belief that power can be acquired and then become the ultimate solution to problems of survival and success turns its Managers into avid readers and literal applicators of the strategies and tactics of political and military conquest.

Beneath the rhetoric of customer respect and the priority of customer service, the Galley is trying to speak incantations to put customers under its spell. The Galley believes that if you say it right, customers will come, and they will believe in the product without noticing its defects or its inordinate cost. Eventually, enough of the market is monopolized to deprive customers of a choice. The Galley wants to be more than vendor of choice — it wants to be the sole vendor.

The Galley's strong internal orientation to its environment keeps it on a quest for dominance rather than interdependence. It is not in the nature of the Galley to survive by service — it seeks to survive by getting the world to serve it. As an organization, the Galley makes a poor partner, always seeking to take advantage of others while disguising their intention as benevolence. Behind the benevolence is the assumption that the Galley can afford to give (or should give) because it is the richer and more powerful party in the relationship.

The extremity of the Galley culture's belief in the necessity of control and dominance makes it insensitive to its environment. The organization is actually a collection of insensitive departments struggling against each other for dominance and control of resources. Huge amounts of energy are expended in this internal political power play. At the organization's boundary with its external environment is a hard, scaly hide studded with needles, horns, and barbs. It walks through the world perceiving itself to be the author of all good change — considering the objects of change to be shameful and undesirable.

Representative Organization's Extreme Particularism (Dilemma #3)

The only thing tempering the Galley's individualism and keeping it from becoming a Dory Regatta is its particularism. Clusters of individuals divide into pecking orders to form cliques, departments, divisions, regions, business groups, sectors, and corporate staffs. Within each of these subsections, individuals are subjected to others (both formally and informally). The bonds of subjugation include the requirement of loyalty in exchange for the group's protection and special privileges.

Each subsection covertly bends the organization's policy and procedure to exaggerate its rewards and diminish its disciplines as they apply to loyal members. Overtly, however, the same policies and procedures are used to hold everyone outside the loyalty circle to the "letter of the law." This is a common tactic for seeking advantage in the intergroup struggle for resources. Each group wants all the advantages of equal consideration in resource distribution mandated by the organization's policy; each also wants full penalty for violation of policies and procedures levied against everyone else.

In addition to a liberal interpretation of the organization's overall policies and procedures as they apply to their loyal members, each group creates its own set of rules. It creates unique, upgraded job classifications. It redesigns procedures to make itself exempt from certain constraints. It establishes its own system of metrics for performance — both technical and economic. It isolates itself from the interference of other groups by adopting its own set of tools and software systems. Desirable work sites and workplace furnishings are distributed. Special awards are established for group members. Unique perks, including off-site meetings, professional associations, and "edutainment" are provided. The unique set of rules applying to loyal members is both formal and informal. In either case, rules serve to promote the group's unique identity and to reward members for making the group's welfare their primary focus.

Leaders of these loyal bands know of the restlessness of their subjected members. They respect striving for control and dominance as positive forms of energy — as ambition and drive. The Leader's task is to convert this energy to loyalty, defined as surrender of one's autonomy to the authority of the group. The essential accomplishment of Leadership is the ability to secure rewards, advantages, and privileges sufficient to pay for such loyalty. Leaders go to the arena existing at every intersection of the Galley's hierarchy as representatives and champions of their loyal band of subjects. Failure to return from such contests with trophies and booty pours solvent on the glue holding the group together.

Representative Organization's Extreme Individualism (Dilemma #6)

The Galley's culture nurtures and elevates individuals who internalize the belief in control. Dominance and control are the attributes of good Leaders — and are essential to the definition of competence. Those who take small portions of the organization's resources and drive them into larger enterprises, while fighting off competitors both inside and out, receive the laurel wreath of victory.

If, as some suggest, the development of human maturity progresses from dependence, to independence, to interdependence, then it must be surmised that individuals who win in the Galley are arrested in their development. They do not know the difference between dependence and interdependence, and their flight from dependence also makes them resistant to cooperation. When autonomy is surrendered, it is seen as a situation of forced choice — a moment of aggravation and a reminder that ultimate success still lies ahead. The pinnacle of status is achieved when one answers only to one's self.

Summary

Chapter Six recognized the dominance of Representative organizations in the industrialized world, and identified the absence of the Key Management Practices and Basic Assumptions that make Representative organizations less effective than Change-ABLE organizations.

1. Representative organizations encourage their Managers to make the success of their various departments the supreme objective, assuming the organization will thrive as a cumulative effect of the strong departments. In the past, and especially since World War II, Representative organizations have worked well enough to become the dominant form in private enterprise.

2. The structure of Representative organizations is a fragmented hierarchy reflecting the conflict of internal forces seeking autonomous control over resources. It is a structure in which interdepartmental channels of communication are weak and insufficient for maintaining integrated organizational performance.

3. Planning is essentially used as a weapon for declaring domains of autonomy and for laying claim to organizational resources in competition with other departments.

4. Performance feedback is actually communicated through one-on-one channels between superiors and subordinates as in bureaucracy, though this is disguised by the conduct of such communication in group settings. All Regular Meetings in Representative

organizations are actually Nominal Groups — all items on the agenda, including "performance feedback," are used by the members as a means of assuring their own departments' continuing autonomy.

5. Decision-making in Representative organizations is irrational — a process of voting in which some members have more than one vote. Over time, the irrationality of the decision-making is reflected in the organization's growing conservatism and denial of the need for change.

6. Individual Contributors are often left to manage themselves, since Managers are distracted by the politics of departmental survival. Individual Contributors are often found working in informal groups that include their first-line Managers. These groups govern themselves to their own advantage, sometimes in competition with other groups, and often in resistance to upper level management.

7. The management practices of Representative organizations are the habitual expression of three Extreme Assumptions:

    •   Representative Organization's Extreme Internalism (Dilemma #1) — a belief that survival depends upon conquering the rest of the world.

    •   Representative Organization's Extreme Particularism (Dilemma #3) — the belief that survival depends upon securing favored status for the members of one's own department and the establishment of a double standard to assure such a distinction.

    •   Representative Organization's Extreme Individualism — the belief that if everyone takes care of themselves, the whole community will eventually be supported.

Section

III

Practices of Change-ABLE Organizations

7

Memo to Alice: Welcome to Our Change-ABLE Organization

Overview

This chapter is an introduction to the third section of this book. Within this section, the Key Management Practices and Basic Assumptions of the Change-ABLE organization are viewed in detail. Before examining each of these elements in isolation, it is important to appreciate how they go together to reinforce each other in a system of organizational governance.

1. You are invited to assume the role of Alice, who is welcomed to a position of management in a Change-ABLE organization.
2. The welcoming "Memo to Alice" briefly describes the expectations for her management role. These expectations include all five of the Key Management Practices of Change-ABLE organizations: participation in the system of Linked Teams, Performance Plans, Work Reviews, Group Decision-Making, and the maintenance of Breakthrough Systems for the Individual Contributors working in her section.
3. Note anything in the Memo that is disturbing. These areas of discomfort are often indications of certain Basic Assumptions the reader holds that are challenged by the Key Management Practices of the Change-ABLE organization.

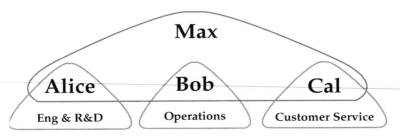

Figure 1

Memo to Alice: The Integrated System of Practices and Basic Assumptions

MEMORANDUM

TO: Alice
FROM: Max
RE: Welcome to the Team

I am delighted that you have accepted the position of section supervisor. We carry a large responsibility. We secure and deploy the technical expertise the company uses to design, evaluate, and maintain its products. The complexity of our work and the speed at which it must be done require cooperation. The purpose of this memo is to suggest some of the ground rules we use to maintain this cooperative effort.

Your Role as Section Supervisor

Everything else I talk about in this memo is intended to create a system of management that will support the people in your section as they do their work from hour to hour each week. If we are successful, we will create a work environment in which Individual Contributors are: clear about the results expected from their performance; able to monitor their own performance against these expectations continuously and reliably; and in control of the resources necessary to meet the expectations. We refer to this set of conditions as "Breakthrough Systems."

It is only from Individual Contributors working in Breakthrough Systems that we get reliable and timely information about the organization's status, issues, and opportunities. It is their good self-management that empowers us to coordinate their work to accomplish the organization's goals. So, at all times, you will be expected to perform the role of section supervisor, the essence of which is to ensure that your people are working in Breakthrough Systems.

Your Role at Department Team Meetings

The weekly Team meeting is the time during which we act to ensure that the resources of our department are properly focused to accomplish our goals. The meeting exercises the *department's* formal authority over all its resources.

I am personally accountable for the department's performance, but I do not exercise the authority alone. The operational issues of the department are exposed to Team discussion. Rational disagreement is not only welcomed, but required. I use the Team members as consultants in the consultative mode of Group Decision-Making.

As Team Leader, I will facilitate and participate in the discussion. In the end, based on what I have learned from the discussion, I make the decision and take personal accountability for it. (I always share the statement of the decisions with the Team members before putting them into action. This gives you another chance to question my understanding, to get feedback from me about how I am responding to your ideas, and to be sure that, as a Team, we are consistent in explaining the reasoning behind the decisions.)

Consultative decision-making is a waste of time if the consultants are ineffective. There are two common forms of ineffectiveness:

1. A Team member may be biased by a narrow concern for the advantage of the section he or she supervises.
2. A Team member may be uninformed beyond the specialties of his or her own section.

Departmental strength depends upon highly

rational coordination—the constant evaluation of priorities and willingness to reallocate resources among the sections. Competitive politics among sections must be confronted and forbidden.

A consultant's advice increases in value only to the extent that it considers all the variables, possibilities, and resources that operate at the departmental level. So as soon as someone joins the departmental Team, he or she must immediately undertake a serious effort to understand all the sections of the department.

It is the responsibility of the departmental Team Leader to protect the Team from any behavior in the mode of "section representative." You can count on me to reward those who most effectively perform as departmental consultants.

Requirements for Your Consultant Role

Your value as a consultant is in direct relationship to your knowledge of your section plus all of the sections managed by your peers. A general familiarity with the other sections is not sufficient. You need to promote your understanding of the other sections to the same depth you already have for the one you supervise! This is not easy—I am still working at it myself. I need your help. Get on this learning curve immediately so you can assist in a responsible process of departmental decision-making.

Your most immediate opportunity for getting on the learning curve is to master the information provided in your peers' Work Reviews at the weekly Team meeting. Each format is tailored for the work being done, but all the reports graphically display the section's current performance and include the following information:

1. The few key results that represent at least 80 per cent of what the section plans to do;

2. The relative priority of each key result;
3. Current status of performance against the section's goals and standards (presented graphically);
4. The current issues affecting the section's performance; and
5. Recommendations for what the Team can do to resolve the issues.

Knowledge of each section's expected results and whether or not they are being achieved provide two immediate advantages:

1. You will be able to follow the discussion of these reviews in the weekly meeting—so the meetings will promote your learning of the other sections.
2. Knowing the expected results will give you a place from which to work backward in understanding each section's key processes.

You are expected to show interest in the sections managed by your peers, and you will find that you are welcome to drop in for observation and/or discussion. Your welcome generally increases in enthusiasm as you demonstrate the sincerity of your interest by doing your homework. Reading and interviewing with subject matter experts is crucial to getting beyond superficiality.

You will notice many opportunities to serve on cross-functional Task Forces and Project Teams. These are excellent ways to get operational familiarity with the personnel and specialties of the other sections. I will work with you to structure these opportunities so you will always be able to make a contribution and push the edges of your organizational understanding. In a while, you will also be given responsibility for leading some of these groups.

During the next few weeks, be sure to spend some one-on-one time with each of your peers listening to their perceptions and advice about the needs and opportunities of your own section. Some of your peers have been on the department Team for years. They know a lot about your section and can speed the process by which you learn to manage it. Please do not assume that you are currently the best informed person for managing your own section.

Toward the end of this first month, you will take your first turn at leading the weekly Team meeting as it reviews your section's work. By then, you will have seen how the procedure goes. I will assign one of your peers to coach and rehearse you for some of your first reports.

During the meeting, make a full and accurate disclosure. Avoid salesmanship. Try to stay off the defensive. Encourage all the members of the Team to evaluate your section's performance. I think you will find we enjoy celebrating your success and are genuinely concerned about and able to help you meet your section's goals. Your success is ours, too!

As you grow into your supervisory position, teach the rest of us what you are learning. Your respect for our concern about your section is demonstrated by questioning and correcting our perception of what goes on — especially during your Work Review.

In addition, you should take the initiative to encourage your peers to visit your section both to observe and discuss current developments. Also, use these visits to broaden the exposure of your subordinates and reinforce their good performance.

Your Boss's Role as Your Link to the Division

Let me assure you that the requirements I have outlined for you are the same as those my boss requires of me. I have been serving on the division Team for three years now.

I am required to maintain considerable expertise in all functions of the division. In the process, I am also developing a large network of personal relationships with people at all levels of the division. I will make these resources available to you for the coordination and implementation of your section's performance. Don't hesitate to ask for such help.

This is a Requirement for Your Performance Evaluation

I want to be explicit about the fact that your role as a consultant during the Team meetings is a performance requirement. It will be an item appearing in your performance review and will be weighted as 20 per cent of your overall rating during this first year. The weight on this part of your performance will rise in subsequent years.

The 20 per cent weight suggests the amount of time you will probably have to spend developing your Team competence. That's about one day a week! If you give the task this kind of effort, it usually takes about two years to reach minimal competence.

Your Introduction to the Team

Finally, I want you to know that we will discuss these ground rules of Team membership as the first item on our agenda at your first Team meeting. It is part of the "ritual" by which we initiate all new members. It reminds us all of our shared authority and accountability for the performance of the whole department.

Again, welcome to the Team.

This memo is an invitation to manage in a Change-ABLE organization. Notice that all the practices are woven together by the way Max expresses his expectations of the Team. His Team is only one in a hierarchy of Linked Teams. All Team members are working with

Performance Plans. Work Reviews are at the heart of Team meetings. Decision-making is the purpose of Team meetings and the process is defined as "consultative decision-making," one of the two forms of Group Decision-Making. Most important is the acknowledgment, right at the front of the memo, that the purpose of the management Team is to support the performance of Individual Contributors.

After imagining what it would be like to fulfill the expectations expressed in this memo, you may feel uncomfortable. Underlying these expectations are some unspoken assumptions — a theory of what it takes for an organization to succeed. The assumptions you are operating from at the present time may be different, and you may find your assumptions being challenged.

If you have any concern for your ability to manage in a Change-ABLE organization, let us offer this assurance. Once you commit to the Change-ABLE organization's particular purpose and put your talents to work on its behalf, the other Managers will surround you with a system that is extraordinarily supportive. Your peers in the Change-ABLE organization will exhibit high levels of competence and may be initially a bit intimidating in this respect. But you will learn that their accomplishments and abilities are largely a function of the Change-ABLE organization's system of governance. It makes the most of all its human assets.

With this glimpse of what it is like to manage in the Change-ABLE organization, you should know that it is a uniquely integrated system of the five practices, and that some of the uniqueness is due to its unusual, underlying Basic Assumptions. Without forgetting this necessary, systemic integration, we will introduce the specific practices and assumptions one at a time.

Summary

Chapter Seven attempted to immerse you in the entire system of Key Management Practices characterizing the Change-ABLE organization.

1. You were invited to assume the role of Alice as a new Manager in a Change-ABLE organization.

2. All five of the Key Management Practices were presented as a system of management responsibilities: participation in the structure of Linked Teams, the use of Performance Plans, involvement in Work Reviews, the requirements for participation in Group Decision-Making, and the assurance of Breakthrough Systems for the Individual Contributors working in Alice's section.

3. You may have experienced moments of discomfort while playing Alice's role as recipient of this Memo. These moments should be noted — they are often symptoms of Basic Assumptions you currently hold that are not aligned with those of Change-ABLE organizations. With this self-assessment, you are prepared to derive greater value from this section of the book.

It is important to remember that all five Key Management Practices are required before a system of governance emerges that accounts for the speed, intelligence, and flexibility of Change-ABLE organizations. While these practices can be described in isolation, as they will be in the following chapters, they do not operate in isolation. In considering each practice, try to keep the whole system in mind.

Linked Teams — Structure of the Change-ABLE Organization

Overview

This chapter describes Linked Teams, the Key Management Practice by which Change-ABLE organizations accomplish the function of structure. It emphasizes the following points:

1. The structure is a hierarchy, made relatively flat by large spans of control and by the use of information technology — integrated networks of computers.

2. The hierarchy operates as a system of Linked Teams — it is a system of synchronized Regular Meetings.

3. Each Team meeting is focused on achieving the Leader's/Team's goals.

4. The Leader and members link all Teams together through multiple Team memberships.

5. Through multiple role performance, i.e., people reporting to more than one Team Leader, the structure supports a very complex matrix of authorities.

6. This structure is explained in "Max's Change-ABLE Organization."

A Flat, But Still Hierarchical Structure

The first thing to appreciate about a Change-ABLE organization is its hierarchical structure. Popular and somewhat romantic theories require the complete removal of hierarchy to make an organization fast, advanced, and flexible. They imagine a truly flat organization in which everyone knows about everything through various sorts of information technology, such as E-mail. Individuals spontaneously contribute ideas and resources according to their own interests, self-assessed competencies, and availability. This isn't happening in Change-ABLE organizations, which have clearly defined levels of authority and roles at each level performed by clearly designated individuals. The faster and more complex the organization's tasks, the more important this clarity of designation becomes.

In Change-ABLE organizations, hierarchy is used as a network of channels through which information is processed by Managers to coordinate and focus the organization's resources. The Change-ABLE organization accepts hierarchy as necessary since the coordination of its work is so complex that it transcends the ability of Individual Contributors.

Traditional hierarchy, as discussed in the chapter on Rafts (bureaucracies), tends to overload its channels of communication, making the organization slow and stupid. The Change-ABLE organization diminishes many of the problems of traditional hierarchy through two practices. First, the span of control is increased, and the hierarchy is flattened through the use of information technology. Messages travel with greater reliability through fewer levels of management. Technology allows more of the organization's management decisions to be confidently made by Individual Contributors at the hierarchy's base— eliminating the need to route many messages to upper management.

Second, each Team of Managers reporting to the same Leader performs the Leader's decision-making task as a group. Within the Change-ABLE organization, there are many meetings — successful meetings — that function as clear channels and decision points in the

Linked Teams

- Hierarchy of Linked Teams;
- System of synchronized Regular Meetings;
- Each Team meeting focuses on the Leader's/Team's goals;
- The Leader and members link the Team to all other teams; and
- Structure supports complex matrix of authorities and multiple role performance.

organization's structure. The best way to understand Change-ABLE organizations is as a system of regular, decision-making meetings. As we shall see, the use of groups for decision-making enlarges the database with which the decisions are made, while improving their quality. This practice also provides an opportunity for participants to understand decisions and prepare for their implementation, thereby speeding up the organization's decision implementation process.

A System of Synchronized Regular Meetings

The Managers of the Change-ABLE organization work in Teams. The point is to have the right people take action on the right things at the right time. The right people are those who, as a group, have the authority and influence to control the resources necessary to achieve the Team's goals. The right action involves determining that the Team's goals are still appropriate, and then providing the resources needed to ensure their achievement. The right time is at a regularly scheduled and frequent meeting, so that the rest of the organization knows how to access the group's authority for dealing with emergent issues.

In the Change-ABLE organization, meetings are held with great regularity. Other organizations may have such meetings scheduled, but an audit will show that often less than half of the meetings take place. In such organizations, meetings are often cancelled at the last minute when not enough members are available to make the meeting worth holding. Decisions must then be delayed, or they must be made by a process less informed and less understood than if they had been made by the right authorities.

But in the Change-ABLE organization, meetings are a well-respected discipline. They are a very high priority because members know that many other people depend upon the quality and timeliness of their decision-making. Managers make these meetings the place and time where the work is done. Their reliable attendance turns the meetings into something the whole organization knows about and counts on — like a strong and steady heartbeat.

Meetings are roughly synchronized with all the other higher and lower level meetings affecting goals and allocation of necessary resources. Lower level meetings are held quite frequently — often daily. Usually on a Friday or Monday, lower level meetings will be held just prior to the meetings at the next level up the organization, until the issues roll up to a level high enough for appropriate action. If necessary, a problem at the Individual Contributor level of perfor-mance can typically surface for decision-making at the executive level (four or five levels higher) and be in the process of solution within 10 calendar days. Most of the time, however, problems are solved much sooner at much lower levels in the hierarchy. (An illustration of this process is offered in Chapter Ten on Work Reviews.)

Meetings Are Focused on the Leader's/Team's Goals

Each Team has a Leader. The Leader's Performance Plan (or at least some part of it) is the statement of the Team's goals and is the Team's charter. The Leader is the Team's formal authority. Team members report to the Leader and are peers to each other. The Leader is individually accountable to the rest of the organization for the quality of the group's work. Usually, the Leader is the group's "de-cider" in a process of consultative decision-making. (This process is discussed in Chapter Eleven.)

The Team of Managers gathers to evaluate the appropriateness of the Team's goals and priorities. They begin evaluating progress toward goal achievement and decide what actions are required to sustain or further support progress. Managers are not there simply for information sharing. They are there to make decisions regarding resource allocation relative to the needs of their Team's goals.

Though Team members have unique roles to play in the imple-mentation of the Team's plans, they do not see themselves as respon-sible for only a piece of the Team's work. They accept responsibility for the entire Team's accomplishments and problems. During the meeting, the more mature members act as though they were the Team's Leader. They engage in discussion from the perspective of the Leader's do-main of authority and accountability, evaluating themselves and everybody else in terms of how well their ideas serve the accomplish-ments of the whole Team. These members address the Leader as a peer and advise him or her as to the particulars of running this part of the organization. The mature Team members are able to do this because they have taken the time to learn other or all parts of the Team's business. They can speak with almost the same depth and breadth of knowledge as the Leader can. Members come together intending to help exercise the Leader's domain of authority, and they are well-prepared to do so. The Leader listens — not out of politeness, but because the subordinate members offer truly valuable advice!

Members raise well-informed questions about each other's parts of the business. As a new member takes over a previously existing role on one of these Teams, such questioning can be a bit intimidating. New members are challenged by example to accelerate their learning of the Team's business as a whole. It is clear the Leader and the other members expect such learning, are willing to support it, and are evaluating each other's level of mastery in every meeting. These Regular Meetings are on-the-job management seminars and focal points in the organization's governance system.

With increasing frequency, Change-ABLE organizations are expressing this upward thrust of accountability in management through incentive pay and bonus programs. Instead of rewarding Managers for the performance of the Teams they lead, bonuses are based on the success of the Teams where they are subordinate members. The effect is dramatic! It becomes very clear that the members of each Team are accountable for the whole Team's performance, and they must constantly be concerned about integrating the work of the Teams they lead into the success of the whole Team. In this system, you can't win by simply "pulling your oar." You must turn around in the boat and make sure everyone is paddling in a balanced and integrated way to ensure the Canoe goes where it is supposed to go.

This concern for the whole Team's performance is probably the key distinction of Managers in the Change-ABLE organization. Instead of looking down the hierarchy and seeing all below in their domain of authority, Change-ABLE Managers turn around and look up to the next level of authority as the position from which they are expected to think and act in every management meeting. One member of a Change-ABLE organization's executive Team described the group as "We're 10 in a box," — meaning that when the meeting is held, all the members climb up into the Leader's box on the organizational chart. In our watercraft analogy, this looking upward is akin to paddling while facing the front of the Canoe as opposed to sitting backward in the boat and rowing. Accepting responsibility for the whole Team's performance is the source of the Change-ABLE organization's extraordinary integration, unusually well-informed Managers, and intelligent decision-making.

All Teams Linked by Leaders and Members

To function well as the channel for organizational communications, each Team is carefully linked into the whole hierarchy. The Leader is the link for the upward, vertical communication process. He or she carries issues and recommendations upward when higher level authority for resolution is required, and brings decisions downward from higher levels of management for compliance in the lower Team. But each member also performs the linking function, bringing Team decisions downward in their capacity as Leaders of lower level Teams. Within the Team meetings, members link the Teams they lead horizontally to the Teams led by their peers.

The linking person is obliged to carry accurate descriptions of issues and the rationales for decisions. But the linking person is not just a messenger. This person is also expected to be a proactive participant in all the decisions made by any of the Teams he or she leads or attends as a member.

This linking role demands particular skills. Leaders must be active listeners in both their Team and upper level meetings. Being an effective listener involves more than attendance and note taking. It requires the skills of rapid rapport building — making oneself friendly and easy to approach. It requires the self-confidence to ask the questions that reveal one's own genuine lack of knowledge. It also involves asking the kinds of questions that help others get off the defensive and make themselves fully understood —including the disclosure of sources and the admission of known limits to the validity of their information. Over time, these listening skills make the Managers real experts in the business and contribute to an important part of the reputation they need to be effective — the reputation for being respectful, supportive, and approachable.

In addition to honing their listening skills, Managers must be skillful advocates. They must have quick access to their own and the organization's memory systems — people and databases — to support their evaluation of issues and alternative solutions, and to effectively express their preferences. Instead of being salespeople and persuaders, Managers must be efficient teachers and advisors. Persistent demonstration of these discussion skills increases their influence throughout the organization, and adds other essential elements to their reputations — reliability, insight, and integrity.

Once Managers participate in a Team's work, they are expected to represent that Team's work whenever its decisions affect the concerns of other Teams. Everywhere Managers go, they carry with them concerns of all Teams of which they are members as well as Leaders.

Cross-Functional Teams Requiring Multiple-Role Performance

The discussion about Linked Teams might appear to apply to three levels of Teams: the level above, to which the Leader links the Team; the level of Team members or peers; and the level of the Teams below, through the member's leadership. Like shingles on a slate roof, these three levels are linked vertically and horizontally. However, it is not characteristic of Change-ABLE organizations to stop at this level of complexity. There are, additionally, a large number of cross-functional or "Network Teams" woven into the hierarchy. Managers are expected to be effective links for these Network Teams, as well.

Cross-functional Teams have become essential to the integration of organizational performance. A hierarchy that serves only one purpose in each of its vertical structures locks up too many underutilized resources and encounters the problem of "handing off" its part of the work to other divisions. Integration of organizational performance is needed to serve several different purposes simultaneously, using common resources and eliminating or speeding up "hand offs" that are delaying the movement of products and services through their necessary stages of processing.

In particular, there are four different purposes organizations need to serve simultaneously. They must develop, maintain, and apply their technologies (sometimes called basic functions). They must pull products through the stages of their development. They must serve customers, adapting to their unique needs and balancing their demands for attention. And, they must manage their operations in different geographical areas. Matrix management is the typical response to this need, and in most organizations, it has not worked very well. The Managers of the structures designed to serve any one of these purposes usually seek to clarify their unique accountabilities and claims to resources by defending their autonomy. In the contest for resources, one or more of the purposes always loses. Change-ABLE organizations, by contrast, demonstrate an unusual ability to serve all four purposes in a highly complex matrix of authorities. The instrument of this cross-functional work is what we call Network Teams.

In some cases, the Change-ABLE organization uses Network Teams to sustain its basic technologies (what is usually called the functional organization). More often, however, it will let its basic technologies be the backbone of its structure. The Network Teams will then cross these structures to focus the technologies on the other three purposes. Some of the Network Teams will control resources of a line of products. Another set will combine resources for service to specific customers. Still other Network Teams may form a system for controlling the organization's performance in various geographic locations.

All four types of Teams will function simultaneously within the same organization, while sharing resources for their various purposes. This resource sharing is not necessarily a matter of controlling a dedicated part of the organization's budget, though this will be the case to some extent. Most Managers serve on several Network Teams weekly, and often share the same Individual Contributors, equipment, and working areas.

In a Change-ABLE organization, every Network Team is a fully authorized element in the organization's structure. Like other management Teams, it will adopt a portion of the Leader's Performance Plan and have its own allocation of resources. The Leader carries the same responsibility for linking the Team upward to another Team in the next level of hierarchy.

Subordinate members of the cross-functional Team come from other Teams in which they are members or Leaders. They may also come from different levels of the hierarchy, occasionally from a level higher than the Leader of the Team on which they are participating.

Network Team members study the specialties of the other members of each Team to become competent consultants to the Leader's decision-making. They link the concerns of all the Teams into every discussion in which they participate.

Membership in many different management Teams completely disregards the idea that everyone must report to only one boss. In Change-ABLE organizations, Managers and many Individual Contributors report to several different Leaders. The reporting relationships depend upon which Teams a person serves. A Manager in this system usually relies upon a Performance Plan, the key results of which require participation in several different structures of authority. Conflicts in the priorities are constantly worked on in every meeting and must occasionally be escalated for resolution. The presence of these conflicts is not seen as a failure in the system, however, it is seen as the substance of managerial work. (We say more about Performance Plans in Chapter Nine, and also discuss managerial evaluation for purposes of pay and promotion.)

Linking Network Teams into the hierarchy enables Change-ABLE organizations to act quickly in well-coordinated change. Every Team in the hierarchy is well-informed regarding the intentions, accomplishments, and problems of every other relevant Team. This information is gleaned not from newsletters, communications meetings, or rumors, but by having the information reliably reported into Team deliberations by a member participating in another Team. Because Team members are links to so many other Teams, they supply immediate access to facts relevant to their own acts of governance. They also provide an immediate channel through which to communicate their interdependence and influence the work of the other Teams.

Team members are fully authorized to speak for any of the Teams of which they are members. They take responsibility to prevent these Teams from countering each other's actions. Most of the time, conflicts are identified and immediately resolved. When that is not possible, there are ready-made channels (linking members) through which the issues can be escalated to the appropriate level for resolution. This fully authorized linking of Teams through their shared members keeps the network from waiting for all the Teams to "get lined up" through the shuttle diplomacy of powerless messengers. Change-ABLE organizations skillfully design the membership of management Teams to ensure this ready-made, fully authorized channel of coordination among Teams. This enlarges the number of short channels of communication, keeps decision-making low in the hierarchy, ensures the integration of all the Teams' work, and speeds the reallocation of resources necessary to solve problems and respond to new opportunities.

When the hierarchy operates in this system of Linked Teams, functional and cross-functional performances are constantly guided and reinforced by every managerial decision. Information flows freely as a result of the multiple memberships of Team members. In each meeting, members form a pool of information that eventually becomes the group's resident database. Decisions are enriched by broad knowledge of the organization's business. This is in stark contrast to hierarchies operating as one-on-one chains of command. There, the database is usually limited to two participants — with one participant inevitably dominant. The Change-ABLE organization's Teams are much better informed and managerial decision-making is quick and intelligent.

Cross-Functional Task Forces

The hierarchy of the Change-ABLE organization is characterized by one other kind of meeting or group—the Task Force. It is important to make the distinction between a Task Force and a Network Team. The Task Force is a temporary group formed to study a uniquely complex problem, decision, or plan. Like a cross-functional or Network Team, a Task Force is linked to the hierarchy by its Leader and may take its members from any level or function of the hierarchy. But the Task Force, unlike the Network Team, is not endowed with formal authority to act. It has only the resources necessary to perform its study and its output is a recommendation to the Team sponsoring it.

Task Force membership is comprised of the various subject matter experts relevant to its task. Members form their recommendation and then assume the position of teachers to the Managers who are most affected by their recommendation. Managers are thus prepared for their roles as decision-makers when the recommendation is finally brought back to the sponsoring Team for action.

This use of temporary Task Forces puts the organization's most qualified minds to work on its complex issues. It lightens the burden of information processing otherwise falling on individual Managers. In Change-ABLE organizations, Task Forces perform many of the functions for which other organizations form permanent staffs.

Max's Organization: an Example of Change-ABLE Structure

Now let's illustrate the Change-ABLE organization's fast, flexible way of exercising formal authority by considering Max's organization. For purposes of simplicity, each Team consists of a Leader and three subordinates. (In reality, most of these Teams have at least 7 and often as many as 14 members.) Max's subordinate, Alice, leads Design Engineering and applied R&D; Bob leads Operations (Process Design and Manufacturing), and Cal leads Customer Service Engineering. (See Figure 1 below.)

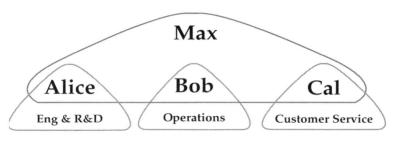

Figure 1

The organization usually develops three generations of its product simultaneously, and we will refer to these product generations as G100, G200, and G300. Each new generation begins under the leadership of Alice, who forms a Network Team. This Team includes Dan and Ed's design technologies from Engineering and R&D, picks up Gil from the Operations Team, and acquires Joe from Customer Service. (See Figure 2 on page 125.) Involving Bob's and Cal's Teams from the start reduces cycle time and smooths out the hand-offs as the product design matures.

When the product design moves into production (G200 is currently at this stage), Bob takes over project leadership. Bob uses the

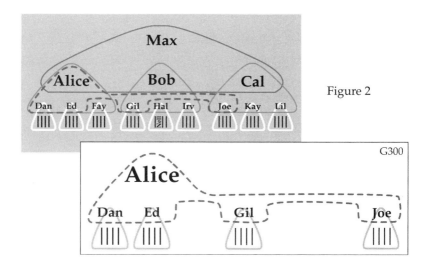

Figure 2

engineers in Hal and Irv's Teams, but continues to involve Design Engineering through Fay, while preparing Customer Service through Kay (Figure 3). As product begins to ship out to customers (G100 is in this stage), Cal takes over. He is using Joe and Lil from his own Team, and continues to coordinate with Operations through Irv (Figure 4).

The business is growing, and the Engineering department must now move into an additional building. Alice and Cal will take their

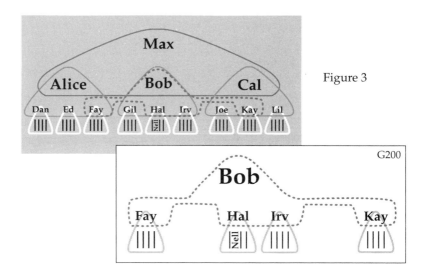

Figure 3

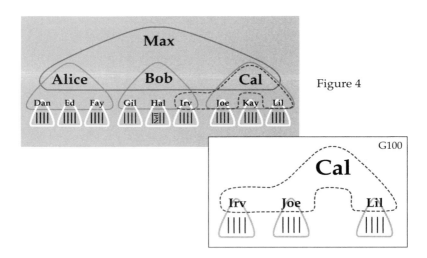

Figure 4

Teams into the new space; Bob will be left to expand into the current facility. Max puts Alice in charge of the relocation project (R1). She plans and coordinates this through Ed, Hal, and Kay. A number of Task Forces are chartered by this relocation Team to study special needs, review floor plans, and schedule the move (Figure 5).

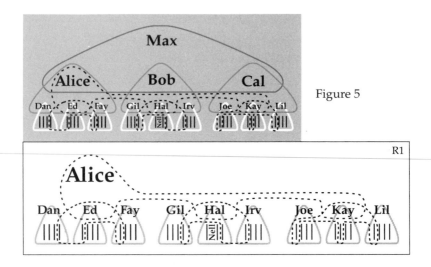

Figure 5

Max's organization is forming a partnership with another organization to develop a completely new line of products (H100). The partners will jointly design the product, it will be produced in Bob's part of the organization, and it will be distributed and serviced by the partner. To manage this partnership, Max adds a new member to his Team, Mei, who will coordinate her work in Max's organizations through Dan and Hal (Figure 6). Mei will also be a member of the

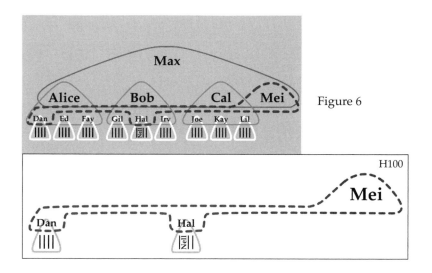

Figure 6

executive Team in the partnership organization .

An especially important customer wants a customized version of the Generation 200 product. This new project (G210) is led by Fay, with Irv and Kay as subordinate members of the Team (Figure 7).

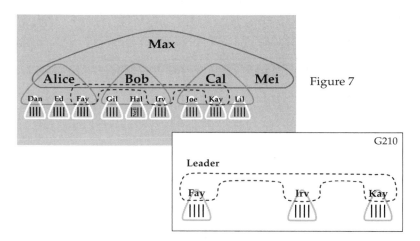

Figure 7

Each of these Teams (with the exception of the Task Forces) is a fully authorized, formal element of the structure. The Teams may last for a few months or a few years. The importance of each Team is not determined by its longevity, but by the priority assigned to its goals. Furthermore, functional groups are likely to change more rapidly in this organization than in others. Whole technologies may be phased out or rapidly dispersed among other groups. No part of the hierarchy is seen as more permanent than any other part.

The ultimate forum for integrating these efforts and resolving issues of priority and resource allocation is Max's Team (Alice, Bob, Cal, and Mei). Hal will not be torn between his commitments to G200 and H100, because Bob and Mei are bound in accountability for the success of these projects at Max's level. Nor will Hal be torn between these projects and the relocation effort, as Alice is bound in account-ability with Bob and Mei for the successful outcome of the work.

This example demonstrates an organization dealing with all four of the traditional rationales for organizational design: Function/Technology (Alice, Bob, and Cal's original Teams); Product (G100-300); Customer (G210 & H100); and Geography/Facility (R1). The use of Network Teams provides simultaneous and fully integrated perfor-mance for all four of these concerns (Figure 8).

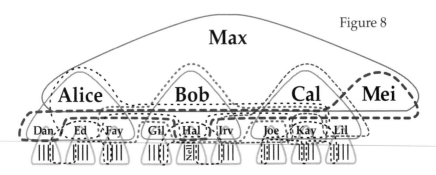

Figure 8

In Change-ABLE organizations, the hierarchy works like a stadium score board, with the capacity to light up any configuration of its bulbs. Individual Contributors are these light bulbs, and the man-agement network provides the capacity to reconfigure quickly the organization's human resources for a great variety of performances.

Summary

Chapter Eight described the Key Management Practice in the way Change-ABLE organizations structure themselves — Linked Teams. It emphasized five characteristics of this practice and offered an illustration.

1. Change-ABLE organizations have a well-defined hierarchy kept relatively flat by the use of large spans of control and an integrated network of computers.
2. The hierarchy operates as a system of Linked Teams — it is a synchronized system of Regular Meetings.
3. In each Team meeting, members show an intense commitment to the achievement of the Team Leader's and the Team's goals. Members share accountability for Team goals and quickly share resources to assure Team success.
4. The Leader and members link all the Teams together by participation in several Teams and by carrying the concerns of each Team to all the others.
5. Through multiple-role performance (i.e., people reporting to more than one Team Leader) the structure simultaneously integrates the exercise of authority over the organization's technologies, products, customer services, and geographical zones of operation.
6. This Key Management Practice of Linked Teams was illustrated with "Max's Change-ABLE Organization."

Managers in Change-ABLE organizations keep their hierarchy flat, their communication channels short, push decision-making to lower levels in the hierarchy, and make the processing of information rapid, intelligent, and well-integrated through the Key Practice of Linked Teams.

Performance Plans — Keeping the Organization Focused

Overview

This chapter describes Performance Plans, the Key Management Practice by which Change-ABLE organizations accomplish the function of planning. It emphasizes the following points:

1. There are six essential characteristics of a Performance Plan:

    - It is a simple, emphatic statement —stating less than seven key results that can be said from memory in less than two minutes.
    - It is comprehensive —identifying how the resources under the influence of a Manager are going to be employed during the next few months.
    - It focuses only on results — it does not attempt to describe processes.
    - It describes the results in specific and concrete terms.
    - It declares the relative priority of each result.
    - It identifies the few people who are key partners in accomplishing the result.

2. A process for writing a Performance Plan is suggested.
3. Three functions of the Performance Plan are emphasized:

    - It establishes the goals of the Team(s) a Manager leads.
    - It facilitates instant role clarification and role alignment in all the Teams of which Managers are members.
    - It provides the foundation for Work Reviews in all Team meetings.

4. An illustration of the function of Performance Plans is provided in "Mei's Story."

Performance Plans as a Key Element in Change-ABLE Planning

A Performance Plan is a verbal statement identifying the key results a Manager expects to accomplish over the next year. In Change-ABLE organizations, Managers "introduce" themselves with their

Performance Plans as soon as they discover a relationship has the potential of being work-related. The stark specificity of the statement creates an impression of high task orientation. The brevity of the statement implies a sense of urgency. The pause that follows the statement seems to ask, "And what are you going to do?" It is a verbal tactic by which these Managers habitually provoke the rapid formation of functional working relationships.

Performance Plans are not the whole story regarding planning in the Change-ABLE organization. The organization also engages in mission identification, strategic planning, process design, and project planning — and generally does all this very well. These items constitute a written database, with which the organization validates the probabilities of its hopes, assigns specific tasks, and assesses progress. In all its planning, however, the organization does not cherish the illusion of being able to predict the future beyond the next 90 days.

Change-ABLE Managers know that planning is a way of expressing intention and testing the realism of those intentions. They plan with urgency and in great detail for the short term — the next three months. Beyond this, the future is staked out in terms of major milestones. Managers become impatient with anyone detailing plans beyond six months. They expect unknown change and know they will have to replan their way through the future. The mindset is not "plan," but "replan, replan, replan."

Performance Plans

- Seven or fewer statements;
- Comprehensive — covering 80% of one's resources;
- Focuses on results — not process description;
- Results described in specific and concrete terms;
- Relative priority distributed over 100%; and
- Aligned with key partners.

These concerns for the near term and the expectation of constant change get expressed in the behavior we call Performance Plans. Managers have learned they must quickly make clear what they are trying to accomplish and what they want done with the resources they influence, which may include other Managers. They know lots of tactical adaptation will be required, and since they want everyone involved in the work to initiate these tactical adaptations, they must make the intended results clear. They also have learned that clarity of purpose requires constant repetition of the expected results, especially under constantly changing conditions. A Manager must know how to quickly project the whole picture to meet this requirement.

Performance Plans are required management practice. Behind this verbal behavior are all other forms of planning. What makes the Plans a psychological reality for human cooperation is the Manager's ability to name the expected results in a "sound bite." A Manager's Performance Plan is the key planning practice translating the Change-ABLE organization's detailed planning tapestry into the living reality of a flexible and well-focused organization.

The Six Characteristics of Performance Plans

There are six essential characteristics of the Performance Plan that make it a causal force in the life of the organization:

Simple and emphatic.

Each plan describes less than *seven* key results the Manager intends to accomplish during the next year. The originator has the Plan memorized. It can be recited in less than two minutes, usually in less than 90 seconds. If it is written down (as it often is), it fits easily on one page. Generally, Managers don't "show" their plan to people, they "say" it.

Hearing (or reading) this statement provides a clear idea of the Manager's intentions. It states the Manager's knowledge of what he or she is about in the organization and usually expresses an intense and focused commitment.

Comprehensive.

Though the plan is brief, it must be comprehensive. The results it describes will require 80 per cent of the resources the Manager controls or influences in the organization. When the plan is shown to any subordinates to the Manager, they should see their work represented somewhere in the set of results. The goals of all Teams of which the originator is a member also should be represented.

The plan is not only a statement of new initiatives to be undertaken during the year. It also describes the routine actions to be accomplished again this year. The statement describes the results of the whole performance to which this Manager is committed. Only by being comprehensive can the plan help Managers clarify their roles for others. Anything not represented creates mystery and confusion.

The plan also states what the Manager really believes is going to happen. It is not deliberately inflated to show ambition, nor is it deliberately couched in such minimal terms as to be a "sure thing." As soon as a Manager discovers the originally expected results are unrealistic, the plan is altered to reflect the new understanding. Usually, the original Performance Plan is kept on file as a "plan of record" for reference in later efforts to understand planning errors, organizational performance problems, and surprise successes. A Performance Plan is an honest statement of what the Manager currently thinks is going to be accomplished — its credibility must not be damaged by intentional "stretch," "sandbagging," or denial of new realities requiring changed expectations.

Describes Results Only, Not Process.

The plan is only a list of specific results. A *result* is a concrete deliverable. It is an output visible to and verifiable by anyone concerned with the desired outcomes.

The Performance Plan deliberately avoids trying to give any explanation of how the results will be achieved. It doesn't describe the specific resources required to deliver the result and focuses attention entirely upon the desirability of the result. It provokes others to answer the question, "Do you agree that these are the results I should be working for and that we should be working for together?" This is the key to the simplicity and emphatic clarity of the statement. It is also the key to the plan's ability to instantly initiate working relationships. The plan constantly keeps the basic question up front: "What are we trying to do together?"

Specific Description of the Results.

Each result in the plan is described in specific terms of pace and quality. Pace refers to the speed with which the result will be delivered. For highly routine and repetitive tasks, the quantity of the output to be delivered in a specified time period is stated. For instance, "1.2 billion items a year" or "4,000 items per hour." For Projects, the pace is described as the deadline or critical milestones of the current year. For important Troubleshooting tasks, the pace is described as response time and average solution times — "pick up the phone before the third ring and answer the customer's questions about billing in five minutes," or "be on the site of the equipment breakdown within 15 minutes of receiving the service call; have 80 per cent of the cases up and running in less than an hour."

Quality requirements are also to be described for each result. Often these requirements are so numerous and technical they must be dealt with by reference to the document in which they are defined — "according to the contract," or "as listed in the production specifications." Sometimes the required quality is described by naming the customers who must be satisfied with the output — "so that the board of directors can use it for determining compensation policy," or "so that 80 per cent of the target population is using the database at least once a day."

Sometimes the specifications of the results will refer to several different measurements of pace and quality. It is important for the Manager to anticipate two things — the ability to say the plan and its specific measures from memory, and the ability to use the plan as the basis of Work Reviews in management Team meetings. If it can't be said from memory, it is too complex to have psychological effect on day-to-day performance. If the measures are not verifiable by a graphic display of information, they are probably only wishful thinking and empty promises.

Describes the Relative Priorities of Each Result.

There are two ways of talking about priorities: ordinal and relative. Ordinal priority lists results in order of their importance. When stated, it sounds like this: "The most important result is..., and the second most important is..." By contrast, relative priority assigns a percentage weight to each result. It sounds like this: "This result is about 60 per cent of my plan..., another 30 per cent is this result..., and 10 per cent goes to this result."

The problem with talking about results in ordinal terms is that people tend only to pay attention to the most important thing. The message received is, "Do this first, and then worry about the rest." But this message is rarely appropriate in complex situations. There are usually several things a Manager wants done simultaneously. Some of them are more important than others and, in case of resource shortages or other emergencies, people are expected to know which results must get priority attention. Given planned resources, however, all the results are to be worked on simultaneously. If, in fact, all the results are equally important, only relative priority allows the Manager to clearly say so.

Managers in Change-ABLE organizations don't avoid talking about priorities. They know the issues of priorities are at the center of their work. The organization's resources will always be limited, and Managers will always be faced with clarifying what is most important to accomplish. The issue of priority is at the center of every organization's most serious conflicts. It is management's function to resolve these conflicts, not to avoid or ignore them. Putting the priorities as they are currently understood into the plan pushes them into the open. Those elements of the plan challenged and changed most frequently are the priorities.

Priorities also are important for building trust and confidence among Managers. As Managers move from Team to Team within the Change-ABLE organization's complex matrix of authorities, they must be careful not to overcommit. By showing each Team their Performance Plans, Managers show each other all the commitments already made to other Teams. This sharpens the Team's awareness of available resources and keeps the members from expecting more of each other than is realistic. In this way, they avoid the misunderstanding and disappointment that can damage their respect for each other.

Identifies Key Partners for Achieving Each Result.

Identifying key partners for each result is the only reference the plan makes to required resources. In this case, the Managers name other Managers whose cooperation they know will be required. To keep the list short (three or four partners), the Managers name only those other Managers who are Leaders or members of the Team meetings they attend.

The purpose of naming key partners is to make explicit the network of contacts and authorities required to accomplish the result. These partners — inside or outside the organization (i.e., vendors and customers, as well as internals) — are the people at peer level who must be aligned with the identified outcome to guarantee its success. Naming them in the Performance Plan is an overt invitation and a reminder to engage in continuing discussion and cooperation.

A Process for Writing Your Performance Plan

Drafting a Manager's Performance Plan should not take more than an hour. Large parts of the plan have usually been written in some other document — the challenge will be to simplify these other statements. Also, Performance Plans are intuitive. Most Managers are already walking around saying these things over and over to themselves. All that remains is to get the thoughts out of the Manager's head and into the world of discussion. If a Performance Plan doesn't seem right at hand, here is a process for putting one together:

> **Step One:** Quickly list all the activities that must take place this year if you are to fulfill your current responsibilities and achieve new things you want to put in place.

Step Two: Go through List I and scratch out all the activities that are managerial processes. Managerial activities are anything done in order to: make expectations clear; provide performance feedback; or provide resources necessary to get the work done. Eliminate from the list anything that has to do with planning, setting up goals or standards, creating data-bases, attending Work Reviews, making reports, budgeting, scheduling, or recruitment and training of human resources. These are the activities taking up all of a Manager's time, so many of the items on List I tend to get eliminated. What should be left are the activities performed by the Individual Contributors in your part of the organization. A Manager's Performance Plan is not about the things Managers do; it is about the results accomplished by those being managed.

Step Three: Think of each activity remaining on List II as a system: What inputs does the activity require? What processes will it perform? What outputs will it produce? Who are the customers for the output? Next to each activity on List II, jot down the last two items: its outputs and customers.

Remember that an output is always concrete. It is an object — something you can point to and that others can see. If the output is intangible, such as giving advice, the output that matters for the Performance Plan may be the *report* that the advice-giving process was done. Name the report.

Don't confuse outputs with customer responses. You may see your result as "satisfied customers," but customer satisfaction is only a response to something you deliver to them. What you deliver is the output. The output provokes a customer response. For now, just name the output — don't yet try to describe what it must be like to provoke customer satisfaction.

Step Four: Now look at all the outputs you have identified with List II, and find a way to compile all of them into no more than seven. The way to do this is sometimes intuitively obvious. If this is the case for you, trust your intuition. Remember, at this point we are only trying to name the key outputs, we are not yet trying to describe what a good one has to be like.

If the key results don't seem to pop out, try one of these methods for grouping the outputs:

- Notice when the outputs of one activity become the necessary inputs for the production of some other output. Line up these outputs in sequence and take the last one in the sequence as the representative of all the others. Getting this last output requires getting all the others, so the others can be dismissed as "implied processes."
- Sometimes the outputs can be grouped together because they have a common customer. They are different parts of a service or a deliverable that enable the customer to do something. Create a name for this set of outputs, or think of the document that names them all — such as a contract or one of its sections.

If you still can't get all your important outputs represented in less that seven key statements, you are probably dealing with the kind of work we call Unpredictables. These are emergency tasks you have reason to believe will come up, but you aren't sure what will be required until the emergency arises. Label these responsibilities with a big letter "U" — for Unpredictable.

Step Five: At this point in drafting the Performance Plan, all we have is a collection of raw outputs. We haven't tried to describe them in any way that would distinguish between a good one or a bad one. Now it's time to add a description of the output letting us know what a good one is like.

The first part of the description is to identify the desired pace for its delivery. How many of these outputs do you want each hour, day, week, month, or year? If the task is a Project, what is the deadline or what is the critical milestone to be achieved this year?

The second part of the description is to indicate the level of quality required. Quality is always defined as how complete and accurate/precise the output must be to satisfy the customer's intended use. These quality requirements often have been carefully specified in some document. If so, refer to the document. Sometimes it is sufficient to refer to the customer's intended use and promise the output will serve that purpose.

For those important but unpredictable outputs you labeled with a "U" on List II, try making this statement: "(Name of task) will be done according to the objectives established with the customer at the time the work is accepted." If this statement seems inadequate, perhaps you can at least state a standard for your expertise as a troubleshooter. These standards state four things: expected response time (e.g., within 15 minutes of being notified of the problem); an average solution time (e.g., 80 per cent of the cases within two working days); a first pass success rate (e.g., 95 per cent of the problems solved well enough so as not to occur again for at least a year); and a description of manners (e.g., politely enough not to provoke a complaint for rudeness.)

Special Functions of the Performance Plan

Many of the functions of the Performance Plan have already been described. Some of these require special emphasis.

Facilitating Team Leadership

When a Manager performs the role of Team Leader, the Team's goals will be among the results described in the Leader's Performance Plan. Sometimes the Leader's entire plan is the Team's plan, and this is almost always the case for the senior executive of any organization. For lower level Managers, often only part of the Leader's plan constitutes the Team's plan. When the Leader performs as a member or Leader in other management Teams, some of the Leader's plan will refer to these other concerns. Even where only part of the Leader's plan states the Team's goals, it is important for the members of the Team to understand the rest of the Leader's commitments. The Leader must show the whole Performance Plan and then indicate which results constitute the purpose of the immediate Team meeting.

The Leader expects Team members to question these goals not only for clarification, but in terms of their appropriateness. Members will question whether or not the goals are realistic, have been assigned proper priority, and have been associated with useful metrics. Such questions are potentially a part of every Team meeting, though in fact, they tend to emerge about every 90 days.

As described in Chapter Eight, the Leader expects the members of the Team to commit to accomplishment of all the Team's goals. The Leader uses the Performance Plan as a way of focusing this commitment. The Performance Plan is a statement of how the Leader is delegating authority. The results are the accountability of all the subordinate members of the Team. No member's accountability can be fulfilled by doing only a part of the Team's plan; it is only fulfilled when the Team's whole plan is achieved.

When Team members understand and commit to these goals, they align their own Performance Plans with each other to ensure resources will be available for their accomplishment. This alignment of Plans is also a constant concern of the Team's and must be revisited whenever any member's commitments change. It is every member's concern that the resources of the whole Team are sufficiently employed to ensure the Team's achievement of the results stated in the Leader's Performance Plan.

When a Manager is leading higher level Teams, it is tempting to list all the Team's sub-goals in the Leader's Performance Plan. This, however, would break the rule of having seven or less key results in any one Performance Plan. The rule should be kept. The place for sub-goals is in the plans of subordinate members. Breaking down the results in the Leader's plan into the sub-goals appropriate for the Team members is part of the alignment process. Of course, subordinate members may also have trouble keeping the rule. They will have to find a way of stating the results summarizing the sub-goals of their subordinates.

This is actually one of the great gifts of the rule of seven: it forces Managers to think about their commitments at the proper level of abstraction. At higher level management meetings, the results are stated in more abstract, summarized terms, such as the total volume of production and the delivery of the final results of large Projects. In middle levels of the hierarchy, Managers state results in terms of specific parts of the organization's production goals or in terms of milestones for certain branches of the larger Projects. Lower level Managers will look at the operations in certain zones of the production facilities or at the specific quantities of work adding up to this month's project goals.

Whenever Managers cannot get their commitments accounted for in seven or less result statements, it is a symptom of confusion regarding the level of authority at which the Managers are expected to operate. They are usually trying to dip down to some lower level of authority, perhaps because it is the level from which the Manager came and at which he or she is still most confident and comfortable. Holding subordinates accountable for the exercise of authority at these lower levels is a subtle balance of letting go and holding on. The rule of seven helps Managers find the right balance and strengthens their abilities as Team Leaders.

The rule of seven may alert Managers to another form of confusion: role overload. In this case, Managers cannot get their plans down to seven key results because the results they are committed to are beyond the scope of the resources over which they have influence. They have no one to whom they can delegate the responsibilities and they cannot do it themselves. The rule of seven works as an alarm for role overload. When Managers can't state their commitments realistically in seven or less key results, they are surely trying to do more than they are likely to get done. They are overcommitted and set up for failure.

Continuous Alignment and Quick Role Change

Performance Plans provide efficient tools Managers can use to align their resources with the other members of their Teams. As they work on their plans, they are actually aligning the work of their subordinates. Once Managers have agreed on this, it is much easier for management in the next level down the organization to cooperate. They understand their work is supposed to be coordinated with other organizational units, and they know they are assisting their Leaders when they go out of their way to make sure such coordination occurs. Everyone understands cooperation is expected by their Leaders and that the Leaders will be disappointed if it doesn't happen. They show greater initiative in relationship to Managers in other units, and are quicker to bring their Leader's attention to cases of poor cooperation.

Performance Plans, because of their simplicity, are also efficient as facilitators of rapid role change. Whenever a threat or opportunity emerges requiring the organization to shift its resources, people in the management structure must change their roles. Performance Plans allow Managers to focus their attention quickly on critical results and priorities. They also point to Teams and relationships requiring Managers to go work things out. Because all Teams are holding Regular Meetings in a synchronized schedule, it is not unusual to see large divisions of Change-ABLE organizations change their direction quite suddenly. In at least one case, we know of an organization changing its worldwide strategy and altering the roles of nearly 3,000 Managers in less than 90 days. They made the turn with the suddenness and grace of a school of fish!

The Foundation for Work Reviews

It is necessary to continue emphasizing the interdependence of the Key Management Practices in Change-ABLE organizations. We've seen how essential Performance Plans are to making an organization's complex structure work — it keeps roles and accountabilities clear while making constant adaptations to the plans. Performance Plans are also essential to the effectiveness of Work Reviews.

In Chapter Ten, we will focus specifically on the Work Review practice. Whenever a Manager is composing a Performance Plan, it is essential to be thinking about how progress toward results is going to be monitored. In Change-ABLE organizations, this progress also will be monitored by many other Managers at several different levels of the hierarchy of Teams. The Manager, therefore, must pay attention to metrics and databases.

The measures of progress, wherever possible, should be leading measures. Managers need to see approaching problems and opportunities as quickly as possible. There is little point in asking Managers to come together to close the barn door after the horses are already gone. A reliable leading measure is a precious and difficult discovery. Managers should borrow and use any such measures already existing and work at discovering new ones for any part of their organization that doesn't already have them.

No measurement becomes reliable until it has been worked with long enough to develop a database. Attention to the collection of information and the design of databases is more essential than ever. Managers must be careful because there is such an ocean of information available! There are so many questions people would like to get answered. To be Change-ABLE, Managers avoid distractions. They keep key results in mind, and ensure information gathering and databases are relevant for governing the performance that yields these results.

Finally, Change-ABLE Managers remember how quickly this information must be made available to their Team members. There is no time to explain what is happening with words. They need pictures that are worth a thousand words, so they develop their skills in the graphic presentation of data. This is largely a matter of computer literacy — knowing how to use the large range of software converting data to charts and graphs. Manual preparation of such displays is out of the question given the Change-ABLE organization's demand for up-to-the-minute current data.

Performance Plans are a first step toward the real scene of action in Change-ABLE organizations, the Work Reviews. Getting these Plans right is essential to the effectiveness of the organization's governance.

Mei's Story: How Performance Plans Can Work

A Change-ABLE organization, with its multiplicity of Teams, easily threatens Managers coming from Galley or Raft cultures. Imagine, for instance, that Mei comes from a Galley culture to join Max's Team (See Fig. 6 in Chapter 8). Even if Max explains the new ground rules (as in the Memo to Alice) and works with her to draft and align their Performance Plans, she may still be confused.

Mei's confusion begins when she finds her subordinates taking time in her meetings to discuss other Projects they are still working on! She is further shocked to find that her "subordinates" are running all over the organization telling everybody about the status of her Project — warts and all. By the time she gives her first Work Review, Mei is embarrassed by her peers' ability to question her about every detail of her work. She feels out of control and overexposed.

Mei's Fiscal Performance Plan		
Objectives	Priority	Partners
• H100 product line design by EOQ2	70%	• Alice
• H100 manufacturability by EOQ4	20%	• Bob
• H100 product line introduction by EOQ4	10%	• Cal

In her attempt to "start taking charge" in the autonomous manner of the Galley, Mei creates a crisis for herself. She goes to Hal with demands for accelerating her Project, H100. Hal resists, making the point that her schedule changes "bump" other higher priority Projects (G200 & R1). Mei sees this as insubordination and threatens Hal with a negative performance review. She soon finds herself being led by Hal into Max's office.

In Max's office, the three associates have a brief review of their Performance Plans — probably to reaffirm Hal's original understanding of priorities and overrule Mei's changes. Then, when Hal has left, Max does some coaching with Mei. Having seen other Managers disoriented when first joining his organization, Max is sympathetic. He goes over the ground rules again and reminds Mei that her commitment to Project H100 must be kept in the context of her commitment to the Team's (Max's) entire Performance Plan. Mei is invited to bring her desired schedule changes to the Team's meeting, where such issues

Hal's Fiscal Performance Plan		
Objectives	Priority	Partners
• Ramp up for G200 by EOQ3	75%	• Irv, Fay, Kay
• Coordinate mfg. relocation (R1) by EOQ2	15%	• Ed, Kay
• H100 mfg. issues resolved by EOQ3	10%	• Dan, Mei

should be considered. And Max also suggests Mei recognize how important Hal is to everyone in the organization and quickly repair her relationship with him.

Mei understands the ground rules this time. She sees her role differently — not just as a Project Leader, but also as someone responsible for all the work being done by Max's Team. Following Max's suggestion, Mei immediately apologizes to Hal and thanks him for his help. They briefly review their Performance Plans and make sure they are in alignment. Sensing her sincerity, Hal sighs with relief and becomes a reliable ally as Mei continues learning to manage in Max's Change-ABLE organization.

Max's Fiscal Performance Plan		
Objectives	Priority	Partners
• Sell 4,500 G100s by EOQ4	30%	• Sr. Team
• Introduce G200 in 3 mkts by EOQ3	20%	• Sr. Team
• Relocation (R1) complete by EOQ2	20%	• Sr. Team
• Test/validate G300 design by EOQ3	15%	• Sr. Team
• H100 product line introduction by EOQ4	10%	• Sr. Team
• Ship first G210 to XYZ Co. by EOQ4	05%	• Sr. Team

Summary

Chapter Nine focused attention on the Performance Plan, the Key Management Practice that distinguishes planning in Change-ABLE organizations.

1. Six essential characteristics of a Performance Plan were noted:

    - It is simple and emphatic — less than seven key results;
    - It is comprehensive;
    - It focuses on results only;
    - It specifies pace and quality for each result;
    - It displays the relative priority of the results; and
    - It identifies key partners.

2. A methodology for writing a Performance Plan was suggested.
3. Three functions of the Performance Plan were emphasized:

    - It establishes the goals of the Team(s) a Manager leads.
    - It facilitates instant role clarification and role alignment in all the Teams of which Managers are members.
    - It provides the foundation for Work Reviews in all Team meetings.

4. Performance Plans were illustrated with "Mei's Story."

Performance Plans are essentially a verbal behavior of Managers — something they say and talk about repetitively. Performance Plans are the tool for maintaining focus while responding to the demands for frequent change. Though they are by no means the only form of planning in Change-ABLE organizations, Performance Plans make all the other forms come alive as causal forces in day-to-day operations.

10

Work Reviews – Central Act of the Change-ABLE Organization

Overview

This chapter describes Work Reviews, the Key Management Practice by which Change-ABLE organizations accomplish the function of performance feedback. It emphasizes the following points:

1. Work Reviews are the central focus of attention in the Regular Meetings of management Teams; they are the heartbeat of Change-ABLE organizations. A Work Review is not just an information-sharing event; the information is used to evaluate the Team's performance and to take corrective action when necessary.

2. There are five essential characteristics of Work Reviews in Change-ABLE organizations:

   - They are focused on the desired results in the Team Leader's and members' Performance Plans.
   - The reports always display both the objectives and the current status, thus facilitating evaluation.
   - The information presented is always current — not older than 48 hours.
   - The current status of all the expected results in any Performance Plan is presented graphically — in less than four minutes.
   - The discussion is issue focused — using the Team's authority to resolve problems and to seize opportunities.

3. A variety of schedules is used to synchronize all the organization's Work Reviews and assure that the right people will be talking about the right things at the right times.

4. Work Reviews in Change-ABLE organizations are supportive. Without denying the importance of problems or practicing any kind of polite circumlocution, the members of the management Teams understand their interdependence and are proactive in assisting each other with problems and opportunities.

5. The function of Work Reviews (also Linked Teams and Performance Plans) is illustrated with "Hal's Story."

Work Review: The Team Evaluates Each Team Member's Work

The Work Review is one of four tasks a management Team performs in its Regular Meetings. (Pass Downs, Recommendation Reviews, and News will be discussed in the next chapter on decision-making.) In Change-ABLE organizations, the Work Review is the most important on-going function of management Teams. This single subject takes up to at least 80 per cent of the Team's meeting time.

During this part of the meeting, Team members look at each other's work and evaluate their progress toward achieving the Team's goals. The assumption is that this discussion determines whether or not some change must be made in the way the Team uses its resources. Members listen with the intent of participating in a decision. They are not listening for the simple purpose of learning the status of each others' work.

Work Reviews

- Focused on desired results in Team Leader's and members' Performance Plans;
- Evaluative — displays objectives and current status of the work;
- Data current to within 48 hours;
- Status presented graphically in less than four minutes; and
- Discussion focused on variance:
    - Problem resolution and
    - Support for surprise success.

In response to its evaluation of performance, the Team will make one of three decisions:

> **Approval**: It may decide the performance is good and should be continued. This is, in fact, the norm. The Team takes a little time to congratulate such work.
>
> **Resource Reallocation**: When actual performance varies from the Performance Plan, the Team will examine the situation to see if some shift of resources is desirable. In the case of problems, it seeks to define the situation and then determine what resources must be reallocated to facilitate the problem solving. When the variance from plan is a surprise success, the Team looks for ways to move resources to fully exploit the discovery.
>
> **Plan Modification**: Sometimes, instead of responding to variance from plan with a reallocation of resources or addition to such reallocation, the Team will change the plan. The Team remains open to the discovery that its plans are unrealistic — either too ambitious, timid, or wrong in their determination of priorities. The Team's commitment does not preclude continuing to question the appropriateness of the plan.

When performance requires corrective action or additional support due to surprise success, the Team always reconsiders its goals. Sometimes the Team learns something that now renders its goals unrealistic. In such cases, the goals will be altered. However, the Teams in Change-ABLE organizations usually do a very persistent and thorough job of exploring options before they let go of any objective.

The point to be made here is that Work Reviews in Change-ABLE organizations are not mere information-sharing events. The members don't come with the question, "How are things going?" Instead they come with the question, "What are we going to do about it right now?" They are impatient with anything distracting them from using the meeting to improve the organization's performance.

Work Reviews process information in order to take action. Their purpose is decision-making. Every meeting utilizes the authority of its Leader and members to advance organizational objectives.

The Five Necessary Characteristics

Work Reviews are focused on the desired results in the Team Leader's and members' Performance Plans

The first essential characteristic of the Work Review practice is its focus on Performance Plans. The Team Leader's Plan is always the primary focus, and at least some part of it is seen as the Team's plan. (Remember, the Leader's plan may also refer to key results that are the accountability of other Teams. All the Leaders' roles are represented in their Performance Plans.) These goals are usually memorized by the members, but are occasionally reviewed to reinforce the Team's focus. Even if the Plan is not actually displayed at the beginning of the meeting, it is understood that the meeting will do a complete job of evaluating progress on all key results in the Leader's plan applying to this particular Team. The Leader's plan is the essential agenda of all the Teams' meetings.

Each member of the Team has a Performance Plan aligned to support the achievement of the Leader's plan. (Remember, the members may also have key results in their plans that refer to accountabilities of other Teams.) The most common Work Review procedure is for members of the Team to take a turn displaying their entire plans, and then reporting against the expectations of Plan as they relate to this Team's goals. In this procedure, members remind the Team of their whole range of commitments, then focus the Team's attention on progress toward the specific commitments made to this particular Team. Sometimes, the Work Review procedure will follow the expectations in the Leader's plan: the Leader puts up one of his or her objectives and all the members take turns reporting the related parts of their own Plans. When this procedure is followed, the last part of the meeting focuses on the other purposes the Leader and members serve by examining each person's entire Performance Plan. Both procedures focus the Team on key results and reinforce the interdependence and alignment of all Team members.

It is important for the Team to briefly review each member's entire Performance Plan to understand the context of priorities in which each member works. Many unforeseen conflicts or duplications of effort are identified and corrected in this way. Looking at everyone's entire plan encourages role linkage, and keeps each Team conscious of how its work integrates with the work of other Teams. This crucial contribution maintains the Change-ABLE organization's precision and performance speed.

The reports always display both the objectives and the current status, thus facilitating evaluation.

In the Change-ABLE organization, Work Reviews always report against the expectations of a Performance Plan. The expectations sometimes come directly from the Leader's plan, or sometimes from the plan of one of the members. These expectations and their accompanying metrics are defined in earlier meetings of the Team. When a member reports for the first time, his or her Performance Plan is displayed and the discussion focuses on issues of definition and alignment. Getting the right metrics is important, and several rounds of reporting are usually required before the Team is satisfied that it is looking at the right information. Once these issues have been resolved, however, each report moves quickly beyond status information to focus on the issues causing variance from the plan.

Making sure the presentation always includes a comparison between expectations and actual performance is critical to Work Review dynamics. The comparison between planned and actual performance ensures the vitality of the Work Review. It instantly empowers every member of the group to evaluate performance. No judgment can be made until this comparison is possible, and without the ability to judge, the Team members are powerless.

When people report their work without a plan or a trend line for comparison, the Work Review degenerates into a series of mere activity reports. Team members are left to politely accept the report (or more likely, ignore it), or attempts are made to evaluate it against many different and conflicting expectations. In the latter case, the discussion gets confusing and frustrating. Managers in Change-ABLE organizations don't tolerate such reports, insisting instead that each presentation make a clear comparison between planned and actual performance, and that Work Reviews acquire focus and efficiency. These concise, accurate presentations lead to informed decision-making.

The comparison between planned and actual performance also renews creative tension. If Work Reviews declare a difference between the actual and the desired situation, they inspire change. The difference may indicate a critical element for survival and success is missing — delivering a call for corrective action. Or the difference may indicate a surprise success requiring additional support — delivering a call for innovation and growth. The organization is motivated to creative change because the differences between desired and actual performance are recognized and dealt with continuously.

The information presented is always current — not more than 48 hours old.

Another distinguishing characteristic of Change-ABLE Work Reviews is current accuracy of its performance data. The least informed groups look at data not more than 48 hours old. This time lag is usually seen only at upper levels of the organization's hierarchy. In the trenches, data is often less than an hour old. The speed with which accurate and actionable information moves through the organization's network of meetings is remarkable.

The effect of having management Teams work in the present instead of in the past is difficult to describe. Vitality and excitement spark group discussion. Group members know they can make a difference; it's not too late. Decisions seem necessary and natural, and nothing contributes more to a sense of urgency and importance than a tight feedback loop! Current information constantly feeds the organization's creative tension.

Information regarding current status is presented graphically — in less than four minutes

Another key contributor to the effectiveness of Work Reviews is the use of graphics. Change-ABLE Managers have the skills required to communicate with charts and graphs. These pictures are literally worth a thousand words, as they can be used to define very complex technical problems in moments. In Change-ABLE organizations, it is not unusual for Performance Plans to be the only written documents displayed — everything else is discussed in relationship to the charts and graphs.

This use of graphics in Change-ABLE organizations has been accelerated in the last few years by software development. There are now many spreadsheet, financial, statistical, scientific, and project management programs with built-in graphing features. Change-ABLE Managers are competent in the use of these features.

Graphic presentation of performance information is not a frill. It marks a level of sophistication in metrics and the management of data that is painfully missing in many organizations. Skilled use of charts and graphs is itself a metric of how thoroughly a Manager understands the work being managed. In Change-ABLE organizations, these skill levels are high. They are required and practiced in every Work Review.

Discussion is issue focused —using the Team's authority to resolve problems and to seize opportunities

Finally, Change-ABLE organizations keep their Work Review discussions focused on issues. We refer to the presentation procedure as OSIR:

O: Objectives — show your Performance Plan

S: Status — State simply which objectives are "On track," "Behind," "At Risk," "Planned," or "Completed."

I: Issues — only for objectives that are "Behind" or "At Risk," state the issue in one sentence and show us the charts and graphs highlighting the difference between planned and actual performance.

R: Recommendation — start the group's discussion by recommending what you want done about the issue and whose help you need.

The objectives and their status are presented quickly. The presenter is prepared to display charts and graphs on any of the objectives, but unless asked to do otherwise, he or she only shows the ones relevant to the discussion of issues.

The presenter selects the issues carefully. There may be so many the presenter must prioritize them and deal only with the top priorities in the meeting. In this case, the presenter usually shows the entire list of issues and circles one or two he or she wants the Team to work on in the present meeting. Corrective action is often already underway, and the presenter must be ready to describe it. The most important question for the presenter to have asked in preparation is, "What do I want the Team to do in response to this issue?" This question causes the presenter to think about the authority of the group and the best way to use it. That is the meeting's purpose.

The one sentence issue statement is always accompanied by a recommendation statement. This statement clearly describes the action the group should take in response to the issue. Its function as a statement is to focus and stimulate Team discussion. In many cases, this recommendation statement, or some derivative of it, becomes the official statement of the Team's decision.

The OSIR procedure is used for every issue the members bring to the Team's Work Review. It is repeated many times during each meeting. When done well, it keeps the meeting focused on using its authority to advance the organization's performance toward the fulfillment of its goals. It keeps the Work Review from being a mere informational meeting. The recipe works out to about one part status reporting and three parts issue resolution.

As we said in the first section of this chapter, the purpose of the meeting is to take action. The OSIR procedure keeps the group focused on doing one of three things: approving the performance, taking corrective action, or reallocating resources to support surprise success. When Work Reviews make these kinds of decisions, they become vital to the organization. The symptoms of their vitality are obvious: the members come to the meetings regularly, on time, prepared, intensely attentive, and actively supportive. They leave each meeting knowing no time was lost — important work got done.

Get the Right People Talking About the Right Things at the Right Time

There are many variations on the schedule and membership of meetings doing Work Reviews in the Change-ABLE organization. However, the principle is always the same: get the right people (the authorities necessary to decide the use of relevant resources) talking about the right things (the issues currently requiring resolution to meet the Team's objectives) at the right time (some regular and frequent time the rest of the organization can rely upon).

The standard practice brings together all of a Manager's functional subordinates on a weekly basis. They then review the work pertaining to maintenance of the organization's technological competencies. Team resources (both human and material) are then allocated to the work according to the priorities.

This practice may vary, however, depending upon the level in the hierarchy of the management Team. Higher level Teams sometimes meet less frequently — often every other week or monthly. This is often enough, providing lower level Teams are performing more frequent Work Reviews. Under these conditions, most of the necessary decision-making is going on close to the work and only the higher level issues of priority and coordination require the attention of senior management Teams. Usually, however, the lower level Work Reviews are held in the presence of upper level Managers (one or two levels higher than the usual Leaders) at least once a quarter, and more often on a monthly basis. These meetings may last all day and will have large scale attendance — members of many different Teams listening in on the other Team's reports.

The meetings have the same basic purpose and follow the same OSIR procedure, but the presence of other Teams and upper level Managers enables other useful actions. Upper level Managers get a view of the competencies in the organization below them. This knowledge guides their future decisions regarding the formation of new Teams and leadership assignments. Lower level Managers get a chance to see peers in operation from other parts of the organization as well, preparing them for better cooperation in the future. They also see how upper level Managers think together and acquire assurance of the cooperation expected everywhere throughout the organization. Finally, the higher level issues of priority and coordination are at once resolved and communicated to a broader than usual range of relevant Teams.

Often another pattern of Work Review is used, especially when a Team's plan calls for simultaneous governance of several programs and functions in a matrix pattern. To capture all the key Managers under the Leader's domain of authority, the Team may have as many as 14 members — three or four functional Leaders, three or four program Leaders, and another three or four members to perform staff functions, such as Finance and Human Resources. Rather than involving all the members in every program review, the Leader divides the Team so that only the relevant functional Managers and one program Manager meet to review one program at a time. The most current and highest priority programs can all be reviewed in separate meetings on separate days of the week. This keeps weekly program reviews small enough to permit thorough examination of their issues. Usually a full staff meeting is held toward the end of the week to clear up remaining issues between the programs and the staff functions.

A further variation on this last schedule is sometimes used when the number of programs is large — seven or more. Some of these programs may be in the early stages of development, utilizing relatively small amounts of the organization's resources. They can be scheduled for Work Review every other week or month, alternating with other programs also in early stages of development. The more mature Projects, however, utilize more of the organization's resources and are approaching their deadlines. These convergent stages of a Project's life always require more management attention. Therefore, they are reviewed once a week at upper levels of management — one program at a time in separate meetings— and even more frequently (usually at least daily) by lower level management Teams. This schedule has an airport analogy. Planes that are approaching or have taken off and are at some distance away from the airport need less attention from the control tower. Those that are about to land or take off, or are taxiing about on the runways, must have constant attention.

These schedules and membership structures are described to show the flexibility with which the system of Linked Teams, Performance Plans, and Work Reviews can be adjusted to handle varying loads of complexity. If the organization keeps requiring everyone to attend every Work Review as the organization grows, the communication channels will sooner or later overload and the governance process will bog down. To deal with such growth, Change-ABLE organizations treat every management Team as a potential set of Teams. Some of the subsets operate some of the time in separate Team meetings, and occasionally the whole Team meets. The frequency of the alternation between subset meetings and the whole Team meetings — in fact, all questions of meeting frequency— are determined by the principle: get the right people talking about the right thing at the right time.

Work Reviews Are Supportive

One of the most frequently asked questions regarding the Work Reviews in Change-ABLE organizations is: "How do people handle their emotions in such meetings — how do they keep from getting beat up?" This deserves some attention.

In the first place, it is important to notice what kind of an organizational culture the person asking comes from. Those coming from a Raft, Dory Regatta, or Galley culture, are justified by experience to assume that questioning each other's work every week is a setup for some nasty fighting. If the assumption exists that Managers are supposed to be able to run their part of the organization autonomously, then any inquiry into their operations will be seen as, at least, implied criticism. Asking questions is also seen in these cultures as an expression of distrust — to ask is to show doubt regarding the Manager's ability to do the job. So, the usual response is defensiveness and a fight for rights and dignity.

Because the Basic Assumption is different in the Change-ABLE organization, much of this familiar scenario is avoided. People don't expect to operate autonomously. They expect others to cooperate with them, to make commitments, and to work together continuously in the fulfillment of these commitments. Cooperation means interdependence, and that means working at maintaining relationships. Part of maintaining relationships is asking, "How are we doing?" In the Change-ABLE organization it seems natural to ask the question, and it feels supportive when others ask it.

Even with the different assumptions, Change-ABLE organizations still have to deal with negative emotions. The problems are real, frustrating, and frightening. The Managers care about them, and can't help personalizing them. They feel guilty about the problems they have and angry about the problems others have. Failure to solve the problems has real consequences — the failure of the Team and the demotion or removal of Managers contributing to the failure. There is a lot at stake, and all the Managers feel it, but Managers in Change-ABLE organizations have at least two very significant advantages.

First, the Change-ABLE organization processes information so much more effectively its Managers are able to stay ahead of problems, learning of them while they are still in the early stages of their development. The corrective actions required are usually less dramatic or risky. Furthermore, no Manager is asked to face even these problems alone — the experience and knowledge of the other members of the Team are constantly available. These facts keep the emotional tone of the Work Reviews at a fairly low pitch. This lower emotional tone also allows the members to think more creatively — to be less driven by the habits of panic mode. This increase in creativity makes for better, longer-lasting solutions.

Secondly, Change-ABLE organizations experience so much more success than other organizations, their problems and failures seem less important. This is not to say the Managers ignore or deny their problems, it is just that in the context of the Change-ABLE organization, the problems are not fatal. The organization is so healthy, it overcomes the consequences of most of its failures. This allows the culture to be a bit more rational in its review of failures, and a bit better in learning from them. This way of seriously examining failures brings a higher quality of justice to the evaluation of those involved. This reliable environment keeps Managers feeling safe while under the continuous scrutiny of their colleagues.

Even with all this going for them, Managers in the Change-ABLE organization do sometimes get hurt. Individual human beings have very different thresholds for emotional pain, and inevitably, work with other human beings to find a way of climbing over that threshold. The Change-ABLE organization does not spend much time trying to be polite, nor is it very permissive. The Managers and Individual Contributors care about the work and have little tolerance for any behavior that isn't positively related to getting the work done. They tend to hurt those people who appear careless, and they will especially punish those they discover hiding a problem belonging to them all.

Hal's Story: How Linked Teams, Performance Plans, and Work Reviews Function as a System

To illustrate how the hierarchy of Linked Teams, Performance Plans, and synchronized Work Reviews work together for speed and flexibility, consider the case of Hal. Hal is a first line Manager brokering the talent of software engineers for process design in manufacturing. Seventy five per cent of Hal's Performance Plan is to deliver the software that will manufacture a new product called "G200," crucial to the company's sales plan for this year. G200's launch is 20 per cent of Max's (the Leader two levels above Hal) Plan.

The software is a very complex piece of work and it hasn't been going well. In the prior week's Work Review, the G200 project was put on the critical path and work has continued around the clock ever since. However, at this week's regular Work Review, 8:00 A.M. Monday, it is reported the software failed its milestone test for a third time earlier in the morning. Nell, the lead Engineer, thinks they are at a dead end. They may have to back up and come at it with a whole new approach. That could take two months!

Hal doesn't wait for his boss's 10:00 A.M. Work Review. He immediately takes Nell and the bad news with him to Bob's office. Together they review the problem, then alert two other members of Bob's Team, Gil and Irv, to come prepared for in-depth discussion at their 10 A.M. meeting.

The meeting begins with Hal's report. He is assisted by Nell. Gil and Irv have also brought some of their best engineers. Together, the Team generates two or three technical alternatives to the one Nell offered, and Bob immediately charters a small Task Force, to be led by Nell. Some Task Force members come from Gil's and Irv's groups, another is a renowned design engineer from one of the equipment vendor's shops.

Bob and Hal then go immediately to Bob's boss, Max. He soon calls in Alice and Cal, Bob's peers and key partners for positioning the G200 in the marketplace. This group suggests another technical alternative for Nell's Task Force and adds to its membership a materials scientist from Alice's R&D group. In case the Task Force is unable to cut down the delay, they also commit to having contingency plans ready to discuss at Max's Work Review on Tuesday morning.

By Tuesday morning, Nell's Task Force has successfully completed the first steps of a promising new technical solution, though it still calls for a delay of three weeks. After Bob reports this to Max's Work Review, the Team begins reallocating resources to reduce other steps on the G200's critical path. The revised plan is recommended by Max in his boss's Tuesday afternoon Work Review and approved. Before the sun rises on Wednesday, the Performance Plans of seven lower level Managers (in four different sections of the organization) and the assignments of 13 Individual Contributors have been altered to keep the G200 on schedule.

Hal's case illustrates how the Leaders of each management Team link the resources within the Team to the rest of the organization's hierarchy. It also demonstrates how Performance Plans align Managers on accountability for all the goals and resources within each Team's domain of authority. The disciplines of Work Reviews — focus on issues and the graphic display of current data — make the meetings efficient. The synchronized schedule of Work Reviews causes the entire decision-making process to be readily available to support the performance of Individual Contributors.

Summary

Chapter Ten described the Key Management Practice by which Change-ABLE organizations accomplish the function of performance feedback — Work Reviews. The following points were made:

1. Work Reviews are occasions for decisive action — a time when management Teams evaluate their performance and take action to solve problems or seize opportunities.
2. Work Reviews in Change-ABLE organizations have five essential characteristics:

   • They are focused on the desired results in the Team Leader's and members' Performance Plans.

- The reports always display both the objectives and the current status, thus facilitating evaluation.
- The information presented is always current — no more than 48 hours old.
- The status of all the expected results in any Performance Plan is presented graphically — in less than four minutes.
- The discussion is issue focused — using the Team's authority to resolve problems and to seize opportunities.

3. Several Work Review schedules were described — ways in which Change-ABLE organizations assure that the right people (the authorities necessary to determine the use of relevant resources) are talking about the right things (the issues currently requiring resolution to meet the Team's objectives) at the right time (some regular and frequent time the rest of the organization can rely upon for quick action).

4. Work Reviews in Change-ABLE organizations are supportive — no energy is lost on polite circumlocution. Members recognize their interdependence, and they are proactive in helping each other with problems and opportunities.

5. The function of Work Reviews (also Linked Teams and Performance Plans) was illustrated with "Hal's Story."

Though all of the five Key Management Practices are necessary to make an organization Change-ABLE, Work Review is the practice distinguishing this organizational culture from all others. Whether or not Managers recognize their interdependence and mutual accountability for their Team's success is most clearly displayed in their behavior during Work Reviews. It is the heartbeat of Change-ABLE organizations.

Group Decision-Making — Making Organizational Governance Intelligent

Overview

This chapter describes Group Decision-Making, the Key Management Practice by which Change-ABLE organizations accomplish the function of decision-making. It makes the following points:

1. In Change-ABLE organizations, the purpose of Regular Meetings — especially the meetings of management Teams — is to make decisions. The action-orientation of these meetings clearly distinguishes them from the passive information sharing that wastes so much time in most other organizations.

2. The Regular Meetings of Managers make decisions in four areas:

    - Pass Downs — they decide to commit;
    - Work Reviews — they decide to approve, reallocate resources, or modify plans;
    - Recommendation Reviews — they decide to approve, table, or take corrective action; and
    - News — they decide how to adjust.

3. The Regular Meetings of Managers follow a basic process for each issue requiring a decision:

    - Issue presentation;
    - Issue review/discussion;
    - Decision; and
    - Commissioning.

4. Group Decision-Making is defined as: a discussion procedure allowing a group to reach resolution utilizing the knowledge and opinions of its members, without requiring them to agree.

5. Members use five disciplines that allow them to engage in group discussion:

    - They come prepared and expecting to disagree.
    - They seek to understand and be understood — not to agree.
    - They expect to come to resolution — not agreement.

- They are willing to commit *and* disagree.
- They learn to resist group pressure to agree.

6. The Teams use two forms of decision-making to arrive at a rational Group Decision:

    - Consultative Decision-Making, or
    - Consensus Decision-Making

7. Group Decision-Making is essential to sustaining organizational flexibility and management credibility.

Making Decisions as the Purpose of Management Team Meetings

While most of this chapter focuses on specific processes for Group Decision-Making, we must first emphasize the important assumption that meetings are about decision-making. In most organi-

---

Group Decision-Making

- Four areas of decision-making:
    - Pass Downs;
    - Work Reviews;
    - Recommendations Reviews; and
    - News.
- Basic process for each issue:
    - Issue presentation;
    - Issue review/discusson;
    - Decision; and
    - Commissioning.
- Teams arrive at decisions without needing to be in agreement.
- Teams use two forms of rational decision-making:
    - Consultative, and
    - Consensus.

zations, this is not the assumption. Management meetings are most often justified as "opportunities to share information." When we observe these meetings, we often find that more than 80 per cent of meeting time is spent dealing with issues labeled, "FYI" — for your information. The intention of the presenters is to inform, not to ask for the group's action.

We think there is ample evidence to support the proposition that informational meetings are a waste of time. Less than 20 per cent of what is talked about in these meetings lodges in the minds or data-bases of the attendees. The most abundant evidence is the testimony of the attendees themselves when we ask them about the meetings afterward. "A waste of time," is the general conclusion. Information does not get communicated in these meetings because the human nervous system is designed to discard information without immediate usefulness. Our brains literally reject information as soon as it is determined that the information is not about a threat or opportunity requiring a response. If there is a lot of this useless information, the brain invokes the pain of stimulus deprivation — boredom. Most management meetings are a setup for such pain.

In addition to being boring, these decision-less management meetings produce another damaging result. They are a ritual teaching Managers to be powerless. Each meeting calls Managers together so that they may watch each other be inundated with information regarding happenings in the organization they are not asked to influence. The more the Managers sit together and do nothing, especially in the presence of their Leaders, the more likely they are to conclude there is not much they are expected to do.

By contrast, the Change-ABLE organization expects every management meeting to accomplish the work of governance — to make decisions about how its resources should be employed. The brains of the Managers absorb the information in meetings because they know they are expected to use the information for an immediate act of authority— probably within the next 30 minutes. Meeting Leaders make sure this is the case. They screen the Team's meeting agenda to make sure every item requires the action of the members. During the meeting, they redirect the discussion whenever it seems to drift from its decision-making task. Leaders consider mere information sharing to be an abuse of their Teams' time and authority. These meetings are a precious opportunity to do the work of management — to make decisions about how the organization's resources are employed. Their rule of thumb is: *never allow anything on the Team's agenda that does not require the members of the group to exercise their authority in the form of a decision.*

The Four Areas of Decision-Making

In Regular Meetings, Managers make decisions in four different areas:

> **Pass Downs** are decisions made at a higher domain of authority in the hierarchy now being passed down the structure for commitment and implementation. In the Change-ABLE organization, Pass Down decisions are usually made with prior input from the lower level Teams, though emergencies may make a Pass Down new to the receiving Team. The decision to be made in response to a Pass Down is *commitment* — to bring the resources of the Team into compliance with this higher level decision. (We discuss the full meaning of "commitment" later in this chapter.)
>
> **Work Reviews** have already been discussed in detail in Chapter Ten. Here the action is approval, reallocation of resources, or modification of plans.
>
> **Recommendation Reviews** also result in decisions to approve, disapprove, or employ corrective action. These Recommendation Reviews may be brought to the Team by Task Forces, staff members, Individual Contributors, or outside experts. Once a recommendation is accepted, it stops being just a good idea and becomes an operational reality invested with organizational authority and resources.
>
> **News** is often the least active part of the meeting agenda. News is a report from a member of the Team regarding changes taking place that affect at least two other members of

the Team. (If it only affects one other member, the News item is handled outside the meeting.) These are usually brief announcements in headline form, not lengthy reports. They serve as a reminder and early warning system regarding adjustments that may be required in the near future. There is often no discussion required, but members may sometimes need to briefly confer to make immediate adjustments or to put the item on a future meeting's agenda for more serious consideration.

No other forms of information processing are required at the management meeting in Change-ABLE organizations. If a suggested agenda item doesn't fit in one of these categories, then the item doesn't belong on the meeting's agenda *at all*.

The Basic Process for Decision-Making

Every item coming to the management meeting for decision is treated with a four-part process. Sometimes all four steps only take a couple of minutes, sometimes the process is extended over several hours and several meetings. These are the four steps:

Presentation: Issues are presented to the group and are usually accompanied by a recommendation — a statement of what action the presenter wants the group to perform. In the meetings of the Change-ABLE organization, the meeting's pre-published agenda includes these issue and recommendation statements. The presentation is brief and efficient, refined by the use of charts and graphs whenever possible. If much reading is required, documents are distributed in advance of the meeting. Questions for clarification are answered as part of the presentation, and there are often many questions.
Review: Once Team members are satisfied and they understand the issue and the presenter's recommendation, they begin discussing it among themselves. At this point, they will probe to discover the sources and validity of the presenter's data, the criteria by which the recommendation was deter-

mined, and the consequences the presenter believes will follow the implementation of his or her recommendation. Members may also offer additional information and may suggest other options for the Team's consideration. Disagreements are expressed and clearly defined.

Decision: The discussion is summarized and a decision is made. The decision may be made by either a consultative or a consensus process. These processes will be discussed later in this chapter.

Commissioning: Once a decision is made, the Leader takes a little time to make sure members understand the specific requirements for implementation. This may be in the form of Action Required (AR) assignments to specific members, the formation of Network Teams or Task Forces, or in other forms of resource allocation. Sometimes, this part of the procedure is a discussion the Leader conducts to make sure all members are able to explain the decision. This is especially wise if during the review part of the procedure some of the members express strong preferences contrary to the final decision.

Having discussed the four areas in which Change-ABLE management Teams make decisions, and the basic process by which each decision is approached, it is now time to put the microscope on the unique nature of Group Decision-Making. Be assured there are many irrational ways for groups to make decisions. In fact, most groups rarely use rational Group Decision-Making procedures. Instead, groups are usually used as a disguise for what is, in fact, autocratic decision-making by the Leader. More often, groups are manipulated into their decisions by the pressures of a few influential members — known as "minority railroading." Minority railroading is prevalent when the group makes its decisions by voting. And there are hundreds of ways in which the participation habits of individual group members throw a wrench into the group's thinking processes prior to making the decision. There really is a phenomenon known as "group think," which is fairly stupid. Groups can make worse decisions than any of the individual members would have made by themselves.

There is also, however, a real phenomenon known as "group intelligence" — the ability of groups to make better decisions than any of its members would make alone. There is no magic in this phenomenon. It comes from having at least a few members in the group who know the skills of Group Decision-Making.

Group Decision-Making can be defined as *a discussion procedure allowing a group to reach a resolution utilizing the knowledge and opinions of its members, without ever requiring them to be in agreement.*

The Disciplines Required for Group Decision-Making

Come prepared and expecting to disagree

The key to Group Decision-Making is finding a way to use and preserve member disagreement. Very few people understand the first requirement, which is that participants never allow themselves to feel any obligation to reach agreement!

Agreement has two components: intellectual and emotional. The intellectual component of agreement is to perceive a similar set of facts and to arrive at the same interpretation of those facts. The emotional component of agreement is feeling the comfort and confidence that comes from sharing this common perception with another person — the feeling of relation and acceptance instead of isolation and loneliness. The emotional component is very powerful and desirable, and most of us work at intellectual agreement to gain the emotional component. The intensity of the emotional component increases with the number of people holding the same intellectual perception. Groups *always* play on this emotional component. It is used to affirm the group's identity, and the threat to withdraw this good feeling is used to discipline the thinking process of group members. It is difficult for most of us to imagine a group in which all members feel no obligation to agree. What would be the point of such a group?

The point might be to promote each other's thinking and learning! Membership and the emotions of acceptance would then be based upon the precision and uniqueness of each member's thinking, rather than upon the similarity of it. Group respect and status would be based upon individual diversity of thought. Such diversity would not just be tolerated, it would be required.

It is this peculiar sort of group that is best suited for Group Decision-Making. The quality of the decision-making is directly related to the diversity, not the similarity, of the members' thinking. More, different, yet relevant, facts, and more differences of interpretation of those facts, yield better decisions. Without this diversity, there is little reason to expect the group's decision to be any better than one of its agreeing members could have made alone. In fact, without diversity, there is no rational group decision. What is produced instead is an emotional affirmation of the members' conformity. Group Decision-Making requires the group to perpetuate member diversity.

Diversity means disagreement. If we look for it, it is not hard to find. In fact, we know that no two people actually perceive anything in quite the same way. Language masks much of this diversity — we have learned to label our perceptions by the factual names common to our culture. As soon as we press language to greater precision, we find ourselves describing facts others have difficulty noticing. And our interpretation of these "facts" is even more different. Interpretation is based upon life experiences, and no two people share the same history. It is not hard to be in disagreement, but it is often difficult to admit it.

Whether or not we are comfortable admitting our disagreement depends upon the norms (ground rules) of the group. If the group's norms expect and encourage disagreement, most of us have little difficulty expressing unique ideas that are both carefully considered and sincere. When a group permits it, members almost always enlarge the database with a rich mixture of knowledge and opinion. These are the ingredients from which better decisions are made.

In Change-ABLE organizations, Teams operate from these peculiar norms. Their standards for membership are different. The first requirement is *disagree*.

Seek to understand and be understood — not to agree

The second requirement for participation in Group Decision-Making is *understand and be understood.* Participants go to Team meetings not expecting to reach agreement, but to be understood and to understand the other members. Understanding each other is not the same as agreeing.

Understanding is being able to identify the facts another is attending to and the interpretation made of those facts. To be able to do this, a participant must listen actively — ask questions and test understanding with illustrations and summaries. As members of the Team get behind each other's language, they discover they are not looking at the same facts. Nor will they find that, even looking at the same set of facts, they arrive at the same interpretation! Many people interpret this discovery as misunderstanding. They expect understanding to lead to seeing and interpreting the facts in a similar way. But this is not a realistic expectation. In reality, we live in different worlds of perception. To understand each other is not to come to a common perception, but to notice the distinctions.

For a member to understand others is not enough. Each member must also insist on being understood. To be understood requires assertiveness. Members can't wait for the group to ask for their ideas. They must learn to express their ideas more than once, never assuming people "get it" the first time. They must also learn that a response of silence followed by a change of the subject is not acceptable. Nor is being interrupted an excuse for allowing oneself to be ignored. Members have to operate from the attitude that if they don't get understood, they have failed to perform their role as a group member. They were made a member of the Team because their ideas and authority were needed, and unless they persist until understood, their membership responsibilities have not been fulfilled. However, it is also important for members to recall that being understood is not the same as getting others to agree.

Another way members discipline themselves to promote understanding is to always engage the entire process from the Leader's perspective. Members hold themselves accountable for making the group's decision. It is as though they say to themselves, "If I were the Leader of this group, given this presentation and discussion, what else would I want to know and how would I make the decision?" This attitude keeps the members from falling into representational thinking — simply representing, advocating, and defending their special concerns. It requires them to climb up into the Leader's role and view the Team's work from the Leader's domain of authority and account-ability. This attitude keeps every member struggling to really understand the entire discussion. It also contributes to a better group process, making every meeting a classroom in Leadership.

To fulfill the requirements for understanding, members must know how to test for it. The test is simple and quick. A member understands another's idea when he or she can describe it in such a way that the other member affirms the description. Sometimes discussions get a bit too excited in the Change-ABLE organization. Members start repeating themselves with louder and louder voices — as if they were talking to someone who was hard of hearing. This is usually because members have forgotten that they have no obligation to win each other's agreement. Some other member then comes to the rescue by running the test of understanding. The question is asked, "Can you two summarize each other's point of view?" As the participants take the test, they assist the group in summarizing its thinking, one of the essentials of group work. It also diminishes passions and rationalizes the discussion. All members should know how to run the test for understanding whenever they suspect the group is missing or ignoring their ideas.

We do not mean to imply that to understand is necessarily to disagree. Members are not obligated to stick stubbornly to their starting positions. A genuine effort to understand others almost always leads to learning — the alteration of one's own perceptions. Sometimes this learning moves people to agreement — a new and common perception of reality. Usually, we learn from each other but still disagree. This is acceptable. Coming to agreement doesn't have to be the test of learning. The point is, in Group Decision-Making, only understanding each other is important. Agreement is irrelevant.

Expect to come to resolution — not agreement

When a Team in the Change-ABLE organization reaches resolution, it has not reached agreement. The resolution will be the group's decision, but many of the members may disagree with it.

Resolution does not require the group's agreement to achieve its validity. The quality of the resolution involves three other criteria: it must reflect a respect for the known, relevant facts as identified by the group; it must have a logical fit to the issue it is intended to resolve, and the group should be familiar with this logic; and it must be consistent with the goals of the Team (assuming the Team's goals are aligned with the organization's overall goals.)

During the presentation and review stages of the decision-making procedure, members will have identified a body of facts. Members will not likely agree that all the facts are relevant, and will probably have an even greater range of disagreement regarding the validity or relative importance of those facts. There is usually an uneven level of understanding of the facts as well. Still, a body of information called facts has been accumulated and considered. The first test of the validity of the group resolution is the degree to which it displays a consideration for this body of facts. If it is not consistent with some interpretation of these facts, then it has obviously come from some other source than the group — perhaps the unexpressed mind and preferences of the Leader, or from some covert alliance within the group. It cannot be a group decision if it does not reflect the facts proposed by the presentation and review.

The second test of the validity of group resolution is whether or not it addresses the original issue in a way made apparent by its logic. When the resolution does not have an obvious, logical relationship to the issue, it is usually a sign of some dominant prejudice at work in the group. In these cases, the group usually has a history of solving every problem with the same hammer. Furthermore, the logic of this resolution will have been thoroughly explored during the presentation and review. If the resolution is a" brand new" interpretation of the data, it is probably not a product of the group's work. This often occurs when the Leader does not understand the process of Consultative Decision-Making and therefore sits silently through the discussion, dismissing one member's opinion after another until it is time to make the decision. Then, for the first time, the group hears the Leader's opinion and finds it surprising. In Group Decision-Making, the resolution must have a logical relationship to the issue it addresses, and because it was put to the test of their understanding and disagreement during the presentation and review, that logic must be familiar to the group.

The final test of the validity of the decision is its alignment with the Team's goals — its obvious intent to advance the Team toward the accomplishment of key results in its plan. Any mystery regarding this relationship is dangerous! Failure of the Team to make sense of its decisions in light of its stated objectives will damage its credibility with subordinates. Such decisions are invariably interpreted by Individual Contributors as power plays at the expense of their work effectiveness. Individual Contributors eventually withdraw their consent to be managed by such Managers. Then management discovers who empowers whom — often at the expense of their own careers. When the whole Team accepts its accountability for all of the Team's goals, as is the case in Change-ABLE organizations, every decision relates directly and obviously to the accomplishment of those goals.

Valid resolutions respect the information and opinions expressed by the group during its deliberations and are relevant to the Team's goals. The validity is not dependent upon the Team members' agreement. This is an important distinction. When it is forgotten, the group's process moves toward emotional intimidation and subversive voting. Resolutions become compromises or the irrational affirmations of dominant power blocks. Such resolutions are typical of other organizational cultures, but they are less likely in Change-ABLE organizations.

Be willing to disagree <u>and</u> commit

An extremely important discipline for participants in Group Decision-Making is that of disagree and commit. In Change-ABLE organizations, commitment is not confused with agreement. Commitment is a two-part behavior.

First, each member must be able to explain the rationale of the group's decision — to explain it in a way the other members of the group would agree is accurate and complete.

Secondly, members must strive to make sure the resources under their control are employed in compliance with the decision.

Understood in this context, member commitment can be easily demonstrated and evaluated. It also clearly does not require agreement. In fact, in Change-ABLE organizations, disagreement doesn't stop with resolution. Once resolution has been reached, members commit *and* continue to disagree. The particular benefits of this feature of disagreement are discussed later in the chapter. As we shall see, this continuing disagreement is not disloyalty or failure to commit. On the contrary, it is the expression of a genuine concern for keeping the organization thoughtful and responsive.

There are many who just cannot believe this sort of commitment is sufficient. It is popular, for instance, to call it "mere compliance." This argument suggests that commitment must be characterized by enthusiasm and conviction. The argument rests on the assumption that group process can and should lead to a resolution to which all the members can intellectually and emotionally agree. We've already stated our case against this assumption. We can also add that we have seen better group work and more intelligent decisions made in organizations operating from the requirement that Teams disagree *and* commit.

Learn to resist group pressures to agree

Though we have said this already, we want to reemphasize it: participants in Group Decision-Making are required to resist group pressures to agree. It is common for groups to enforce cohesion and conformity by intimidating their members with threats of disapproval and exclusion. Each member must learn about his or her susceptibility to group intimidation — the subtle ways groups will use an individual's needs to enforce compliance. This learning is intensely personal; our susceptibility to group pressure is unique and profound.

Sometimes, the group plays on our need to be dependent and tempts us to revert to early stages of our personal development. Sometimes, it plays to our rebellious need for independence and keeps us ineffective in cooperation with others. Rational group work requires members to push themselves in their personal development toward the stage of maturity called interdependence. In this stage of development, members learn it is possible to understand and respect each other without being in agreement, and that interdependence is both smarter and more reliable. Members also discover that interdependence feels different — it is intensely communal, yet freeing. As groups persist in the effort to do rational group work, members are pushed toward this stage of maturity. They can then think rather than feel their way toward group decisions. Diversity of knowledge and perspective is then invested in the decision-making process, and the quality of decisions improves.

Two Forms of Group Decision-Making

Consultative Decision-Making

Consultative Decision-Making is the most commonly used process in Change-ABLE organizations. This process is preferred because, unlike Consensus Decision-Making, it can be used in situations where the status quo is not a legitimate option. Consultative Decision-Making also reinforces the authority of the management Team Leader, and clarity regarding authority keeps an organization empowered.

In a Consultative Decision-Making process, members present issues to the Leader to inform the Leader's decision. It is understood ahead of time that the Leader will be the decider. The effectiveness of this process depends upon two things: the group's ability to bring a full database and a reasonable set of alternatives to the discussion, and the Leader's ability to learn.

There is no magic in good group work. Getting people together to talk about things will not automatically lead to more effective decision-making. Members must know the business, be prepared, be active listeners, and be verbally efficient as participants. It helps if they have the maturity and self-confidence to think critically and to effectively challenge all the others' ideas, including the Leader's. The group can be smarter than all of its individual members, but it is best if the ingredients for the process include smart, well-prepared members. The role of the members is to educate the group's decider (usually the Leader). If the members are not up to this task, the process suffers.

The Consultative Decision-Making process allows the group to reach resolution through the learning and decision-making of its decider. The decider does not use member agreement as a measure of the decision's validity. Rather, the decider uses his or her own reasoning as the means to a quality decision. The first obligation of the decider is to learn from the discussion and to deal reasonably with all information and opinions made available by the group. Using this database, the decider arrives at the decision and explains it to the group. At this point, the Team's decision is made — it is not the decider's decision; it is the Team's decision. Members are now expected to commit — probably to disagree *and* commit.

Deciders are obliged to teach the group the rationale they finally use to reach their decisions. This is an important ingredient of the last step in the decision-making procedure — commissioning. This final part of the discussion is usually accompanied by further questions from the members. Some of the questions are simply for clarification; some are raised as final expressions of disagreement and warning. Commissioning assures that the members are able and ready to commit to the Team's decision — to explain its rationale faithfully and to bring the resources under their influence into alignment with it.

Few Teams start out with wonderful participants and great Leaders. Fortunately, the frequent repetition of the group process creates the classroom in which members learn their skills. The better the group gets, the better its members get. To observe a group that has been at it two or three times a week for a few years is literally breathtaking! It proves that, as individuals, we are all capable of a high degree of intelligence, and all we need is the opportunity to work in a few good Teams to actualize this potential.

Consensus Decision-Making

Consensus is now commonly defined as providing all group members with a respectful hearing and then going along with the majority's preference. This misunderstanding usually causes the consensus process to achieve the same irrational conclusions typical of voting — a Nominal Group process. When voting is the explicit or implicit decision-making process, members usually vote at the end of the discussion exactly as they would have without it. The decision would have been the same without the pretense of group involvement.

A proper understanding of Consensus Decision-Making follows this rule: if any member of the group believes the status quo is better than any proposed alternative, the status quo will be the group's decision. The consensus process invests each member with the power to veto change. Remaining with the status quo must be a legitimate option if consensus is going to be used — and it will often be the group's resolution. Staying with the status quo is not a failure to achieve consensus, it is a legitimate outcome of the process and must be understood as the group's resolution.

One of the strengths of Consensus Decision-Making is that it gives such serious consideration to the status quo. It forbids the group to operate from the unchallenged assumption that change must be made, and often enriches the group's thinking by establishing a well-documented baseline from which to compare proposed changes. It also frequently protects the group from the risks of choosing unnecessary or exaggerated proposals for change.

Consensus can lead to one person causing the group to resolve in favor of the status quo when all other members want change. Consensus also can lead to a resolution for change without full agreement from the group. For instance, all the members may accept the premise that Proposal A is better than the status quo. However, the members may not all agree that A is the best possible change. Team members may have advocated Proposals B, C, and D, but were unable to demonstrate to all the other members that any of these options were better than both the status quo and A. In the end, Proposal A is the group's decision, while many members still prefer the options B, C, and D. In the Change-ABLE organization, these somewhat disappointed members will be expected to disagree and commit to the Team's consensus decision.

Group Decision-Making Sustains Organizational Flexibility and Management Credibility

Sustaining Organizational Flexibility

Earlier in this chapter we mentioned that the principle of disagree and commit applies not only to the decision-making discussion, but also after the decision is made. Members are encouraged to commit *and continue to disagree.* They are expected to manage the resources under their control in compliance with the decision, but they are not expected to pretend that they are in agreement with the decision or its rationale. Managers are to maintain their intellectual integrity and are encouraged to express their disagreement whenever they are asked about their opinions, especially when asked by subordinates. It is not always possible for them to explain how their ideas were not accepted without showing disappointment and irritation. Whereas other organizations consider this kind of disagreement to be dysfunctional and disloyal, Change-ABLE organizations perpetuate it, tolerate the emotional grit in its bearings, and get significant rewards for doing so.

Disagree and commit serves the Change-ABLE organization not only by enriching the intelligence of the decision-making process, but also by keeping all organizational options alive. No idea is ever finally discarded. All decisions are carefully evaluated throughout the life of their implementation. Subtle adjustments in the implementation of ideas are easier and quicker when appropriate disagreement is maintained. When, in spite of full commitment, a decision proves to be seriously inadequate, dramatic alternatives are often immediately at hand as contingency plans. The alacrity of the Change-ABLE organization is due in part to its perpetuation of disagreement. Disagreement maintains options to the organization's current commitments.

Maintaining Management Credibility

One further benefit of disagree and commit is its contribution to management credibility. Requiring Managers to act as cheerleaders for every group decision during its implementation erodes confidence in their intelligence. If a Manager consults with subordinates before attending the upper level decision-making meetings as he or she should, subordinates are left with a good idea of the Leader's frame of mind. If the Leader keeps coming back from higher level meetings with enthusiasm for a significantly different set of ideas, and with careful attempts to suppress opposing ideas, subordinates will create a theory to explain such peculiar behavior. Either their Leader is a mindless wimp, or his boss is one horrible autocratic SOB who rams everything down the throats of his subordinates and expects them to do the same! A third theory is that only the people at the top are really smart and well-informed, and the rest of us, including our immediate Leader, are pea-brained!

These destructive interpretations of management are common in Raft or Galley organizations. But in Change-ABLE organizations, Leaders are seen as thoughtful and a bit on the scrappy side. They are known as people who speak up and insist upon being understood. They also have a reputation for being able to recognize another person's good ideas. They are trusted to make sure every decision is carefully and reasonably achieved. Such a reputation contributes mightily to trust and confidence in management. Empowered by such consent from the managed, Managers keep an organization fast and flexible in its performance.

Summary

Chapter Eleven described the Key Management Practice that makes Change-ABLE organizations distinctive and unusually intelligent — Group Decision-Making. The following points were made:

1. In Change-ABLE organizations, the purpose of Regular Meetings is to make decisions — information-sharing that is irrelevant to making a decision is not permitted on the agenda.
2. Regular Meetings make decisions in four areas:

    *   Pass Downs — they decide to commit;
    *   Work Reviews — they decide to approve, reallocate resources, or modify plans;
    *   Recommendation Review — they decide to approve, table, or take corrective action; and
    *   News — they decide how to adjust.

3. A basic process is followed for each issue requiring a decision:

    *   Issue presentation;
    *   Issue review/discussion;
    *   Decision; and
    *   Commissioning.

4. Group Decision-Making was defined as: a discussion procedure allowing a group to reach a resolution utilizing the knowledge and opinions of its members, without ever requiring them to be in agreement.

5. Five disciplines for engaging in rational group discussion were described:

    - Come prepared and expecting to disagree.
    - Seek to understand and be understood — not to agree.
    - Expect to come to resolution — not agreement.
    - Be willing to commit *and* disagree.
    - Learn to resist group pressure to agree.

6. The two forms of rational Group Decision-Making were described:

    - Consultative Decision-Making, and
    - Consensus Decision-Making.

7. The importance of Group Decision-Making to organizational flexibility and management credibility was explained.

While Change-ABLE organizations seem to make more good decisions than other organizations, they do not always make the best decisions. Change-ABLE organizations don't wait until they have achieved a perfect decision. Instead, they just take the next step forward as intelligently as possible. Then they learn from the consequences what further adjustments are required. Because Change-ABLE organizations use Group Decision-Making processes, they are able to learn more quickly than other organizations, and to secure rapid, organization-wide commitment for each new step.

12

Breakthrough Systems — Acknowledging the Real Managers of Work

Overview

This chapter describes Breakthrough Systems, the Key Management Practice through which Change-ABLE organizations accomplish the function of managing Individual Contributors. Here we will briefly summarize these observations and emphasize their important contribution to organizational speed and flexibility. The chapter makes the following points:

1. Change-ABLE organizations fully acknowledge the fact that Individual Contributors process most of the information required to manage the organization's work. They know how important it is to pay attention to the way Individual Contributors manage themselves and each other.

2. Breakthrough Systems is a term used to describe the self-management methods enabling Individual Contributors to sustain high levels of productivity. These methods assure a work environment characterized by:

   • Clear expectations regarding the results expected from performance;
   • Immediate, self-monitored feedback showing comparison between actual and expected performance; and
   • Control of the resources necessary to meet performance expectations.

3. A Task Grid is used to identify four types of tasks, and the different methods used to apply Breakthrough Systems to each type are described:

   • Breakthrough Systems for Routine Tasks;
   • Breakthrough Systems for Projects;
   • Breakthrough Systems for Troubleshooting Tasks; and
   • Breakthrough Systems for Negotiable Tasks.

4. The various forms of teamwork used by Individual Contributors to manage themselves and each other are described.

5. The informality of Breakthrough Systems is emphasized and the ways that Change-ABLE organizations protect this informality are described.
6. The interdependence of Breakthrough Systems and the other Key Management Practices is discussed and illustrated by the "Project Team's Story."

Individual Contributors Are Acknowledged as the Real Managers of Work

In any organization, thousands of decisions must be made by Individual Contributors every hour to manage the on-going performance of the organization. Researchers have found that most Individual Contributors talk to someone in "management" only about twice a day — for a total of four minutes per day. But they talk to each other about work on average, about 20 times an hour. If it is understood that management is a matter of processing information to coordinate the organization's performance, then it becomes clear that Individual Contributors do most of the management task.

In Change-ABLE organizations, the role of Individual Contributors in managing work is fully acknowledged. The rest of the organization's practices are viewed as support to the management going on among Individual Contributors. The objective is to create very distinctive work environments for each Individual Contributor: Breakthrough Systems.

Breakthrough Systems for Individual Contributors

- Clear expectations about the expected results;
- Self-monitored feedback systems; and
- Control of the resources necessary to realize the expected results.

Three Requirements for Self-Management in Breakthrough Systems

Breakthrough Systems were first described by J. M. Juran in his writing regarding quality control in organizations. Juran emphasized that no process design was complete until it took into account the requirements for self-management of the Individual Contributors operating the process. He identified three requirements for self-management, and named the following combination as performance Breakthrough Systems:

- Individual Contributors know what results are expected from their performance. These expectations are explicit regarding the pace and quality of the outputs desired.
- Individual Contributors are able to determine for themselves, on a continuous basis, how they are doing in relationship to the expectations. They have an immediate and reliable means of performance feedback.
- Individual Contributors are in control of the resources necessary to meet the expectations.

When the rest of the organization's governance system makes Breakthrough Systems possible, Individual Contributors' management of the work vastly improves. The quality of their decisions rises because they are focused on appropriate and clear expectations. The timeliness of their decisions improves because they have continuous and reliable performance feedback. When these two conditions are met, Individual Contributors manage themselves, each other, and the organization's resources much more effectively, guaranteeing a significantly better return on the organization's investment in physical assets.

The productivity of Individual Contributors in Breakthrough Systems seems incredible to other organizations, who usually receive only about 50 per cent utilization of the resources made available to their workforce. Through Breakthrough Systems, Change-ABLE organizations get about 80 per cent utilization on a regular basis, moving up from there when temporary peak performance is required.

It was this dramatic difference in the productivity of Individual Contributors — this 30 per cent leap in productivity — that inspired Juran's dramatic label: Breakthrough Systems. This everyday increased return on the assets managed by Individual Contributors gives the Change-ABLE organization a frightening competitive advantage.

Adapting Breakthrough Systems to Various Task Types

There are many different Task Types performed in any organization. For convenience, we look at two work variables to create a simple Task Grid. On one axis is the variable of predictability. Some tasks, especially the ones performed by an organization for a long time, become quite predictable. But there are always tasks that are Unpredictable. Customer emergencies, faulty products, process breakdowns, and surprise shortages of critical raw materials can interrupt even the most basic and familiar work.

On the other axis of the Task Grid is the variable of delay-tolerance. Many organizational tasks require performance on very exacting schedules. For instance, high volume production requires

Task Grid

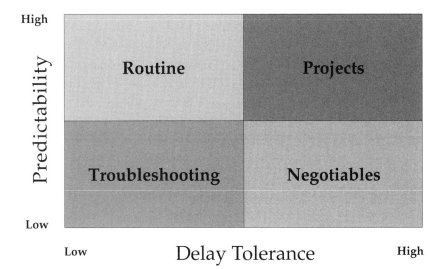

split-second timing between process steps, while other tasks are much
more flexible in their start and end times. Sometimes, when planning
performance, we deliberately inject slack time into these tasks to give
them more tolerance for delay.

The tasks that make up a Task Grid are as follows:

> **Routine Tasks** are defined as high in predictability, but low in
> delay tolerance. We do not use the term to connote work a
> person does all the time, as some people do Projects and
> Troubleshooting all the time.
>
> **Projects** are defined as high in both predictability and delay
> tolerance. This kind of task is always intended to produce a
> unique output — to cause a change. It is not repetitive. But
> through the techniques of planning, these unique tasks are
> made predictable and delay tolerant.
>
> **Troubleshooting** is defined as low in both predictability and
> delay tolerance. It is always a surprise and an emergency.
>
> **Negotiables**, like Troubleshooting, are also unpredictable.
> They are a response to some demand that cannot be com-
> pletely foreseen. But, unlike Troubleshooting, Negotiables
> have some delay tolerance. Responding to a request for a
> special cost study could easily become a Negotiable Task.

Dividing the organization's work into four kinds of tasks helps
select the most effective methods for getting them performed in
Breakthrough Systems. Because the tasks are fundamentally different,
the methods are also quite different. But once the Task Types have been
identified, there are no tasks for which it is impossible to create Breakthrough Systems.

It is important to notice, however, that Breakthrough Systems are
always task specific. In order to get an Individual Contributor's entire
job into Breakthrough Systems, the job must first be broken down into
its component tasks. They will then experience their jobs as moving
from one Breakthrough System to another, shifting their attention from
task to task.

Routine Tasks

We will now briefly describe the various methods that make Breakthrough Systems possible for the performance of each task type, beginning with Routine Tasks.

> **Expectations for Routine Tasks**: It is always important to establish both a pace and quality specification for each task. In the case of Routine Tasks, these specifications always take the form of a standard describing how fast the work should be done and the quality expected for each output. The expectation is stated as a standard — a level of performance to be maintained. For instance: "two cases/hour, filling every blank in the form without more than one audit error per week;" "one machine load every 40 minutes, each load according to its specified recipe."

> **Self-Monitored Feedback Methods for Routine Tasks**: Because of the volume of outputs usually involved in the performance of Routine Tasks, constant attention is required to monitor the process. Any lapse of attention may allow large amounts of wasted material and/or damage to the equipment or processes, resulting in costly delays. Therefore, the ideal performance feedback systems for Routine Tasks are those which operate on a continuous basis.
>
> The three most common methods used for self-monitored feedback when performing Routine Tasks are: Batching, Tally Sheets, and Checklists.
>
> - *Batching*: This is the preferred self-monitoring system because it doesn't require anything that looks or feels like administrative work. The Individual Contributor's input materials or finished outputs are arranged or stacked in small groups of some well-known number. As Individual Contributors perform the task, they can count these batches to monitor the pace of their work. The tools or

samples necessary to check the outputs for quality should be near at hand.

- *Tally Sheets*: This is a commonly used method for self-monitored feedback regarding Routine Task performance. A Tally Sheet is a chart on which people make a mark each time some defined unit of output is completed. It is a way of displaying the completed task count. There are several types of these very simple forms. Some are designed to cover two or three different kinds of Routine Tasks, enabling Individual Contributors to use only one form as they move from one task to another. Others are designed for only one task. There are usually places on the Tally Sheets for start and stop times, which allow Individual Contributors to account for interruptions.

- *Checklists*: One of the most versatile self-monitoring methods is the Checklist. Such forms list all the steps that need to be done each time a Routine Task is performed. Checklists are especially useful for repetitive tasks consisting of several subroutines, for instance, cleaning the rooms in an office building. In each room, there may be as many as 15 different things that need to be done — trash removal, dusting, vacuuming, rearranging the furniture. The Checklist reminds the Individual Contributor to do all the sub-tasks. The Checklist also can specify the sequence in which the sub-tasks should be done when sequence is important. It also can be tailored to indicate which tasks are to be done daily, weekly, and monthly.

Resource Control for Routine Tasks: To be in Breakthrough Systems, Individual Contributors must have control over the resources necessary to perform the task in conformity with the expectations. A variety of resources must be considered, including materials, equipment, and other tools. Skills, access to information, and definition of authorities must also be assured. Anything making it impossible for Individual Contributors to take corrective action when their feedback systems indicate they are not meeting expectations should be explored as a resource-control problem.

Change-ABLE organizations surround the Individual Contributor with the configuration of resources required to meet performance expectations. Putting Individual Contributors to work in Teams, as we discuss later in this chapter, greatly increases the degree to which resource-control problems will be prevented or quickly resolved. At least once a month, Change-ABLE supervisors lead meetings devoted to identifying resource problems, deciding on appropriate corrective actions, and reviewing recommendations from previously chartered Task Forces. Individual Contributors are rarely able to solve all the resource-control problems without the support of higher management. Supervisors are their links to the larger system of organizational governance, in which resource problems and performance expectations are reviewed.

Projects

Expectations For Projects: Project expectations are established through the project planning process. In Change-ABLE organizations, the planning process is highly participative — a meeting we call Chart Day. Every part of the organization affected by the Project sends its most important people to this meeting. For a new product development Project, the meeting lasts a full day, and there are often as many as 70 people in attendance — marketers, designers, manufacturers, customer servers, human-resource specialists, budgeters, and schedulers. Before the meeting has ended, attendees will have worked together with Post-its™ and markers to make a project flow chart that can reach 70 feet in length. The chart schedules everything from design, to sales, to service. And, most important for our immediate consideration, the deliverables for the first four weeks of the first month are specified. With these weekly deliverables in place, Individual Contributors currently working on Projects can begin designing their Breakthrough Systems.

Change-ABLE organizations have discovered the folly of asking anyone to work on a planning horizon longer than one week. The more complex and uncertain the tasks in the Project are, the more important it is to get short-term deliverables identified. Sometimes, the deliverables will merely be the creation of one's notes on the basis of documents read or conversations held with other experts during the week. At other times, deliverables will be as specific as an engineer's drawings, or the lines of code created by a software designer. The emphasis, however, is on making the expectation a concrete deliverable. Deliverables pass the "Look Ma!" test — you can show them to your mother and say, "Look Ma, this is what I did this week." At the end of the week, Individual Contributors can say their deliverables are "Done" or "Not Done." (No qualification, such as "80 per cent done," is considered relevant. Such a task is reported as "not done.")

Many Individual Contributors working on Projects are highly professional. They typically have been asked to estimate their performance in terms of months. They do the best they can to respond to these requests, but very few are able to make such estimates with reliability. As they approach the milestone, usually about two weeks before the due date, Individual Contributors are genuinely surprised to discover they are not going to make it. Their failure damages their own belief in planning and their credibility with others.

By asking for short-term commitments from professionals, Change-ABLE organizations maintain confidence in the planning process and in each other. This brings performance problems to light much earlier, when corrective actions require less effort and are taken in time to prevent catastrophic schedule surprises.

Self-Monitored Feedback Methods for Projects: Expectations stated in terms of weekly deliverables are not yet sufficient to create the psychological realities of Breakthrough Systems. The expectation must be in small enough increments to allow Individual Contributors to check themselves against it at least every two hours. Individual Contributors must use weekly deliverables as the milestones from which to back up into the present hour of work. They do this with the simple mechanism of "to-do lists." For instance, they will take a weekly commitment to "deliver eight devices drawn and validated" and break it up into what "to-do Monday," "to-do Tuesday," etc. The feedback loop gets closed often enough to be useful for managing one's own performance.

The supervisor checks a couple of times a week with each Individual Contributor to see how things are going and to ask whether or not there is any doubt about achieving the weekly deliverables. As early as mid-morning on Monday, most Individual Contributors can give a valid answer. If there is any doubt, the supervisor can start work on the necessary adjustments.

Resource Control for Projects: At the end of each week, each supervisor working on a Project holds a brief meeting with his or her direct reports. This meeting is often held standing up — there is not too much work to be done. The Individual Contributors take turns reporting which of their deliverables are done or not done. When the deliverables are done, the supervisor and group members look for opportunities to compliment each other. When the deliverables are not done, the supervisor will usually be forewarned because of checkups held earlier in the week. When it is appropriate, the supervisor may ask the Individual Contributor with the problem to share it with the group — both to inform the group about the nature of the problem and to seek help in solving it.

This meeting is an important way to demonstrate the cooperation the organization expects of its Individual Contributors. Without this weekly encouragement, many professionals (engineers for instance) will work for months without talking to each other about what they are doing. Such isolation slows down their learning and the application of their talent to the organization's work. Isolation makes Individual Contributors overly possessive of their ideas and encourages a defensive mentality. Ideas grow by being shared, played with, and tested. By encouraging a weekly disclosure of what Individual Contributors have done and not done, Change-ABLE organizations remind people to utilize each other as resources, thereby accelerating the performance of their Projects and the organization's learning.

Troubleshooting

Troubleshooting Tasks can easily be seen as frustrating interruptions and a scene of unpleasant human interaction based on fear, disappointment, blame, and conflict. Change-ABLE organizations encourage Individual Contributors to see them as opportunities for demonstrating their creativity, making immediate contributions to productivity, and bringing peace and solace to those in distress. Their respect for Troubleshooting Tasks is reflected in their effort to make sure they are performed at a very high level of expertise — in Breakthrough Systems.

We will discuss Breakthrough System methods in the usual order, i.e., expectations, self-monitored feedback, and control of resources. With Troubleshooting, however, it is often necessary to start by setting up feedback systems for collecting the data necessary to establish appropriate expectations.

Expectations for Troubleshooting: Since Troubleshooting Tasks are by definition unpredictable emergencies, it is not possible to set standards for the expected outputs of the work. Instead, the effort must focus on setting standards for the level of expertise expected from individuals responding to these emergencies. As always, the standards must address the issues of pace and quality. There are usually four metrics in the statement of the standard: *response time, average solution time, a first pass solution percentage,* and *manners.* For instance: "pick up the phone before the third ring (*response time*); answer the customer's question in less than five minutes, in 95 per cent of the cases (*average solution time*); well enough that they don't have to call about the same problem again in 90 per cent of the cases (*first pass solution percentage*); and be polite enough so that no customer ever files a complaint about your manners."

Self-Monitored Feedback for Troubleshooting: The two most common forms of self-monitored feedback for Troubleshooting are: 30-Second Reports, and Checklists.

• *30-Second Reports*: This form is a 3X5 index card (usually of a special color) on which the Individual Contributor records four items of information about every Trouble-shooting event: date; time of day; identification of the problem; and time required to solve the problem. The date is usually entered on several of the cards at the beginning of the day. As soon as a Troubleshooting event occurs, the Individual Contributor reaches for the card, enters the time, puts the card aside, and begins listening to under-stand the problem. When the problem is solved, the card is taken up again and some phrase or code number is written to identify the nature of the problem. This entry is not intended to take more than 10 seconds — just enough of a message to remind the Individual Contributor of the nature of the problem a month later. Finally, the time required to solve the problem is written down — as accurately as possible.

These 30-Second Reports are stacked in an obvious place each day for a month. The visual feedback regarding how much Troubleshooting is being done is very important to the psychological impact of this performance feedback method. We will talk about the analysis of these reports in the next section on resource control.

- *Checklists*: Checklists are used when the Troubleshooting Tasks are better known and can be at least roughly categorized by symptom. The Checklist specifies the sequence of steps required to complete the diagnosis of the problem and lead to its solution. Troubleshooting Checklists are usually a set of forms, each form designed for a particular kind of Troubleshooting Task with pace standard for the task prominently displayed. A packet of these forms, considered one of the Troubleshooter's tools, is always at hand. As the Troubleshooter performs the task, the Checklist is filled out. It includes blanks for the date, time of day, and required time for solution. Like the 30-Second Report, each completed Checklist should be stacked in an obvious place.

Resource Control for Troubleshooting: At the end of the month, Individual Contributors sit with their supervisors and/or other Troubleshooters to summarize their month of Troubleshooting. The cards can be dealt into stacks for various kinds of analysis. One kind of analysis establishes the solution time required to solve 80 per cent of the problems. Pareto analysis is another way to organize the cards: stack them by similarity of cause and identify which causes account for 80 per cent of the problems.

This meeting often leads to corrective actions Individual Contributors can implement for themselves — the invention of new procedures and the development of new skills. It also provides information the supervisor and Team will want to use to alert the organization to new threats and opportunities and to make a case for change in product and process designs. Troubleshooting is one of the most important sources of innovation in Change-ABLE organizations.

Negotiable Tasks

Just like Troubleshooting, Negotiable Tasks are performed in response to unforeseen demands, but they do not require immediate response. The demand is usually for a study or investigation related to a potential threat or opportunity. Engineers are asked to look into new technologies. Marketing people are asked to do a preliminary study for a new product idea. Accountants are asked to do special cost studies, and financial experts are asked to make projections based on new variables.

The Tasks tend to look like short-term Projects. They often use underutilized resources allocated to other planned work and, therefore, have staggered, opportunistic schedules of performance — people work at them when they can. But the task type is important. It is another source of the Change-ABLE organization's innovation— one of the ways it nurtures options for the future.

> **Frequency Determines the Methods Used for Negotiable Tasks**: There are no new methods to introduce for Negotiable Tasks. The appropriate methods are determined by the frequency with which the Negotiable Tasks are demanded. Methods used for Troubleshooting are used when these Tasks are demanded as frequently as once a week and require completion within a few days time. If the frequency of demand is lower and the performance periods are estimated to take weeks or months, the methods described for Projects are used.
>
> When a large part of an Individual Contributor's work consists of working on Negotiable Tasks, it is especially important for him or her to have a Performance Plan. Others tend to get confused about the role of such individuals and start treating them like a "slack resource. " To avoid overload and promote the organization's understanding and respect, the individual must be able to state the key results they seek. The Performance Plan is an important tool for Individual Contributors to use for maintaining control of the resources necessary to accomplish Negotiable Tasks.

Individual Contributors in Teams

When describing Breakthrough Systems in the Change-ABLE organization, the focus is on improving the way individuals manage their performance. But the management task expected of Individual Contributors does not stop with self-management. Individual Contributors are also expected to make sure their performance integrates with that of others. Change-ABLE organizations expect, support, and encourage Individual Contributors to participate in managing each other. Instruments for this influence are Teams and meetings.

There are several kinds of Teams that will include Individual Contributors as members. In all cases, the Teams are work focused — they are not formed for the purpose of promoting camaraderie and improving morale. It is assumed that knowing you are productive results in self-esteem and morale at work. Teamwork keeps the performance expectations clear and relevant, to stimulate intelligent use of self-monitored performance feedback, and makes sure all the resources are efficiently employed. Teamwork reinforces Breakthrough Systems. In fact, the combination does contribute to high levels of morale, which Change-ABLE organizations enjoy as a side-effect.

Functional/Technology Teams

One kind of Team still common among Individual Contributors in Change-ABLE organizations is the basic Functional Team. Individual Contributors are grouped together by their common specialty, such as design engineers, manufacturing assemblers, or salespeople. Often, Individual Contributors see this Team as their Home Team.

The purpose of the Functional Team is to promote the development and application of the member's specialty to the organization's work. Participants use this Team as a "learning group" for further personal development of their technical skills. It is also the place where members find innovative new ways of applying their technology to the organization's work.

However, the actual performance of work will be done in the context of other Teams. Members of Functional Teams are often assigned by their Leaders to other work Teams. Their day-to-day direction and supervision will take place under the leadership of these other Teams. Individual Contributors are also involved in "multiple role" performance, as we discussed for Managers in Chapter Eight on

Linked Teams. In the Functional Team, Individual Contributors are held accountable for their personal development as specialists and for their contribution to improving the application of the Team's functional specialty. In other Teams, they are accountable to that Team's specific production objectives.

Self-Sufficient Teams/Integrated Production Teams

In Change-ABLE organizations, it is very common to find Individual Contributors participating as members in what is called a Self-Sufficient Team or an Integrated Production Team. Here, members are grouped according to the various specialties required to produce a particular output. Such a Team might have Individual Contributors who are materials handlers, process engineers, specialized operators, maintenance engineers, quality specialists, and customer service representatives.

The purpose of the Team is to take charge of an entire process (usually a fairly complex one) and ensure its efficient delivery of a particular product. The concept is to collapse the hierarchy of functions into a set of Self-Sufficient Teams. The Individual Contributors in the Teams have full authority to apply their specialties to the production of the particular product. Members manage all the details of coordination among themselves and make the hand-offs between specialties as seamless as possible. When the Teams are properly designed, they don't need much help from upper level Managers; they are in control of all the resources necessary to accomplish their task. This complete control of necessary resources for the entire process gives the Teams their name — "Self-Sufficient" and/or "Integrated Production Teams."

The Leader of the Self-Sufficient Team is usually a full-time, first line Manager. That same Leader may also hold another role as Leader of a Functional Team. It is not unusual for Leaders of self-sufficient Teams to find themselves directing the work of people from entirely different specialties. For instance, a supervisor with a background in design engineering might easily find herself leading a Team including assemblers and maintenance engineers. The role of the Leader is to assure cooperation among the members of the Team, to link the Team to upper-level management through Work Reviews, and to get upper level management action whenever the Team confronts an issue reaching beyond the limit of its self-sufficient authority.

Self-Managed Teams

A Self-Managed Team is defined as a group of Individual Contributors assuming authority for all the functions usually performed by a first line Manager. The functions may include selection, orientation, training, work assignment, coaching, evaluation, benefits, and representation in higher level management decision-making. Any time a significant portion of these functions is delegated to the group of Individual Contributors, the Team becomes "Self-Managing." In fact, most Self-Managing Teams in Change-ABLE organizations pick up only the functions of selection, orientation, training, work assignment, coaching, and evaluation. First line Managers are still used to performing the administrative aspects of many of these delegated functions, and they are responsible for all the others, including compensation, discipline, transfer, and termination.

From the standpoint of definitions, a Self-Sufficient or Integrated Production Team also could be Self-Managed. In fact, it is the Self-Managing aspects (orientation, work assignment, coaching, and inter-specialty coordination) that make the Self-Sufficient Teams effective.

Change-ABLE organizations always acknowledge the role of Individual Contributors as part of management. But Individual Contributors usually express a preference for limiting the extent of participation. They don't want to be distracted from their work by too much managerial activity, as they usually have a low threshold of tolerance for issues of schedule and budget. Given the chance, Individual Contributors almost always "delegate upward" the administrative, disciplinary, and linking functions of management.

Upper Level Management Teams

There are two other forms of group work in which Individual Contributors frequently participate, both of which are related to making higher level management meetings more effective. First, they are often invited to present in the Work Reviews of higher level management Teams. These invitations are always authorized in advance by the management Team's Leader. They attend only that part of the meeting dealing with an issue for which they are a relevant source of information and opinion. Their participation is usually necessary and important, so these events are seen by Individual Contributors as an opportunity to make a difference. It is a useful and positive experience for everyone.

A second form of participation in higher level management meetings is membership in Task Forces. These groups are expected to think on behalf of a management Team. When they have collected the relevant information and formed a recommendation, Task Force members act as tutors to the members of the management Team that originally chartered them, preparing the Managers for their Team decision. They then participate in the management meeting as present-ers in a Recommendation Review procedure. Again, these recommen-dations have significant impact upon the organization's course of action, so Individual Contributors are usually willing participants on Task Forces.

This discussion regarding teamwork for Individual Contributors can be summarized by saying Individual Contributors are not ex-pected to work alone. Their management of themselves, through the use of Breakthrough Systems, is the foundation upon which they participate in managing each other and the members of higher level management Teams. The teamwork reinforces the Breakthrough Systems, keeping expectations clear and relevant, encouraging atten-tion to self-monitored feedback, and taking action to make efficient use of resources. In Change-ABLE organizations, Individual Contributors are expected to be members of a Team and managing themselves well in Breakthrough Systems as a criterion of membership.

Breakthrough Systems Only Work Informally

Breakthrough Systems are informal. They are a simple set of methods Individual Contributors use to manage the work they do. This is not the official information gathering process by which the organization evaluates individual performance and determines the pay and promotability of that individual. Change-ABLE organizations make this distinction, and it is an important distinction to make.

Breakthrough Systems are immediate and personal — they must be if they are to sustain Individual Contributors' beliefs in their validity. When such immediate and personal methods are made to produce information for the organization's formal process of evaluation — for the official files in the Personnel department — Individual Contributors start to feel like they are in straitjackets. Individual Contributors understandably resent such intrusions into their work life. Their resistance is both active and passive under such conditions, and very effective at rejecting the methods. To protect the informality of Breakthrough Systems, Change-ABLE organizations pay attention to the bridges built between the information as it is used by the Individual Contributors and by the rest of management's formal decision-making processes.

One of these bridges is the determination of expectations. Ultimately, these expectations must be consistent with the organization's formal planning system. The expectations are determined with as much participation from Individual Contributors as possible. In a variety of ways, Individual Contributors are consulted regarding the practicality of pace and quality requirements given the organization's priorities and resource constraints. Once expectations are defined, it is understood that changing the standards will require formal decision-making processes. Otherwise, the expectations will not support coordinated performance throughout the organization.

Change-ABLE organizations build bridges between the informal and formal systems of performance feedback very carefully. Once in Breakthrough Systems, Individual Contributors generate and evaluate their own performance data. The methods are always simple and not very intrusive. In this way, Individual Contributors use them on a nearly continuous basis — at least every two hours on the job. When the informality of these methods is protected, performance data becomes abundant and accurate. It is very tempting to process designers, continuous improvement Teams, human resource analysts, and other observers (such as MBA students looking for a thesis) to collect this data. However, as soon as the original records are taken out of the Individual Contributors' hands and preserved somewhere else in the organization — regardless of all assurances of benign intentions—

Individual Contributors begin to resist using the methods. Even in Change-ABLE organizations, where the levels of trust and confidence between workers and Managers are unusually high, Individual Contributors will not generate such information without retaining complete control over the use of it.

Two bridges between the Individual Contributors' performance records and the organization's formal information systems are usually necessary.

First, the Change-ABLE organization mandates self-monitored feedback methods. Keeping records is essential to sustain high levels of performance. Relying on the memories of Individual Contributors as a feedback system is very unreliable and does not yield high level productivity. Without an objective record, the high level performance doesn't occur. So the formal system of governance has an interest in ensuring that Individual Contributors keep such a record — the practice is part of the Individual Contributor's job expectations. Supervisors check frequently to make sure self-monitoring systems are used. They check twice a day with Individual Contributors performing Routine Tasks and twice a week for all other Individual Contributors. These interfaces are very brief; their only intention being to reinforce the Individual Contributor's maintenance of the record.

Supervisors never take the initiative to use the Individual Contributor's information as a takeoff point for evaluative inquiry, advice giving, or problem solving. Only the Individual Contributors can use their Breakthrough System feedback records to initiate problem solving. Managers and Individual Contributors must be in agreement about these ground rules so that this checkup bridge serves its purpose without crashing the Breakthrough Systems.

The second bridge between the performance feedback records in Breakthrough Systems and management's formal decision-making processes deals with the daily or weekly summary meetings supervisors hold with Individual Contributors. These meetings are sometimes referred to as "Done/Not Done Meetings." They are often held while standing up in a hall way. The supervisor goes down a Checklist of deliverables due from the group of Individual Contributors at the time of the meeting. The Individual Contributors tell the group which of their deliverables are Done or Not Done. The meeting is brief, usually less than 15 minutes, and sums up the record of deliverables done or not done as a group. No individual's performance is identified in the record the supervisor takes away from this meeting. The supervisor will use this group summary as data for updating the organization's formal information systems, including any public display of production data in the work areas.

How does a supervisor get the information necessary to evaluate an individual's performance for purposes of coaching? First, they use any of the information systems built into the production design process. For instance, most machinery now generates an electronic database about its own performance that is useful for analyzing problems of pace and quality. This information may bring to the supervisor's attention the need for coaching, training, or discipline. When a group of Individual Contributors is not meeting its production commitments, supervisors ask the Team to meet (sometimes without the supervisor in attendance) and submit suggestions for corrective action. Most often, however, Breakthrough Systems give Individual Contributors the information they need to initiate their own performance improvement. Supervisors in Change-ABLE organizations usually find themselves barely able to keep up with the suggestions and requests for help that come at the initiative of the Individual Contributors.

How does the supervisor get the information necessary to evaluate an individual's performance for the formal personnel record? There is nothing especially unique about these processes. Supervisors keep incident files on each direct report; they hold regular (usually monthly) one-on-one dialogues with each Individual Contributor; they get reports from other Managers and Team Leaders who work with the Individual Contributor; and they participate in Ranking and Rating meetings with other supervisors, comparing their Individual Contributors to others doing similar work. This information is then used in evaluation forms, which are discussed with the Individual Contributor and submitted to Human Resources for filing. These processes are taken very seriously, and are used as a way of assuring Individual Contributors that there is no secret or illegal criteria used in the evaluation process affecting their retention, pay, or promotability.

Supervisors do not try to make this formal process a major performance coaching event, knowing that effective coaching has to be done immediately on-the-job. As we said, there is nothing especially unique about the formal performance evaluation process, including the fact that most Managers and Individual Contributors, as in all other organizations, find the process emotionally uncomfortable and do it out of necessity rather than out of any sense of inherent satisfaction.

The Interdependence of Managers and Individual Contributors

The other Key Management Practices (Linked Teams, Performance Plans, Work Reviews, Group Decision-Making) of the Change-ABLE organization make Breakthrough Systems possible for Individual Contributors. Creating an environment in which Individual Contributors work with clear and relevant expectations, pay attention to their own informal systems of performance feedback, and control the resources necessary to meet their expectations, requires an extraordinarily effective system of organizational governance. Management must be operating as a system of Linked Teams, focused with Performance Plans, informed by Work Reviews, and making decisions with Rational Group Processes. Unless this is happening, very few Individual Contributors will be working in Breakthrough Systems. In fact, the percentage of Individual Contributors working in Breakthrough Systems is itself a very reliable metric for the effectiveness of the organization's management. Good governance from the Managers in Change-ABLE organizations makes Breakthrough Systems possible for a large percentage of their Individual Contributors. Managers empower Individual Contributors to increase the economic and social value of their talents through the multiplier of large scale cooperation.

It is also important to appreciate the reverse statement: all other management practices of the Change-ABLE organization are dependent upon Individual Contributors managing themselves with Breakthrough Systems. Only Individual Contributors provide reliable data regarding the organization's performance status. Like the sensory system of the human body, Individual Contributors act as the eyes, ears, and fingertips of the Change-ABLE organization — alerting it to its threats and opportunities and making possible its strategic and tactical plans. Well-informed Individual Contributors load management's linked and synchronized Work Reviews with current and valid information — the necessary foundation for rational decision-making and continuous reevaluation of Performance Plans. Finally, Breakthrough Systems give Individual Contributors self-confidence, mutual respect, and trust for each other. This results in a resilient and flexible workforce, and makes possible the rapid implementation of management's decisions. Individual Contributors empower Managers to plan well, and to swiftly and intelligently allocate resources for unusually efficient achievement of the organization's purposes.

Project Team's Story: Using Breakthrough Systems To Get a Project Back on Track

The contribution of Breakthrough Systems to the rest of the management system was demonstrated to us by a large product-design Team in one of our client companies. They were three months into a nine-month project that would eventually end up costing about $70 million. Management's computerized Project schedule was saying the Project had already slipped its deadline by seven weeks. The customer had made it contractually clear that the deadline was absolute—anything later would be useless to the customer, and they would have no obligation for payments. Our client had to find a remedy within two weeks or cancel the Project—forfeiting the $20 million they had already spent.

The Project Team was well-managed in terms of the other four practices. The structure was a system of Linked Teams, Performance Plans, and Work Reviews, and the Managers were good at Group Decision-Making. We were not sure, however, if they were using Breakthrough Systems. We urged management to go immediately to their Individual Contributors and explain the situation. Management thought the 100 or so engineers involved in the Project already knew of the situation and were doing everything possible to remedy it. They took our suggestion only because they were feeling desperate.

An all-hands meeting was immediately called. When the Individual Contributors learned of the crisis, they were appalled and angry. "Why didn't you tell us earlier?" they exclaimed. Management discovered Individual Contributors didn't know the deadline was a "drop dead" deal. Furthermore, the Individual Contributors disagreed with what the computer was reporting. They were not, however, able to prove they were on schedule — they were not working in Breakthrough Systems.

The meeting resolved to implement Breakthrough Systems and verify the status of the Project. The new Project plan required every engineer to work on a specific set of deliverables due each Friday. With these specific expectations, the engineers were now able to manage themselves on a day-to-day basis with to-do lists.

At the end of the first week, Individual Contributors were able to prove that things were not as bad as the computer reported, but the Project had, in fact, slipped its schedule by four weeks. With the fully informed participation of Individual Contributors, however, Managers were now confident they knew exactly what they had to do to restore the Project to its demanding schedule. At the end of the fourth month, they had done so.

The entire system continued to demonstrate its resilience when it was later confronted with two additional delays due to failure of the design tools. In spite of these unforeseen delays, the Project was completed a week early!

This case demonstrates how no other source of information is more important to the organization than its Individual Contributors — its planners, designers, manufacturing operators, sales and service people, and personnel and marketing specialists. These people are the sensory system by which the external condition is judged. They are also internal sensors of the organization's potential for action. As soon as Individual Contributors are in Breakthrough Systems, the sensory systems of the organization are restored to health. Changes ranging from corrective action in tactics to full-scale strategic reorientation are made with confidence because management knows what is happening and what can be done about it.

Summary

Chapter Twelve described Breakthrough Systems, the Key Management Practice by which Change-ABLE organizations accomplish the management of Individual Contributors. The following points were made:

1. Change-ABLE organizations acknowledge the fact that Individual Contributors manage the organization's work and pay serious attention to the way Individual Contributors manage themselves and each other.
2. Change-ABLE organizations maintain high levels of productivity by making sure Individual Contributors manage themselves in Breakthrough Systems. This environment is characterized by:

   - Clear expectations performance results;
   - Immediate, self-monitored feedback showing comparison between actual and expected performance; and
   - Control of the resources necessary to meet the performance expectations.

3. Breakthrough Systems were described for four Task Types:

   - Breakthrough Systems for Routine Tasks
   - Breakthrough Systems for Projects
   - Breakthrough Systems for Troubleshooting Tasks
   - Breakthrough Systems for Negotiable Tasks

4. The various forms of teamwork used by Individual Contributors to manage themselves and each other were described.
5. The informality of Breakthrough Systems was emphasized and some of the ways in which Change-ABLE organizations protect this informality were discussed.
6. Finally, the interdependence of Breakthrough Systems and the other Key Management Practices was discussed and illustrated with the "Project Team's Story."

13

Basic Assumptions of Change-ABLE Organizations

Overview

This chapter explores the Basic Assumptions underlying and supporting the Key Management Practices of Change-ABLE organizations. The following points are made:

1. It is important to become conscious of Basic Assumptions. If they are incompatible with the Key Management Practices, they cause vague but strong feelings that inhibit learning and mastery of the practices.
2. Change-ABLE organizations use Reconciled Assumptions — they find a way to preserve and find synergy between both alternatives in the Survival Dilemmas confronting all human communities.
3. We will state the individual Basic Assumption that reconciles each of the seven Survival Dilemmas listed below, and show how that assumption is expressed in the Key Management Practices:

-   Survival Dilemma #1: Internal or External control of the environment?
-   Survival Dilemma #2: Past, Present, or Future orientation?
-   Survival Dilemma #3: Universal or Particular rules?
-   Survival Dilemma #4: Ascribed or Achieved status and power?
-   Survival Dilemma #5: Affective or Neutral expression of emotions?
-   Survival Dilemma #6: Individualism or Communitarianism?
-   Survival Dilemma #7: Diffuse or Specific commitments?

The Importance of Basic Assumptions in Change-ABLE Organizations

All organizations learn and perpetuate management practices that promote their survival and success. These practices must solve the common, constantly recurring survival problems presented to organizations by their external social and economic environments and their internal dynamics of cooperation.

An organization learns its management practices through a process beginning with experimentation. When it finds a practice that seems to solve one or more of these problems in a reliable way, the practice is refined through repetition. An important part of the refinement process is learning to recognize all the conditions in which the practice works and the subtle variations of it that will make it most effective when confronting various combinations of conditions. This refinement relies upon memory of previous efforts and assessment of their consequences.

The knowledge regarding these conditions, probable consequences, and preferences becomes a strategy: to survive under these certain conditions, you should do this! If the strategy and the practice keep fitting together and reinforcing each other over a period of time, the strategy begins to operate as a Basic Assumption. At this stage of its development, the practice becomes an unconscious response — a survival habit. The practice occurs without the interference of further critical thinking — adding to the speed of its application. When the organization completes the process of learning a management practice, it is then triggered and guided by these unconscious survival strategies, i.e., the Basic Assumptions.

As Basic Assumptions are formed, the most critical choices are those made when the organization confronts a Survival Dilemma — a choice between what appear to be exclusive alternatives. Choosing either of them will mean suffering the consequences of not having chosen the other. Along the path of learning, these Survival Dilemmas act as forks in the road. When the choice is made to go one way, all the territory along the other path is left unexplored. Each time an organization makes one of these critical choices, its range of survival strategies is limited. It will continue to develop more and more refined practices to enact its chosen strategies, but it will not explore or benefit from any of the strategies and practices lying along the path not chosen. The Basic Assumptions an organization makes when resolving Survival Dilemmas tend to set limits on its ability to generate new management practices.

Basic Assumptions have an important influence upon an organization's management practices. Many people assume that to change the organization's practices, it is first necessary to "fix" its Basic Assumptions. The authors do not agree. These Basic Assumptions were initially formed as conclusions based on experimentation with practices. An organization's current Basic Assumptions can be changed by encouraging the organization to continue experimenting with new practices — practices that could prove to be even more effective in promoting its survival and prosperity. The path from behavioral experimentation to Basic Assumptions is actually the more natural order of organizational learning and change.

It is easier to discuss management practices because they operate at the empirical level of consciousness. Management practices can be seen, heard, touched, recorded, and agreed upon far more readily than can the more intangible and less obvious stuff called Basic Assumptions. As a result, a fundamental approach to organizational change is to first deal with its management practices — to get it experimenting with Linked Teams, Performance Plans, Work Reviews, Group Decision-Making, and Breakthrough Systems. When these Key Practices are adopted, the organization starts to change at less obvious levels as well — the levels of its Basic Assumptions.

Since Basic Assumptions are unconscious, very few organizations ever talk about them, and Change-ABLE organizations are no exception to this generalization. People in Change-ABLE organizations have not taken the initiative to report their Basic Assumptions. Upon first seeing the statements explored in this chapter, Managers in Change-ABLE organizations have often been surprised. Not until they spend some time in reflection do they recognize their organizations as expressions of these assumptions. Yet without ever mentioning these Basic Assumptions, Change-ABLE organizations accept thousands of new people into their membership every year and soon have them comfortably using the Key Management Practices.

If organizations become Change-ABLE just by focusing on the Key Management Practices, why should they talk about their Basic Assumptions?

Key Management Practices are resisted when introduced to organizations operating from incompatible Basic Assumptions. Sometimes the resistance is expressed by distorting the Key Management Practices into conformity with the old assumptions that keep the organizations stuck. More often, Managers start the Key Management

Practices but soon feel like they are going through some kind of empty, meaningless ritual — they feel cut off from the certainty and familiarity of their old survival strategies. Or they sometimes find themselves caught between their perception of how much more effective the new practices are and a deep suspicion that they aren't supposed to work so well. In all these cases, the old Basic Assumptions inhibit the growth of confidence in the Key Management Practices and slow development of these new habits.

Because such resistance operates unconsciously, people have difficulty articulating why they are uncomfortable when they first use the Key Management Practices. Organizational Leaders help the learning process by taking the initiative to uncover the source of inner conflict and resistance. By talking about the Basic Assumptions of the Change-ABLE organization, people can be made more comfortable while accelerating the understanding and use of the Key Management Practices.

The Contribution of Reconciled Assumptions in Change-ABLE Organizations

Before exploring the seven Basic Assumptions of the Change-ABLE organization, consider the unique way in which Change-ABLE organizations deal with Survival Dilemmas. Most other organizations tend to choose only one of the alternatives presented in these dilemmas. Many of them take the refinement of their strategy and its expression in management practices to the extreme — including the denial that alternatives exist, or learning to deny the alternatives as fundamentally incorrect, dangerous, and punishable. By making these Extreme Assumptions, the organizations simplify and clearly define themselves, but they also define themselves more rigidly, with limited survival options. Change-ABLE organizations, by contrast, avoid these extremes by resolving the Survival Dilemmas through Reconciled Assumptions.

A Reconciled Assumption goes beyond a mere middle position between the horns of the dilemma. It is not a compromise seeking to minimize both the beneficial and harmful consequences of alternatives. Instead, a Reconciled Assumption finds a way to preserve both alternatives and find synergy between them. When a Basic Assumption is Reconciled, every exercise of one of the alternative strategies stimulates a greater appreciation of its apparent opposite and enlarges the organization's ability to access the positive consequences of both.

Understanding of the seven Reconciled Assumptions operating in the Change-ABLE organization uncovers the uniqueness of its Key Management Practices. Seen as expressions of these Reconciled Assumptions, the Key Practices take on an even more distinctive profile. Many of their subtle differences come to light, and their advantages as instruments for organizational survival become more obvious. What may have initially appeared to be ambiguous and confusing about the behavior of Change-ABLE organizations starts to make a little more sense. Operating from Reconciled Assumptions, Change-ABLE organizations avail themselves of a broad range of survival habits, remain self critical, and continuously generate creative new responses to their problems and opportunities.

Change-ABLE Reconciliation of Survival Dilemma #1: Internal or External Control of the Environment?

This dilemma presents the organization with a choice between submission to the forces in its environment (external control) or control of these forces (internal control). The choice of external control limits action to the simplest and most obvious forms of adaptation. It encourages everyone to make the most of the status quo and whatever else fate will bring. It achieves peace through passivity. The choice of internal control assumes that the organization has the right, obligation, and power to secure its own destiny. However, it throws itself into continuous struggle against forces it does not yet understand and sometimes hastens its own destruction. It achieves tentative security through conquest and domination.

Change-ABLE organizations find a reconciliation between these alternative assumptions that can be stated as follows:

> Everything — including nature itself — is constantly changing. We participate in making the change creative.

The Change-ABLE organization assumes its internal and external environments are constantly changing in a contest between entropy and renewal. The organization assumes it can contribute to the environment's creative renewal through intelligent adaptation. To fail at adaptive change is to surrender to chaos and destruction.

Obviously, nothing like this appears on any organization's statement of values, nor should it. But without this basic orientation to their internal and external environments, few of the successful organizations we have observed would be doing the things they do.

The first assumption shows in the diligence with which so many Change-ABLE organizations study the sciences and humanities. It shows in their self-perception as creative and inventive people. It shows in their lack of surprise when things don't work and in their delight with the challenge of new problems. Change-ABLE organizations expect change; they also respect it. They see its important consequences, some of which must be avoided, and they believe in their ability to make a big difference. They are proactive, but they do not pretend to be "masters of the universe."

This Reconciled Assumption about the environment is also reflected in the Change-ABLE organization's structure. It is understood that there is survival advantage in large scale cooperation, and that the advantage requires some system of governance, but the hierarchy is not seen as a Holy Order — no particular structure is dictated by natural law. There is a natural need to be organized, but the system can be designed according to the member's perception of what works best. This Reconciled Assumption shows in the Change-ABLE organization's huge respect for authority, its clear identification of authority figures, and the principles of commitment. At the same time, this Reconciled Assumption urges the Change-ABLE organization's constant redesign of itself as a system of linked meetings to make sure the right people are talking about the right things at the right time. It appreciates order; it intends to make that order more effective.

The Change-ABLE organization's planning dances with its environment. Its strategy is always tentative — an acknowledgment of what it doesn't know and a genuine fear of uncertainty. It knows it is guessing about the future and keeps everyone armed with a simple statement of intentions — Performance Plans — that will permit rapid adaptation to what it "learns as it goes."

The dance with the environment requires vigilance and effi-ciency. Frequent reviews of goals and progress keep the organization conscious of its threats and opportunities and the need to constantly reallocate resources to serve its survival priorities.

Participating in the renewal of the environment requires the highest forms of intelligence. Everywhere, the Change-ABLE organiza-tion seeks to enrich its governance and performance of work with the diversity of Group Decision-Making. Minds are respected as natural gifts; groups are the means to multiplying the blessing.

Breakthrough Systems maximize the inherent ability of Indi-vidual Contributors to contribute to the organization's dance with its environment. Through their self-management, they focus the natural forces of their own minds and bodies to act as the organization's sensory system, enabling it to discover and move in harmony with the creative forces of renewal.

Change-ABLE Reconciliation of Survival Dilemma #2: Past, Present, or Future Orientation?

This Survival Dilemma confronts the organization with alterna-tive assumptions about the rightful understanding of time. To exalt and preserve the past obtains security at the sacrifice of opportunities for improvement in the present and the future. To live only for the present secures immediate pleasure by expending the treasures of the past and sacrificing preparation for the future. To live only for the future denies the pleasures to be derived from the present and may ignore the preservation and utilization of treasures from the past.

Change-ABLE organizations find a reconciliation between these alternative assumptions that can be stated as follows:

There is no time but the present, which is full of our past and contains our future.

The Change-ABLE organization's assumption with regard to time indicates that we must not wait—there is no time but a present full of memories and hopes. Change-ABLE organizations have a real sense of urgency. Time is on their minds in the form of immediate deadlines for the work they are doing. Yet the commitment to these deadlines is tied to a deeper sense of the perishable nature of their work and outputs. In their minds, the value of the work is directly related to the time in which it is delivered—the sooner the better and in many cases the rule is: be first or don't bother. The combined assumptions of continuous change and the urgency of the moment give the culture the feel of a busy, hot kitchen.

It is important to notice, however, that the organization does not ignore its past or fail to consider its long-term future. The past and future are seen as aspects of the present, and they matter because they enrich and guide the action of the present. The preservation of data-bases is only appropriate if there is immediate accessibility for reference and application in the present. The time invested in strategic thinking is only to establish guidelines and constraints for action in the present.

The Change-ABLE organization must close its performance feedback loop from executive to Individual Contributor at least every 10 days. The use of longer feedback loops entails the risk of missing vital opportunities and failing to take corrective action early enough to avoid mishaps. The assumptions are that things are constantly changing, and significant change is happening this week!

In planning, the Change-ABLE organizations keep the long-term loose and tentative while the next 90 days are charted in great detail and the next 30 days are staked out in complete detail. Performance Plans retain their simplicity in order to permit massive, coordinated change in very short periods of time. Plans are expressions of intention—a reflection of organizational strategy. Yet everyone knows intentions will be thwarted by changes in the environment. People don't expect plans to last for more than approximately 90 days without significant changes. They don't spend time trying to calculate the details of interdependencies beyond six months out. All planning will be replanning—continuously.

Work Reviews are characterized by the intention to act — right now in every meeting. People come on time and must leave on time in order to be part of the next scene of action. Information is presented in graphic form to speed up its transmission. Graphic presentation also puts the present in the context of the actual history of performance and the intended future. Information is expected to serve the purpose of immediate and intelligent action.

Group Decision-Making, with its emphatic distinction between agreement and commitment, facilitates a rapid focus of information and human experience. There is no time to waste on political posturing or pretentious camaraderie. The process takes time to understand, but it does not wait for agreement. The organization's sense of urgency can only be served by Managers who have a reliable understanding of the principle of disagree *and* commit.

Breakthrough Systems further express the emphasis on immediate action, but with regard for the past and future. The methods of self-management empower Individual Contributors to assess their own performance at any moment and to take corrective action as soon as a problem emerges. Early and continuous problem solving by Individual Contributors keeps the organization approaching its objectives with remarkable efficiency and speed. The immediate action is managed in the context of well-coordinated expectations that are appropriate to the organization's accumulated resources and competencies.

Change-ABLE Reconciliation of Survival Dilemma #3: Universal or Particular Rules?

This Survival Dilemma confronts organizations with the choice between the assumption that social rules are the same and apply equally to everyone (universal application) or the assumption that the rules of one's own group are unique and take precedence over any other rules. If the organization elects the universal option, then everyone's allocation of the organization's resources and everyone's performance must be governed by the same set of rules. There can be no favoritism in the application of criteria for determining needs or in the application of standards of performance. If the organization elects the particularistic option, it justifies itself as it favors its members in allocation of resources and protects them from judgment by outsiders. But this assumption perpetuates endless no holds barred competition since there are no common rules of engagement.

Change-ABLE organizations find a reconciliation between these alternative assumptions that can be stated as follows:

We play by the rules as long as we participate in making the rules.

The Change-ABLE organization desires a world in which everyone will play by the same rules, while recognizing this is not yet the case. The assumption is that people must be responsible for making the rules. This reflects the assumption that people can be proactive in relationship to their environment, and that rules *should* be made. If people are part of the rule-making process, they have a great sense of obligation to abide by those rules until they are altered by further due process. The sense of obligation to rules, however, is in direct relationship to the amount of participation people have in making them.

Once again, the position is one of reconciliation between universalism and particularism. It is particularistic in assuming the rules only apply to those involved in the process of making them. It is universalistic in the assumption that everyone should be involved in the rule-making community.

This assumption about rules and how they are legitimately made is reflected in the Change-ABLE organization's open embrace of a hierarchy of Linked Teams. This is the system — the network of channels — through which every member of the organization is enfranchised in the organization's governance. It is the mechanism by which all members participate in the organization's decision-making.

The Change-ABLE organization quickly resists decisions made outside this system of information gathering and evaluation. It also resists group Leaders or members who attempt to deny the participation of others or to pollute the rational decision-making process with intimidation and other forms of power play.

In Change-ABLE organizations, Performance Plans and Work Reviews combine to provide a participative process for determining and evaluating common goals. This process gives the goals an unusually current and relevant quality, and it also continually renews everyone's understanding of those goals. This understanding is necessary to maintain member consent, the ultimate source of legitimacy for all rule making and decisions. The culture makes it easy for everyone to evaluate whether or not the organization's resources are being appropriately used to achieve those goals and provides an open channel for influencing the organization's governance.

Group Decision-Making has its own set of rules, the procedures of consultative or consensus resolution. These rules are the due process by which Managers assure themselves and everyone else that decisions result from a reasonable and participative process. With this assurance, Team members are able to manage conflicts, which are the natural outcomes of participation. It is reasonable to expect any Team member to raise concerns that are always acknowledged yet may not be accepted for action. With full involvement, those Team members can disagree and still commit to the outcome as decided.

The Basic Assumption regarding the legitimacy of rules is inherent in the performance expectations of Breakthrough Systems. These performance expectations are produced by an integrated system of planning. Managing oneself in Breakthrough Systems requires influential participation in evaluating both the expectations and the allocation of resources for oneself, for one's Team, and for the organization.

Change-ABLE Reconciliation of Survival Dilemma #4: Ascribed or Achieved Status and Power?

This Survival Dilemma confronts organizations with the choice between the assumption that people's status and authority are inherent in their very being or the assumption that these elements can and must be earned only through useful performance. When an organization assumes that status and authority are ascribed qualities of being, it tends to assign organizational roles based upon a person's race, nationality, gender, family heritage, religion, and age. This preserves parallel strands of functional tradition and resolves (by birth) many of the organization's potential role conflicts. But it confines people to predetermined roles that may be well beneath their potential usefulness to the organization. When the organization assumes that all status and authority must be earned through useful performance, it opens to all the possibility of achieving the organization's highest levels of honor and potentially avails itself of every person's best efforts. It also exposes itself, however, to domination by the most ambitious and ruthless competitors within its ranks, and the organization tends to use people up and throw them away.

Change-ABLE organizations find a reconciliation between these alternative assumptions that can be stated as follows:

> We must respect and reward those whose good works serve our ability to learn and adapt. There are no entitlements to status and authority — only reputations based on performance.

The Change-ABLE organization is a meritocracy. It doesn't care about sex, age, social class, nationality, or religion. It doesn't even care about prestigious schools or degrees. Respect and the other rewards of the Change-ABLE organization must be earned through performance. But "what have you done for me lately?" is not the whole story. Status is also based upon previous accomplishments—a performance-based reputation.

Reputation is not an unimportant issue in the ability of an organization to change quickly and easily. John Kotter, a Harvard University professor specializing in leadership research, makes this point. His studies show that most of what is called the leadership effect, the ability to get people to voluntarily follow a Leader through change, is based on reputation — being known by others as competent and reliable. If people are unknown, their ideas are not taken seriously nor are their suggestions quickly followed. People listen to each other carefully and are open to each other's ideas when the organization is comprised of people who have earned their reputations together. This greatly increases the ability to make and implement decisions for change.

In the Change-ABLE organization, reputation functions like ascribed qualities of age and seniority in other cultures. Reputations preserve the organization's memories of success and, by inspiring confidence, smooth and accelerate cooperation. By honoring performance-based reputations, the Change-ABLE organization once again finds a position of reconciliation between the extremes of achievement and ascription.

This Reconciled Assumption about status finds expression in the Linked Teams of Change-ABLE organizations. Within the network of management meetings, the hierarchical levels of participants are ignored. Those who are "superiors" in one context are often peers or subordinates in another. It is their leadership or membership in the particular Team serving its specific purpose that constitutes their authority at any particular moment. Those who have performed well over long periods of time are often found in the uppermost layers of the organization's hierarchy. But this relationship between performance and position in the hierarchy is not closely correlated. Position in the hierarchy is not an important statement of one's status. Extremely important (in some cases world-famous) and well paid Individual Contributors (sometimes millionaires) are found working as supervisors in the lowest levels of the organization's hierarchy. The achievement orientation of the Change-ABLE organization keeps its system of Linked Teams quite fluid. The organizational design is continuously changing to follow the organization's immediate performance needs rather than the personal needs of its Managers for symbols of esteem.

The achievement assumption of the Change-ABLE organization is clearly expressed in the use of Performance Plans. These statements of intended results are the fundamental means used by all members of the management group to identify themselves. Their declaration of roles is not a set of responsibilities and position titles, it is a statement of results they expect to achieve. The Performance Plan is a "calling card," inviting a relationship focused on cooperation. It steps around the issues of formal position or personality preferences to keep the achievement orientation up front in the organization's working relationships. The focus of the relationship is not "What do we need to *be* for each other?" Rather, it is, "What are we going to *do* together?"

The achievement assumption also shows up in the Change-ABLE organization's Work Reviews, which are not about how to please the boss. Work Review is not a time for people of high political position to "look good" or to display their credentials of age and education. Instead, the Work Review focuses on performance. It is an opportunity for Team members to evaluate how clear they are about what they are seeking to achieve and whether or not their Team's resources are integrated for success. The message is not, "Show the boss, or show the Team your power and glory." It is "Demonstrate to the Team your good judgment, powers of logic, common sense, and your acknowledgment of interdependence and accountability for the whole Team's achievements."

Group Decision-Making requires members to overcome their intimidation by others' reputations and formal status. It also requires members to listen carefully to all other participants regardless of their reputations or formal status. Members are obligated only to understand and be understood concerning the facts and opinions that are relevant to the Team's immediate needs. They are expected to express disagreement regardless of the other members' status, whenever their knowledge and experience dictate that the controversy is appropriate.

Breakthrough Systems are nearly pure expressions of the Change-ABLE organization's achievement assumption. They empower Individual Contributors to control the resources necessary to achieve their performance expectations. Work stations, for instance, carry no symbolism of status. These work areas are a bit Spartan, another indication that the focus is on achieving current objectives. Even the most honored Individual Contributors or highest ranking Managers are given only the specific configuration of resources appropriate to their current performance.

Change-ABLE Reconciliation of Survival Dilemma #5: Affective or Neutral Expression of Emotions?

This Survival Dilemma confronts organizations with a choice between the assumption that the free expression of emotions should be encouraged (affective) or the assumption that their expression should be highly controlled (neutral). If the organization assumes that all emotions should be given free reign, it gains a transparency in human relations that allows people to easily assess each other's moods, be assured of affection, and get early warnings of when relational maintenance or self-defense is necessary. However, it may also encourage careless and spiteful self-expression that injures others' esteem and endangers harmony. If the organization assumes that the expression of emotions should be carefully controlled, it can avoid burdening its communication channels with emotional messages, and it may also avoid the intimidation and distractions that open emotional expression often creates. However, diminishing the expression of emotions may rob communication of the context that completes its meaning, and personal needs may be ignored until they become a catastrophic disruption of relationships.

Change-ABLE organizations find a reconciliation between these alternative assumptions that can be stated as follows:

> We should freely express our joy and approval, yet carefully express negative feelings through problem solving.

In Change-ABLE Organizations, people are intensely emotional. The Reconciled Assumption accepts the existence of the emotions and addresses the ways in which they are to be expressed. Some of these emotions will be expressed spontaneously while other must be expressed more carefully.

The Change-ABLE organization generally approves of authentic expressions of the positive emotions—joy, delight, discovery, approval, affection. But even in these cases, there are some exceptions. There is some disapproval for any sort of mindless exuberance distracting from the accomplishment of the Team's plans, and real resistance to "cheerleading," which is seen as both distraction and manipulation.

The Change-ABLE organization requires a great deal of discipline regarding the expression of negative feelings. It is recognized that the spontaneous expression of negative emotions often harms the organization's ability to remain Change-ABLE. Human relationships become rigid when injected with fear, humiliation, anger, and hatred. When someone erupts with intense negative emotionality, people become instantly defensive. They shut down the cognitive tissues of the brain in order to rely upon the instantaneous habits of personal survival — fighting or fleeing. This is not the mental condition from which thoughtfulness or creativity emerges. So, Change-ABLE organizations limit the ways in which negative emotions are expressed.

There is no pretense that negative emotions can be banned. Change-ABLE organizations cannot exempt people from the dark side of their emotional life. Rather than deny negative emotions, the Change-ABLE organization seeks to employ them, knowing that negative feelings are appropriate. Anger, for instance, is part of how the body focuses its resources to remove an obstacle to its control. It is, in fact, an appropriate emotion for anyone who discovers that things are not going according to plan. Failure to feel anger in this situation would indicate the person doesn't recognize the problem, or is not actually committed to the plan. Change-ABLE organizations expect people to experiences anger in this case.

But it is not desirable for the person to make a scene to demonstrate "I am angry!" It is especially undesirable for Managers to make such a scene. When a formally empowered Manager erupts in anger, a serious distraction is created. Attention is diverted from the actual problem and is focused on how to protect oneself from the Manager's emotional assault. In fact, most people will try to avoid having anything to do with the actual problem because it is associated with the danger and pain of the Manager's emotional outburst. It is best for the Manager and the organization to redirect this negative emotion into a more constructive expression. The specific form of such constructive expression is problem solving behavior.

Once again, the Change-ABLE organization's Reconciled Assumption regarding the expression of emotions finds synergy between extremes of the dilemma. It neither approves of "letting it all hang out" nor does it say to its people "keep your feelings to yourself." It reconciles these extremes by accepting all the emotions and providing methods of expression for them through goal-related performance.

Operating from the assumption that it is desirable to redirect the expression of negative emotions is especially difficult in the middle management of the Change-ABLE organization. Like any other middle Manager bearing the special responsibility for the design and implementation of organizational systems, the position requires tolerance for a nearly continuous stream of negative feedback. Lower level Managers are sending the message that the systems they have been given to operate don't work in all cases; upper level executives are sending messages about how the current system certainly won't work in the future. In Change-ABLE organizations, this stream of negative feedback is intensified in that these messages are more frequent, more urgent, and supported by valid and relevant data. Furthermore, the hierarchy is flatter, so there are fewer Managers to share the burden of organizational design, and the life span of any system is much shorter.

Frustration, anger, blame, and a personal sense of loss and failure could easily mount up to an early burnout. Surprisingly, burnout in Change-ABLE organizations is found less often than might be expected. A deeper examination finds Managers in Change-ABLE organizations avoiding the distressful effects of negative emotions through the maintenance of the Key Management Practices.

The structure of Linked Teams keeps the whole organization poised for action. A middle Manager has immediate access to the critical resources — members' knowledge and skills. When these Managers recognize a problem and are ready to work on it, their access to the organization's other formal authorities is well defined — they know when their Regular Meetings will be held — and it is highly probable that they will get a prompt and conclusive response. Middle Managers in the Change-ABLE organization spend little time in the agony of waiting for the ability to act.

Performance Plans give everyone in the organization a way to continually check their alignment on results and priorities with others. This drives the organization's problems and conflicts into the open. Managers in the Change-ABLE organization expect conflict and misunderstanding and don't get hung up in denial. They seem to trust and acknowledge their negative feelings earlier and they take action on problems while these emotions are still at low levels of intensity. They move toward the fire while it is still only smoke in the kindling.

The regular schedule of Work Reviews presents the potentially frustrating issues to Managers early, and in a setting where people are empowered to take immediate corrective action. Work Reviews, like Performance Plans, get the issues into the open so that the most distressful form of conflict, covert conflict, is minimized. Furthermore, the Work Review is specifically designed to make sure the right people are talking together to get these conflicts resolved.

Group Decision-Making, with its encouragement of disagreement, invites all the issues to come into the open. Its disciplines for rationalizing disagreement make the group work psychologically safe while focusing emotions and minds on problem solving — the achievement of resolution. Group Decision-Making is a sort of "reality therapy" for the negative emotions of Managers.

Because of Breakthrough Systems and the use of self-sufficient Teams, first line Managers and Individual Contributors are able to draw downward and away from these middle Managers many of the tasks they would otherwise be required to handle. When these lower level Managers need help, they not only identify their problems, they also provide a steady stream of intelligent recommendations. This takes the pressure off middle Managers by heading off many problems before they come to their attention and by providing resources along with the problems that are passed upward.

The Key Management Practices of Change-ABLE organizations make sure everyone knows about critical issues early, and empowers people to take constructive action. Under these conditions, it is not unrealistic or emotionally hazardous to expect each other to share the spontaneous joy of success, and to discipline the expression of negative emotions through problem solving.

*Change-ABLE Reconciliation of Survival Dilemma #6:
Individualism or Communitarianism?*

This Survival Dilemma presents organizations with a choice between assuming that its survival depends upon every individual looking out for his or her own survival (individualism), or every individual subordinating their personal well-being to assure the well-being of the whole organization (communitarianism). Organizations electing individualism rely on the diversity and conflict of individual needs, abilities, and preferences to "hammer out" a solution for themselves that will also serve the organization's survival. But this assumption often exposes the organization to the tyranny of a few power-grabbing individuals. To elect the communitarian option assumes that by making the organization's survival the primary focus of attention, individuals will find solutions that serve the survival of all the members in an equitable manner. But this primacy of the community often frustrates the actualization of individual uniqueness and loses the cutting edge that their special talents provide.

Change-ABLE organizations find a reconciliation between these alternative assumptions that can be stated as follows:

> Survival depends not only upon skilled individuals but, even more so, upon their cooperation.

This is the most distinguishing assumption of the Change-ABLE organization, especially when compared to other organizations in the United States. The Change-ABLE organization has very high expectations for group work. There is great appreciation for the unique perceptions and competencies of individuals, but the Change-ABLE organization has learned that success is achieved through teamwork. The most brilliant ideas don't come from individuals working in isolation. Instead, outstanding opportunities and ideas emerge from groups of bright people capable of learning together. While only the nervous systems of individual human beings are capable of producing the raw stuff called intelligence, that raw stuff can be lifted to a much higher level of refinement and value through the synergy of group work. This assumption applies to everyone in the organization — Individual Contributors and Managers.

As noted with the other Basic Assumptions, the Change-ABLE organization seeks the reconciled position in which both individualism and communitarianism can be recognized as viable strategies.

The assumptions about cooperation are expressed in the definition of management accountabilities within the system of Linked Teams. Each position of authority is occupied by an individual accountable for the quality of governance in the organization below. Yet it is expected that this individual accountability will be exercised through genuine group work. The Team Leader holds Team members accountable for keeping the Team's goals in top priority as they evaluate each other's work. The Leader also facilitates the group problem solving and decision-making processes, ensuring all members develop the required participation skills. There is nothing "fuzzy" about this exercise of Leader accountability. Leaders will, when necessary, impose requirements for cooperation upon the members and discipline them for failure to comply. In this way, the organization's formal authority is exercised by individuals to ensure effective group work.

In the Change-ABLE organization, Performance Plans are a deliberate invitation to alignment and cooperation. Performance Plans give everyone a quick and reliable way to know what everyone is trying to do, permitting people to determine and manage their interdependencies. This is especially true when people are members of the same Team. In these cases, learning each other's Performance Plans is necessary for understanding one's own accountabilities. Members must know each other's business to fulfill their obligations (individualism) to the Team's common objectives (communitarianism). Used in this way, Performance Plans reconcile the dilemma between individualism and communitarianism.

The most obvious expression of the assumptions regarding cooperation is the vitality of discussion in the Change-ABLE organization's Work Reviews. The reason Team members listen so carefully and evaluate so assertively is because they assume every member's work is part of *their* own responsibility. They assume that any variance from plan in a member's performance is the Team's business and, therefore, the business of every member of the Team. Corrective action must be taken to assure Team success. Members come not only to evaluate each other, but to seek each other's counsel. They assume their individual problems and successes belong to the other members of the Team as well as themselves.

Group Decision-Making expresses a balance of individualism and communitarianism. Disagree *and* commit captures the synergy between individualism and communitarianism. The Change-ABLE organization requires its members to remain strong in their intellectual integrity, to be unafraid of being different from others, to insist on having the uniqueness of their ideas understood by others in the group, and to fulfill the obligation of understanding everyone else. It is the distinctiveness of individuals that makes them valuable as contributors to the group. As individuals, members disagree — during and after the meeting. But once the group's resolution has been achieved, each member commits to the resolution. Commitment expresses the communitarian assumption — that compliance will increase the probability of success as a group and also as individual members of the group. Members disagree as individuals; they commit as beneficiaries of the group —their disagreement *and* commitment discover the synergy that serves both the organization and individuals.

Similarly, Breakthrough Systems are used to express the balance of individualism and communitarianism. Individual Contributors are expected to manage themselves to deliver specific results in short intervals. Acknowledging Individual Contributors as self-managing is a salute to their individuality. The requirement for reporting in such short intervals is an expression of the communitarian assumption. Only when Individual Contributors report in short intervals does their information take on the validity necessary for it to be the foundation of the organization's entire performance feedback system. Breakthrough Systems are disciplines by which Individual Contributors manage themselves and participate in managing the entire organization.

Change-ABLE Reconciliation of Survival Dilemma #7: Diffuse or Specific Commitments?

Diffuse relationships are like traditional marriages in which a couple chooses to share everything in common — "for better for worse, for richer or for poorer, in sickness and in health, till death us do part." When an organization asks its members to make this kind of commitment, its claim upon its members is totalitarian, and its commitment to its members is to permanently provide for their every need so much as is possible given the organization's success. The organization secures its human resources at the risk of finding them inadequate for the demands of the future. Specific relationships are more like entering a limited contract. The parties state their expected contributions and benefits in specific detail and make no further assumptions about their obligations or rights with regard to each other. The relationship is tentative — entirely contingent upon the fulfillment of the contract — and even fulfillment of the contract usually means termination of the relationship. The organization leaves itself free to make whatever agreements are necessary in the future but must accept the risk of not being able to win such agreements when they are necessary.

Change-ABLE organizations find a reconciliation between these alternative assumptions that can be stated as follows:

> We must commit to the organization's purpose, then be explicit about the immediate contribution we will make.

Upon entry to the Change-ABLE organization, many new employees find the environment a bit cold and prickly. The specificity with which performance expectations are established and the short intervals in which they are monitored feel like micro-management and distrust. But two other factors soon counteract this first impression: the clarity and frequency with which the organization's purpose and strategy are reinforced and the genuine reliance upon teamwork. It is soon obvious that once others see your performance as a contribution to the organization's purpose, you are no longer a stranger.

The Change-ABLE organization's claim on its members is limited by its purpose. It expects and rewards the performance that serves its purpose; it makes no other demands or promises. On the other hand, the experience of genuine interdependence in pursuit of a common goal is often the most complex and intensely personal set of relationships employees will ever experience. Over time, as an employee demonstrates competence and reliability, these relationships grow in intensity and satisfaction. Few would describe their relationships in the Change-ABLE organization as family-like, but even fewer would describe their relationships as perfunctory, impersonal, or meaningless. There is a well-defined sense of belonging.

The reconciliation between specific and diffuse assumptions is expressed in the capacity of the Linked Teams to handle extraordinary complexity and continuous change. The human relationships making up the linked hierarchy must be managed with very specific commitments, while constantly aligning all commitment to the organization's overall purpose. This purpose defines the boundary within which the organization's members make their claims upon each other.

Performance Plans define and limit the immediate commitments necessary to serve the organizational purpose. In every management Team the members learn each others' Performance Plans, align themselves with the organization's purpose, then align themselves as a Team to achieve specific results serving that purpose.

Through their Work Reviews, each Team constantly requires the accomplishment of discreet tasks, making the organization appear to be highly specific. But the Teams also manage the integration of their performance. Each Team's members link it to all the other relevant Teams in the hierarchy — they assure attention to the interdependencies and alignments with the rest of the organization. This integrated attention to detail expresses the culture's assumption that human relationships must be both specific and diffuse.

Group Decision-Making also thrives on the reconciliation between specific and diffuse relationships. Group members come to the meeting intending to engage in relationships based on deep, mutual understanding — to make their best knowledge and opinions available to each other, and to seek the Team's assistance to keep all their individual commitments aligned with the Team's. They are predisposed to commit to the group's decisions even when they are personally in disagreement. These are the intentions of people engaged in diffuse relationships. At the same time, each member's commitments are limited by the specific purpose of the Team and the larger purpose of the organization. They try not to intrude on the decision-making process with concerns or issues originating in their personal lives and needs outside the context of the organization's purpose.

Individual Contributors experience this same synergy of specific and diffuse relationships as they manage their personal performance with Breakthrough Systems and integrate it with the other members of their various work Teams. They are expected to deliver very specific and near-term results — so specific that they can monitor their progress toward these goals at least every two hours on the job. But like everyone else in the organization, they are also bathed in the information that makes them conscious of the organization's purpose. They know they are expected to keep their performance expectations aligned with the organization's purpose and that as long as they meet those aligned expectations, their relationship to the organization and to its other members is fully empowered.

When Managers and Individual Contributors operate with this understanding, they are able to engage in complex networks of relations without getting tangled up or stuck in gridlock. They can carry several distinct roles simultaneously—any combination of functional, product, customer, or geographic responsibility. They can report to several different Leaders simultaneously—the Leaders being at any level within the hierarchy. The fluidity with which Managers and Individual Contributors change their roles in the system of Linked Teams is a large part of what makes the organization Change-ABLE. This fluid human interaction depends upon a Reconciled Assumption that acknowledges both the specificity of each relationship's function and the necessity of each relationship's integration with the whole organization's purpose.

Summary

Chapter Thirteen explored the Basic Assumptions underlying and supporting the Key Management Practices of Change-ABLE organizations. The following points have been made:

1. When Basic Assumptions are not compatible with the Key Management Practices, they become a hindrance to learning and mastery of the practices — it is therefore important to become conscious of Basic Assumptions.

2. Change-ABLE organizations operate from Reconciled Assumptions, i.e., they preserve and find synergy between the alternatives presented by the Survival Dilemmas confronting all human communities.

3. The Reconciled Assumptions of Change-ABLE organizations were stated as:

    Everything — including nature itself — is constantly changing. We participate in making the change creative.

    There is no time but the present, which is full of our past and contains our future.

    We play by the rules as long as we participate in making the rules.

    We must respect and reward those whose good works serve our ability to learn and adapt. There are no entitlements to status and authority — only reputations based on performance.

We should freely express our joy and approval, yet carefully express negative feelings through problem solving.

Survival depends not only upon skilled individuals but, even more so, upon their cooperation.

We must commit to the organization's purpose, then be explicit about the immediate contributions we will make.

4. Attention was given to how each of these assumptions is expressed in the Key Management Practices of Change-ABLE organizations.

Any organization can imitate the Key Management Practices we have described in this section of the book. That is exactly what we recommend! We are also aware of the fact that these Key Management Practices will not "feel right" and become fully spontaneous and habitual until compatible Basic Assumptions are formed.

We have concluded this section of the book with a discussion of Basic Assumptions, as we want to accelerate the formation of those that are appropriate to Change-ABLE organizations. The natural process by which people form these Basic Assumptions begins by discovering practices that work — behaviors that promote survival and success. People experiment to discover the range of application and the reliability of these new practices. When the pattern of their utility is understood, people form theories regarding when and how the practices will work. These theories guide more skilled and frequent use of the practices until they become habitual and the theories become unconscious assumptions. By describing both the Key Management Practices and their underlying Basic Assumptions, we hope to make this natural process of integration more efficient and less stressful.

Section **IV**

Becoming Change-ABLE

Recommendations for
Getting Started

Overview

This chapter explores some of the effective principles and methods needed to help organizations become Change-ABLE. The following points are made:

1. Organizational change should not be approached as a Special Event. Avoid these common examples:

    *   The "Turnaround"
    *   The "Restructure"
    *   The "Program"

2. There are three characteristics of a successful effort to make organizations Change-ABLE:

    *   Widespread participation;
    *   Immediate application to the organization's problems; and
    *   Implementation of all five Key Management Practices.

3. One proven sequence of actions is as follows:

    *   Identify and begin linking the Managers' Regular Meetings.
    *   Align the members of Regular Meetings using Performance Plans.
    *   Initiate Work Review.
    *   Use Group Decision-Making every step of the way.
    *   Begin implementing Breakthrough Systems.

4. There are many sequences and starting places — start wherever the organization is able to acknowledge a significant problem.

Do Not Try To Become Change-ABLE Through a "Special Event"

Becoming Change-ABLE is not a "Special Event." It is more like the process of healing after a traumatic illness. It involves the whole body in a continuous process moving from the numbness of shock (a beneficial form of denial) to a recovery of the senses (including pain); the ability to remember and think (including grief work); the gradual recovery of full mobility; and the restoration of the normal immune system that sustains on-going health. Organizations don't get Change-ABLE by taking a magic pill; they become Change-ABLE by getting back in touch with the will to live and the arduous process of getting back in shape. The process can only be hindered by spending time and resources looking for the quick fix — the Special Event that will set it right.

We have participated in many unsuccessful Special Events during our careers. No appreciable organizational change occurred and, in hindsight, it is clear the efforts were wasteful as well as painful. We know of at least three forms of the Special Event that we especially try to avoid.

The first Special Event form we discourage is the "turnaround artist." When the organization is desperately sick, it is very vulnerable to exploitation by this terrorist's promise of a quick fix. But such Leader-dependent efforts at organizational change almost never have a long-term beneficial effect on organizations. The quick results are usually gained at the expense of employees and customers. It often seems as if the turnaround Leader came into the Galley, cut all the oars on one side in half, and then told those rowers to row twice as fast. Costs are temporarily reduced, but the long-term result is a crippled Galley. After a couple of years, the organization is in worse condition than it was before turnaround began.

The second form of Special Event to avoid is "Restructuring." Undoubtedly, one characteristic of a stuck organization is the fact that its structure doesn't work. But the "big restructure" almost never results in making the organization Change-ABLE. The "Special Re-structure Event" expresses the hope that a few right people in the top positions of power will fix everything, perpetuating a dangerous dependency and passivity in the rest of the organization's human assets. Furthermore, no one structure is going to make an organization effective for even the next five years. Many structural changes will be necessary on a continuous basis. No structure will work as a flexible system of Linked Teams unless all of the other Key Management Practices are also a part of the culture. Just focusing on the structure

242 ◆ Change-ABLE Organization

disrupts the whole organization and distracts it from the work it should be doing to renew all its fundamental management practices. It is often a tragic distraction — very much like shuffling the chairs on the deck of a sinking ship.

A third form of Special Event to avoid is "The Program." In this approach, the organization attempts to fix itself by sending everyone to a five-day, in-residence "Change-ABLE Academy." A whole new department must be created to run the program, provide on-going support, and monitor each Manager's progress. (A variation of the approach is the "Pilot Project.") Setting up such parallel structures and taking people off-line for conversion doesn't work. For one thing, it is difficult to find the time for programs regarding goal setting, or Team building, or organizational culture when you feel the organization is about to lose some of its biggest customers and go into Chapter 11. It is also unlikely the organization will tolerate massive programs that operate as separate, parallel organizations. Typically, these programs run into a wall in about three years. They are not seen as essential, but rather as competitors for the organization's vital resources and a distraction from the organization's real work. The Special Program Event is akin to sending the rowers up on deck to build little ships in bottles while the real boat flounders in stormy seas. It just isn't appropriate.

Another subtle form of the "Special Event" is to give attention to only part of the Key Management Practices. Sometimes this is a result of an infatuation with the immediate effects of one of the practices — for instance, the sense of clarity that comes when Performance Plans are first aligned. "This is enough! Thanks!" says the organization, arresting its development at this point and later dropping the whole pursuit when it discovers this wasn't the magic they thought it was. At other times, one of the Key Management Practices is fashioned into a Special Program with the rationale that the organization is already doing some form of all the other practices and just needs to emphasize this one. The emphasis of one Practice, however, tears it out of its systemic context — its necessary integration with the others — and presents it as a broken tool. Getting everyone to write a Performance Plan or getting Individual Contributors into Breakthrough Systems will not make a stuck organization govern itself intelligently. Asking the rowers to consult with the Galley Leader about where the boat is going without first turning them around and giving them a forward view will achieve nothing. Any one of the practices presented in isolation as a Special Program will not be new or effective.

Three Characteristics of Successful Efforts To Make Organizations Change-ABLE

An effective effort at becoming Change-ABLE has to have all three characteristics: widespread participation, immediate applicability, and five core practices.

Management cannot "do change" to the organization. People control their own behavior. They may allow themselves to be coerced into changing their behavior. Coerced behavior, however, is usually slow and awkward, based as it is on latent resentment and fear. Involuntary behavior doesn't have the flexibility and precision representing the practices of the Change-ABLE organization. The needed quickness comes from a person who understands and is committed to the organization's purpose — someone who knows what the organization expects and appreciates anything they do toward accomplishment of that purpose. The Change-ABLE organization is made up of participants, not rule-makers and rule-followers.

An effective change effort has to be immediately applicable so that the change is reinforced with real-world success. The effort should not start with too many off-line, Special Events such as management retreats. Since the change ultimately has to happen on-line, i.e., in the midst of the organization's work, it is a good idea to start the change effort on-line.

If the effort must begin with talking, interrupt talk perpetuating the current ineffective performance and refocus it on solving the real problems. Since the change requires people to alter their own behavior, go to the site where their current behavior is causing problems, interrupt it, and suggest appropriate new behaviors. Since the change requires the use of all the organization's political and social power, get into the organization's politics and power plays right at the start.

Getting on-line to make the change effort immediately applicable is not difficult: join the organization's Regular Meetings. Weekly staff meetings, quarterly Work Reviews, annual planning sessions, and "informal" cross-functional meetings are all effective entry points. It is in these meetings that people are influencing the organization's performance. It is in these meetings that they should be struggling with the organization's Survival Agenda — the big problems on the minds of higher level Managers — as something they must solve in the next 90 days. Go to these meetings and help the attendees adopt the practices that will make the organization immediately more effective in dealing with what it already recognizes as the issues of the day.

Regular Meetings are the way an organization reinforces its current culture. They are the windows to the organization's culture, and the classrooms in which that culture is taught — over and over every week. No training-room program can ever override what is being taught in these real classrooms. When the focus and processes of these meetings are changed, the organization's most fundamental assumptions and practices are immediately changed.

Finally, commit from the beginning to all five of the Key Management Practices. In isolation, none are new or unique. Most organizations do at least one or two of them, but the results are very different when only one or two of the practices is in place. The swift and intelligent performance of the Change-ABLE organization requires all the practices to be done in unison. The practices are not new; it is doing them simultaneously that is altogether new.

One Sequence of Actions We Have Used Successfully

Our experience has taught us that there is no one way to move an organization from a stuck culture to a Change-ABLE one. There are, in fact, many ways. The organizations that were Change-ABLE before we met them had varied histories. Some came to the Key Practices through trial and error, others started out with the whole system as a requirement of their early Leaders. We have had some success changing stuck organizations to Change-ABLE ones, and we have used a variety of approaches — depending upon the organization's understanding of its immediate needs. We know there are many different paths to becoming Change-ABLE, and we offer the following sequences of actions as only one of the ways we have found to be successful.

First Step: Identify and Begin Linking the Managers' Regular Meetings

Begin by doing an analysis of your current organization's structure. (This is just an analysis — don't even think about restructuring!) The objective of this analysis is to understand how the organization *actually* channels its information and makes it decisions. We emphasize the word "actual," because the organization chart — the formal picture of the channels of authority — is rarely reliable.

The most reliable analysis of any organization's structure is accomplished by making a list of the Regular Meetings being held, identifying the attendees, and identifying the issues each meeting is actually resolving. Define a meeting as three or more people — this analysis ignores regular dialogues. Search out all of these meetings — especially look for the "informal" cross-functional meetings, and the "as needed" meetings that seem to be needed on a regular basis. Be on the alert for Task Forces (meetings that were originally intended to solve one particular problem and then dissolve) that have turned into Regular Meetings. A rough test of whether or not you have found all the Regular Meetings is that you will find there are *at least* as many Regular Meetings each month (remember that some of these meetings are being held more than once a month,) as there are employees in the organization you are analyzing. The correlation with the number of employees is not intended to imply that every employee goes to at least one meeting each month, though this may be the case.

Pay attention to whether or not the meetings that are scheduled are actually being held. (Often as many as 50 per cent of scheduled meetings are canceled.) Also, gather as much information as you can about whether or not the meetings resolve issues — actually make decisions. Most meetings only discuss issues and share information — decision-making is not intended or actually accomplished even when intended. Just for shock value, you may want to keep track of how much management time is spent in the Regular Meetings. When you compare the time spent in these meetings with the results they say they accomplish, it will probably look like a poor investment.

Try to picture this set of meetings using the system of loops we used when discussing Linked Teams in Chapter Eight. Use a large flip chart pad. Your picture will be much more complex, and you will probably have to make a set of such pictures, separating out some of the organization's major systems. One way to hasten this analysis is to have the members of higher level Teams make such a picture of the meetings they attend and believe are being attended by their subordinates. It is a good way of getting them involved in understanding how they are actually operating.

Once this listing and picturing of actual Regular Meetings has been completed, many insights into the organization's culture, strengths, and weaknesses will become apparent. The temptation to start over and "clean it up" — to restructure — will be great. Don't! Instead, go for something easier.

Start repairing two kinds of breaks in the linkage between the Regular Meetings currently being held. Look for the breaks that are due to the fact that certain important Managers don't hold or attend the meetings where their authority could make a difference. They are probably trying to exercise their authority in a one-on-one system of dialogues — obstructing the work of the meetings they don't attend. Then look for the breaks in linkage due to a lack of synchronized scheduling — meetings scheduled in such a way that the flow of information and decision-making is awkward and slow. Get the Managers who are "missing links" to start holding and attending the appropriate meetings. Get the schedule of meetings better synchronized.

Just these two corrections may be surprisingly difficult to accomplish. What will help motivate these changes is to relate them to one or two of the organization's "survival agenda" issues. Pay attention to the set of meetings that could and should be dealing with these critical issues. When the two kinds of breaks in linkage between these meetings are repaired, the corrections will be reinforced by immediate, relevant results.

The analysis will indicate many other kinds of breaks in the linkage. Many of these breaks are evidence of problems in managerial competence, and many of them are providing smoke screens and camouflage for covert power play. Be careful. Let it all come into view in its own good time by linking up some of its most important, current Regular Meetings.

Second Step: Align the Members of Regular Meetings Using Performance Plans

Start building the organization's current Regular Meetings as management Teams by getting each group to clarify its goals. (As in step one, this should be done in those meetings that are most obviously relevant to the organization's current understanding of its survival agenda.) Goal clarification can be sped up by having the Leader of the Regular Meeting draft his or her own Performance Plan. Make sure the draft models all the essential characteristics of a good Performance Plan as described in Chapter Nine. Then make this draft of the Performance Plan the main agenda for one of the Regular Meetings. Ask the members to consult with the Leader until the plan states the results they all feel they should be accomplishing as a group. (Notice that the Key Practice of Group Decision-Making is being used.)

Next, the Leader should ask all Team members to draft their own Performance Plans in the same format. They should be encouraged to test their plans, both privately with the Leader and with the members of other relevant Regular Meetings they lead or attend. The group should then set a date — usually about two weeks in the future — when another Regular Meeting will be used to align individual Plans with the Leader and all the group members. This alignment meeting will look for overlaps and disconnects among the Plans. Plans will be revised until they integrate in such a way as to identify the roles each member is supposed to fulfill to ensure the results stated in the Team's plan (i.e., the Leaders's plan).

Start this Performance Plan alignment process with the positive attitude that it can be done in a couple of weeks. Sometimes it can! And don't be discouraged when it takes two months. Big attitudinal and behavioral changes are taking place in this process when working in any of the stuck cultures. This is the right focus of attention — the right set of issues to be talking about — while you challenge the organization's Basic Assumptions. Be prepared to see the group quickly identify and solve some problems long overdue for attention.

These real world solutions are the early success that builds confidence in the new practices.

While engaging the Leader and members in the drafting and alignment of their Performance Plans, stress that the plans must be specific enough that the Regular Meetings of the Team can use them for assessing performance progress. Get them started thinking about how they would display the status of each effort in a chart or graph. Get the Team anticipating its next step — Work Reviews.

Third Step: Initiate Work Reviews

As soon as any management Team has begun the alignment of its Performance Plans, begin doing Work Reviews. Use the Performance Plans of the Leader and members as the standard against which to assess organizational performance. Don't wait for perfect Performance Plans or perfect alignment of the Plans before starting the Work Reviews. The effort to get the plans right and aligned is never going to cease — it will always be an underlying purpose of all the Regular Meetings. As soon as the group accepts one of its member's Performance Plans, schedule that member for a Work Review.

Work Reviews should begin as an agenda item in the Regular Meeting. Set some meeting time aside to review the work of one or two members. These first reviews will often take an hour each. The group will discover the metrics for measuring progress are inappropriate, or that the data displayed is inaccurate. Over a period of a few months, each member's plan and Work Review will come into focus. Eventually, these plans will be able to meet the criteria of displaying the status in four minutes or less, and getting the critical issues addressed in another 15 minutes. The Team will then be able to make a complete round of all its members' Work Reviews within a couple of weeks — as part of two Regular weekly Meetings. But this is the mark of mature Teams. It takes a while — maybe even a year.

Don't be impatient. Not a minute of this time is wasted. Every word, every little correction, every small step in the direction of a more current and valid presentation of the issues affecting the organization's performance is significant progress toward becoming Change-ABLE.

Getting Regular Meetings to focus on Work Reviews and the associated decision-making is the most difficult of the practices to get in place. It is, however, the core issue — are we going to share purposes, accountability, and resources — or not?

Fourth Step: Use Group Decision-Making Every Step of the Way

At every step, apply Group Decision-Making. The Leader of each group must insist on consultation from the Team members regarding every decision, starting with the following questions:

- Should we adopt these practices?
- Is the Leader's plan right?
- Are the members' plans right?
- Are the metrics correct?
- Are the graphics helpful?
- Is the data valid?
- Do we think the performance being reported should be approved, corrected, or supported in some other way?

While these decisions are being made, the Leader teaches the group to check for understanding — not agreement. By modeling and explanation, the Leader teaches the members the importance of inquiry — asking questions to make sure you understand and are understood by others. The Leader then models and teaches Team members not to argue until there is mutual understanding — understanding how much disagreement actually exists. Only then can disagreements be intelligently explored. Disagreement must be made not only acceptable but desirable. And finally, the Leader needs to deliberately follow up in these meetings to make sure the members are exhibiting the behaviors of commitment. Check to see that decisions are being correctly explained to the rest of the organization, and that compliance is defined through the focus and allocation of the organization's resources.

By the time these practices are in place, the organization will already have felt one or more jolts putting it into a more rapid and intelligent level of performance. Don't be fooled. The shift into high gear has not yet occurred — not until the fifth practice is in place.

Fifth Step: Begin Implementing Breakthrough Systems

Once a "critical mass" of Managers — about half of the management meetings — are doing Work Reviews, implement Breakthrough Systems. Begin by putting the idea on the agenda in meetings of first line Managers (i.e., people who manage Individual Contributors). Place it on the agenda as a recommendation for review. Get the first line Managers to consult with their Leaders about whether or not or how the implementation should take place.

Several different ways of introducing Breakthrough Systems have proven effective. Workshops for Teams of first line Managers and their direct reports (Individual Contributors) provide a quick start. In manufacturing settings, such workshops usually introduce the idea through a simulation we call "Chain Gang" — an exercise that allows these Teams to experience what working with Breakthrough Systems is like. The Teams then spend two or three hours deciding how to put Breakthrough Systems in place for their own work —usually beginning the next day.

No organization we have worked with has ever failed to shock itself with the results of getting Breakthrough Systems linked up with the other four practices. The difference this makes is a little frightening. Lots of things begin to change quickly. The organization spontaneously begins redesigning itself for streamlined performance. Customer suspicions and doubts start dissolving and partnerships emerge.

There Are Many Other Sequences and Starting Places

This is only a high level overview of one way to move an organization toward being Change-ABLE. The specific details of all the forms of resistance that emerge and all the possible ways of dealing with that resistance are not being discussed. But it would be untruthful to represent any process we know of as being easy, quick, or certain. The complexity of organizational change is staggering — individuals go through the process of significant role change in their own unique way! And not everyone makes the change. There is nothing sneaky about this process, however. Everyone is asked to reconsider the purpose of the organization, to decide whether or not to contribute to that purpose, and to continuously participate in deciding how to make their contribution. Some choose not to be a part of the new organization. We will attempt to deal with some of the most significant problems of the change process in the last chapter dedicated to "warnings."

The process we have described has all three of the characteristics we believe are required for any successful effort. It involves everyone, it has immediate on-line application, and it ties all the Key Practices together.

The sequence we described seems logical. Pull the organization's hierarchy together as a system of meetings, align Performance Plans, start using Plans for Work Reviews, take each step by using Group Decision-Making, and implement Breakthrough Systems. This apparent logic helps people grasp the concept of what it means to be Change-ABLE and to see the immediate relevance of the Key Management Practices. But we are sure other sequences will work as well. Because the practices make up an interdependent system, it is possible to start with any one of them and work to the others following a variety of paths. Always let the organization's survival agenda point to the best place to start. As long as all the practices are adopted as soon as possible, the change effort will maintain its relevance and acquire more and more of the organization's support.

The process can start at any level in the hierarchy. Of course, the ideal place to start is with the highest level executive Team. Starting there makes the biggest difference in the shortest amount of time. Successful change efforts have been known to begin at the middle or even the lowest levels of the hierarchy — they have just taken longer.

We have seen several large projects transform themselves into Change-ABLE organizations, while nested within an organization that was bureaucratic, entrepreneurial, or autocratic. In such cases, after two or three years, the Change-ABLE organizations are usually cast off — sold, or in other formal ways separated from their parent organization. We consider this result only a partial success.

Finally, we want to make it clear that we do not think organizations must evolve through certain "stages" to become Change-ABLE. It can be argued that there is a historical progression from the Raft, to the

Dory Regatta, to the Galley, but this does not imply a natural course of development requiring replication in each organization. The Raft can go directly to the Sea-Going Canoe without passing through a Galley stage. We think everyone should progress directly to the health and effectiveness of the Change-ABLE organization.

Wherever the change effort has been participative, on-line, and aimed at adoption of all five Key Management Practices, there has been a significant improvement in the organization's performance and an acceleration in its growth. The organizations we have worked with have become noticeably more successful. So we grow in our confidence as we recommend that all Managers and Individual Contributors go for it! Become Change-ABLE now.

Summary

Chapter Fourteen explored principles and methods the authors have found useful when helping organizations to become Change-ABLE. The following points were made:

1. It is important to avoid approaching organization change as a Special Event — especially these common examples:

    - The "Turnaround"
    - The "Restructure"
    - The "Program"

2. There are three characteristics of successful efforts to make organizations Change-ABLE:

    - Widespread participation;
    - Immediate application to the organization's immediate problems; and
    - Implementation of all five Key Management Practices.

3. One sequence of actions the authors have used successfully was described:

- Identify (or initiate and authorize) the organization's current Regular Meetings of Managers — start linking these groups together.
- Align the members of Regular Meetings, beginning with the upper level management Teams, using Performance Plans.
- Initiate Work Reviews in all the management Teams, using the Performance Plans of the Leader and members as the standard against which to assess organizational performance.
- Work each step of the way through Group Decision-Making. Teach these skills as the Teams decide to adopt the Key Management Practices and as you work on operational opportunities and problems.
- As soon as alignment and commitment occur among top level management Teams, move to the bottom of the hierarchy and begin working to get Breakthrough Systems in place.

4. There are many different sequences and starting places — start wherever the organization is able to acknowledge a significant problem and put all of the Key Management Practices to work solving the problem.

Building a Change-ABLE
Organization at
Etec Systems, Inc.

Overview

This chapter explores one organization's experience as it moves toward becoming Change-ABLE. The company is Etec Systems, Inc. of Hayward, California. We are not offering Etec as a model of Change-ABLE organizations — as this book goes to press, it has not yet completed implementation of all the Key Management Practices. But Etec is committed and well on its way, and is able and willing to describe its experience thus far. The purpose of this chapter is to explore the process of becoming Change-ABLE.

The following highlights are illustrated:

1. The advantages of having top level management understand and commit to the process.
2. How understanding grows with experience.
3. How commitment spreads as renewed parts of the organization begin to exert pressures for change on the others.
4. How the delivery of each practice is greater when it links up with the other practices.
5. How the process takes time — but not time "off-the-job."
6. People experience transitional stress.

For Etec Systems, becoming Change-ABLE has been valuable to customers, employees, and stockholders. It is providing a better way for people to govern themselves at work.

Case Study: How One Medium-Sized Company Is Becoming Change-ABLE

Etec Systems, Inc. of Hayward, California is a world Leader in pattern generation equipment for the semiconductor industry. Etec has described its origins as follows:

> "Etec's products include electron- and laser-beam systems that produce high-precision masks, which are used to print circuit patterns onto semiconductor wafers.

Etec Systems was founded in 1970 to provide scanning electron microscopes for scientific, medical, and industrial applications. In 1976, Etec introduced MEBES® — the first commercially available, production-worthy, electron-beam mask-writing system based on a technology licensed from AT&T Bell Laboratories.

In 1979, the company was acquired by Perkin-Elmer, becoming the Electron Beam Technology Division. Within five years, MEBES technology evolved to its third generation. The MEBES III system became the dominant tool in the world of maskmaking, setting new standards for accuracy and reliability. In 1990, Perkin-Elmer exited the semiconductor equipment industry and the company adopted its former name — Etec. The new company was established with the support of a group of U.S. corporate investors, comprised of DuPont, Northrop Grumman, IBM, Micron Technology, Perkin-Elmer, and Zitel.

In November 1991, Etec completed a merger with ATEQ® Corporation, the leading supplier of laser-beam mask-writing systems. With both laser- and electron-beam technologies, Etec provides total maskmaking solutions to serve the pattern-writing strategies of its worldwide customers."

In its first years as a new company, Etec continued as a technology pioneer and equipment producer. It achieved nearly 65 per cent share of the worldwide market but, by late 1992, was still not profitable. In an attempt to improve sales and productivity, management discounted prices, laid off about 13 per cent of the workforce, and reduced salaries for the remaining employees by 10 per cent. Despite these efforts, Etec continued to lose about a million dollars a month and was constantly in need of capital from the consortium.

In 1993, the Board of Directors brought in a new Chief Executive Officer, Steve Cooper. Steve had begun his management career at Intel, where he spent seven years developing his technology management skills. After leaving that company, he was instrumental in bringing other small high-tech companies to profitability. Steve's charge, a major challenge, was to complete the formation of the new Etec.

By early July of 1993, Steve was sounding a consistent and persistent message: "we will be profitable within the next 90 days, we will become self-sustaining, we will be the best in the market!" The company was doing about $56 million in annual revenue, but was operating like a $2 billion enterprise consistent with its former Perkin-Elmer ownership. Steve completed the layoff that should have been done much earlier, but restored the salaries of those who remained and provided stock options to all employees. He began rebuilding the sales effort, eliminating discounts, and raising the prices of Etec's unique products. Etec started earning its way.

Steve also found it necessary to remove the upper levels of management, which comprised two non-communicating, warring camps. Beneath them, he found middle Managers able to release the technical talent of Etec's engineering staff. It soon was apparent, however, that the company had every kind of fundamental problem and needed an injection of management talent from the outside.

This injection began with the employment of Trish Dohren as the new Vice President of Human Resources. In Steve's words:

> "I wanted to rebuild the organization's culture. We needed an open environment that empowered people to make decisions. I knew this would be the toughest part of the challenge. So the first person I hired, in August of 1993, was Trish Dohren. She was people oriented. Her experience in the retail business — Macy's and Brooks Brothers — exposed her to every kind of personnel problem. She had handled thousands of cases a year and was super-competent in all aspects of Human Resources.
>
> We had been friends for a long time, and we trusted each other. I knew that trust among the executives would be important given this organization's long history of internal politics. Trish was a good choice to help lead the organization's cultural change."

Trish brought a positive attitude, too, and she needed it. Etec was really a mess! This is what she discovered:

> "Everyone was doing their own thing, and no one was talking to anyone else. For instance, I found five different performance appraisal systems in operation! Some people in one part of the organization were getting paid $60,000 for doing the same work that others were being paid only $40,000 to do. We weren't doing justice to the people who worked here. We needed to implement 401(k) plans and other employee benefits, such as increasing the number of employees who participated in stock ownership.
>
> People were acting afraid. They'd felt punished for making suggestions in the past. So now the people didn't really care what was going on in the company. The morale was low — a lot of unrest — and employees just did their jobs and went home.
>
> Everybody was going in his or her own direction. There were walls everywhere, and people were throwing their stuff over the walls at each other saying, 'It's not my problem, its yours.'

Steve and Trish began building the executive Team. New leadership was brought in for Finance, Sales, and Marketing. They began confronting people with the need for change throughout the organization. Steve shocked everyone by setting a goal to become a $500 million company by the end of the decade. The executive Team formulated a mission statement and initiated a planning process that they hoped would guide and integrate performance. By 1995, everyone at Etec was beginning to take the new leadership seriously. They knew that change was necessary and possible. But it still wasn't happening fast enough to satisfy the executive Team.

For more than a year, Steve had been hearing about American Consulting and Training (ACT). In July of 1995, he invited ACT's senior consultants to help plan an executive, off-site meeting. The primary purpose of the meeting was to review the plans of the worldwide sales force and to align them with Etec's five-year strategy. The process of planning the meeting helped Steve and Trish gain confidence in ACT's ability to work with the company. During the off-site meeting, the executive Team heard the analogy of the boats, and acknowledged their intention to become a Sea-Going Canoe. They also glimpsed a systematic way for changing the company's 25-year old culture.

It was only a glimpse. As Steve says:

> "One immersion is not enough to understand
> what it's all about. The concept has to be revisited many
> times in the first months."

Or as Trish remembers it:

> "What is this thing? We're getting in a Canoe,
> we're going to go in the same direction. I loved the talk.
> But we didn't have any idea how to implement it, what
> it was going to take, how much time, what the commit-
> ment was going to be."

But the glimpse was enough to get started. ACT began working with the executive Team. Trish accompanied the ACT consultants as they helped Steve with the first draft of his Performance Plan. His plan was reviewed and revised by the executive Team in one of its regular staff meetings. Trish and the consultants then continued working with each member of the executive Team to compose the first drafts of their Performance Plans. All the plans were reviewed in an informal discussion between each executive and Steve. The Plans were then aligned among the executive members in another executive staff meeting. At the conclusion of this process, all Team members agreed they were reaching for results and priorities that, if achieved, would fulfill the Team's plan, i.e., Steve's Performance Plan.

This was not the first time the executive Team had talked about organizational strategy. But it was, perhaps, the first time they clearly recognized their interdependence for addressing the major problems still blocking their success. The ugly problems were now in the open: delayed deliveries; machines shipping to customers with major sub-systems "dead on arrival;" the necessity of reducing cycle times to meet the plans for growth, the misalignment between sales projections and orders; and the failure to recruit and train people in time to meet production and service needs. Now, each of these problems was being addressed in terms of specific results achievable within the next 12 months, and the executives were committing their departments to work as partners in problem solving.

Immediately, Trish and the consultants went to the next level of Managers, coaching them individually as they drafted their Performance Plans. They then facilitated the meetings in which these plans were aligned with their executive Leaders and peers.

It was taking a lot of Trish's time, but she intended to take the entire process internal — to make it Etec's " business system." Trish wanted to thoroughly understand the process and build the staff to support and perpetuate it. By the time she had worked with the two upper levels of the company's management, Trish was ready. She selected Keri Daniels, a member of her group hired a few months earlier, to work with ACT consultants to provide coaching for lower levels of management.

Meanwhile, the executive staff was moving to the next practice, the Work Review. As always, the issue was metrics — in what ways should progress be tracked, and how could this information be displayed effectively for the executive Team's review? Steve wanted a system for providing the executives with some certainty regarding what was getting done in any part of the organization. The key results in the executive Team's Performance Plan had to be translated into the critical smaller results accomplished every day at the base of the organization's structure. In many parts of the organization, attention had never been given to continuous monitoring of work.

Every executive staff meeting was characterized by two problems. First, there was little agreement regarding what measures were appropriate. Second, the executives seriously doubted the validity of the information being displayed.

Lower in the organization, people ran around for days prior to each executive staff meeting, trying to create a new set of charts and graphs. Each time, the information displayed was, at least in part, rejected. Confusion and frustration were rampant.

So much time was taken for questioning metrics and the validity of information, the meetings rarely identified any specific issues or resolved any significant problems. The executive staff was so involved in streamlining their Work Review procedures, they couldn't actually review the organization's performance.

During this time, many questions were raised. Were such meetings necessary? (After all, the company had gotten along without them for years.) Why insist on graphs and charts? (It would be easier just to write a report and answer questions.) Who really needed this information? (Executives shouldn't require such detailed information about what was going on.) Why is our work being criticized by Leaders from other departments? (It isn't any of their business.) Accusations of "micro-management" and "upper level management distrust" were often heard.

Not all the executives showed enthusiasm for the new business process. There seemed to be a lot of other, more important things to do. In August, 1995, Trish was still searching for a new Vice President of Operations, (a new position combining Manufacturing and Engineering) and Steve was performing that role on an interim basis. The company was getting ready to make its Initial Public Offering. Sales were increasing. Orders were backing up. More machines were being delivered with major subsystems "dead on arrival." Parts were in short supply, and this was delaying both production and field service. There were lots of reasons for not following through on Work Reviews.

As Trish reflects on this period, she says:

> "You have those who really believe in it and those who don't. There is a lot of conflict. Those of us who do believe in it do business differently than those who don't. This leads to heated discussions and some people feeling they are not part of the Team. It's painful — there are tears and people losing their tempers. And you lose some people — that's part of it. You should know that up front."

At about this same time, October of 1995, Etec found its new Vice President of Operations, Roy Earle. This is his recollection of what it was like to join Etec:

> "Most of my life was in the Galley. When I came to Etec, I was delighted to hear that I was getting into a Sea-Going Canoe. But as I got familiar with my own part of the organization and with the executive Team, I found out that we weren't really there. There was still a lot of Galley-like behavior and Dory Regattas.
>
> Few of my people could tell me a thing about what the company wanted.
>
> There were many cases where Engineering did not agree with what Marketing wanted and what was in the executive Team's plan. They were blatantly going after something else."

But Steve Cooper persisted. Little by little, it became apparent the executive staff was acting differently. Some were asking the right questions of their subordinates. Significant problems kept showing up for discussion. Some executive Team members began to understand each other's work and its subsequent interdependencies.

Six months after undertaking the work, some of the executive Team members began requiring Performance Plans and Work Reviews at the lower levels of their departments. Trish, Keri, and the consultants were busy providing the coaching necessary for people to comply with these requirements. Parts of the organization began turning around in the boat, giving up their oars for paddles. They would have to paddle for a while, though, before what they were doing began to make sense. Keri describes what it was like on her own Team:

> "We shared and aligned our Performance Plans and started preparing for the Work Review portion of our meeting. For some people this was very, very difficult. And a lot of it had to do with getting the right measurement. But it's a great question to ask: 'Is this

really what we want to measure?' And it's not until you get this far into the process that things 'click' — not until you write your Performance Plan, are living it and using it in Work Reviews. I could talk about it, but actually doing it is a whole other thing. It is very powerful."

Roy Earle speaks of a similar experience as he worked with Engineering and Manufacturing:

"Performance Plans look like MBOs with a twist. I didn't really understand the difference until I began to work with them. It's not driven by one person — there's discussion. And you can change them. But then it really comes into its own when you relate the Performance Plan with the Work Review. I tried linking MBOs to operations reviews before I got to Etec, and it was a disaster — the MBOs couldn't be changed and pretty soon they were irrelevant. But when you start letting the Work Reviews be a time to change the Team's Performance Plans, the process begins to reflect what we actually should be doing. It stays relevant."

Once a few of the management groups started "clicking," a new kind of tension began to develop. Each Team was linked to several others. Members of the effective Teams became impatient with those that weren't focused and active. They put pressure on the members and Leaders of these less effective groups to start using Performance Plans and Work Reviews. Trish describes this stage of development:

"I thought it might be pushed down, might be pushed across, but it wouldn't be pushed up. But it actually gets pushed up. When our maintenance people heard about it they did their objectives before their Manager asked them to. They were getting direction from 300 people and saw the Performance Plans as a godsend. They made their manager hurry up.

People go to cross-functional Teams on which
some of the members have Performance Plans and really
know what they are doing. They go back and ask their
Managers to get with it —to get Performance Plans
done, to get Regular Decisive Meetings. Those that aren't
having them start asking for them."

These upward pressures impact the organization's senior
executives. Steve reflected on this process:

"Not every one on the executive Team came to
the process at the same time. This creates difficulties for
the slower ones. After a while, their subordinates are
having trouble keeping up. Other parts of the organization start solving their problems and accelerate their
pace. No executive can afford to ignore what works.
Eventually they come aboard."

In the spring of 1996, Etec was beginning to notice the difference
in its performance, and so were its closest customers and shareholders.
Its stock, listed on the NASDAQ for about six months, had more than
tripled its value. Etec's people partially attributed this success to their
new business disciplines and started placing greater emphasis on their
implementation. Teamwork continued to mature. Keri noticed that her
Team finally stopped complaining about the meetings and started
focusing on the real issues:

"Our Team started asking each other to stop
talking about the little details and stick to the format we
call 'OSIR' — objectives, status, issues, and recommendations.
We finally came to understand the objective —
instead of just reporting to the manager, we are all
responsible for each other. We stopped being polite —

failing to point out in meetings things that didn't look right. People started looking at each other's charts and saying, 'You say you're on schedule but that line, it looks like you're behind. Why is that?' It was still polite, but there was more challenging of the reports in the meeting. It became more productive. And an incredible amount of camaraderie came out of this."

Trish, the Leader of this Team, describes the same development:

"Now they really do challenge each other. They do so because, like it or not, they have become interested in what other parts of my organization are doing. And they can see how it all interacts. Facilities questions Recruiting: 'Where are we going to put them all?' Or someone asks why we're spending money in Training when we could get it done for less through Corporate Communications.

There are always one or two people who take it very personally, but that's OK. They come back next week and have great graphs and get the Team's praise for having done that. Slowly they get used to all this and take it less personally."

As Etec approached the end of its first year with the Change-ABLE practices, Steve and Trish noticed how the organization was beginning to show flexibility and speed in governing itself. The system put pressure on the individuals and Teams that were not functioning well. Some people eventually left their jobs or were asked to leave. The organization began to spontaneously redesign itself to meet its performance requirements.

New Teams and Task Forces started to emerge. Some became very effective; others were soon stopped for a variety of reasons. For instance, new Teams sometimes emerged because a Manager became alarmed at the decision-making process of subordinates or other departments. The Manager usually found out about the decisions through a Work Review, and felt "left out" of the process. He or she then formed a cross-functional Team or Task Force to better control or monitor subordinate activities. This usually turned out to be unnecessary and redundant, as the worried Manager eventually discovered. Sometimes the Team's members even took the initiative to evaluate themselves out of existence.

As Etec entered the fall of 1996, it looked back on a remarkable year of progress. It had increased its number of employees worldwide by 46 per cent. Its revenues were up by 76 per cent, with healthy profit margins. It had a record backlog of orders. It was investing in acquisitions that gave it new technological and strategic advantages. On the NASDAQ, Etec had bucked the general downturn in high-tech stocks and was holding a value better than three times its initial offering.

But leadership at Etec still isn't satisfied. As the saying goes, "Success breeds ambition." Steve makes this quite clear:

> "This work ensures the organization continues to renew itself. But I think you can only see the true contribution after about 36 months. We're doing things people thought were absolutely impossible — like reducing manufacturing cycle-time from over 52 weeks to less than 26 weeks in less than nine months. Now, they believe they can get it down to less than that. And we've shortened installation times. Performance to schedules is much better. Visibility in all key areas of manufacturing is greatly enhanced. People understand where we are and what the issues are. The idea of continuous improvement is coming alive. We're getting to second-order effects that will make us a really strong organization. We need to take the next steps and keep going."

Roy sees the challenge:

> "We have alignment. We are achieving things we weren't achieving before, just through alignment. We're making our shipments. Cycle times are coming down. We're hitting our timed deliveries. We've taken

our output in nine months and almost quadrupled it. In the last year, we've learned a system that keeps us focused and aligned for achieving our goals. It's so much easier. I don't think we could have done it any other way.

But we're just getting started on this new system. We're only doing Performance Plans and Work Reviews — about two of the five things we should be doing. We still have a lot to learn about Linked Teams and Group Decision-Making. And we haven't really started getting serious about Breakthrough Systems. That's why we're so enthusiastic and passionate about taking it further. There must be so much more we can get when they all come together."

Trish sees the work as a foundation:

"Now we're on our second round of Performance Plans. It's easier to write them this time. People are spending a lot more time on the metrics, to get those right and to make them clear. And they are going to their partners on their own.

I think people are really committed to this process. Our people really want to be successful and they want the company to be successful. They see this as a way to make it a success. And I'll tell you, one thing these Teams do is let everybody see the results, and that gives them a great feeling of satisfaction.

I believe the whole process has contributed to people taking ownership for the company, being responsible, and feeling like what they do is very important. It makes a difference that contributes to the overall goals of the company."

Keri looks at it from a slightly different perspective:

"People are using the tools that have been given to them, which is fabulous. So many of these things are fly-by-night; they come in and go out. And that's what people expected. Well, this one is here to stay, and I think people like that — it's becoming a routine."

Etec is building the cultural foundations of a Sea-Going Canoe. It is being led by people who knew a dramatic change was necessary and had begun the change process before ACT became part of the Team. During the year with ACT, Etec has discovered a way to systematize its change efforts. By persisting in its practice of Performance Plans and Work Reviews, it has started renewing the organization's performance feedback and governance system.

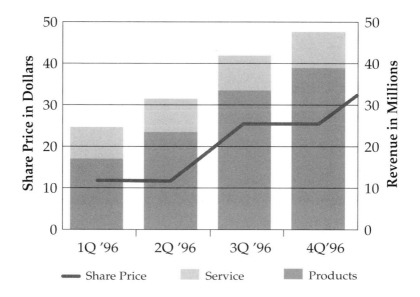

At all times, the new disciplines are applied to Etec's operational problems. The organization's staff meetings are the classrooms in which Etec's Managers learn the new methods. These same meetings, with their Work Review procedures, are the ceremonies by which the organization reinforces its new culture.

As Etec has picked up each new practice, all of the other practices are reinterpreted. Performance Plans become something else when they are the center of Work Reviews. The plans and Work Reviews focus meetings on work and decision-making. New structures emerge and are quickly put to the test: do they add value or not? Will they make it easier for the organization to focus its resources or will they just cause delay and confusion? As Etec begins putting its Individual Contributors into Breakthrough Systems, it will experience a whole new range of possibilities and receive a new injection of productive energy. The interdependency of the practices reinforces them, making each of them, in turn, a greater force for cultural change.

From the beginning, the focus has been to get Etec's problems solved and its work done. There has never been a "program" of cultural change — each new behavior is learned because it seems appropriate for what has to be accomplished. In the process of practicing these new disciplines, Etec's most fundamental assumptions and values are challenged. The old assumptions change because they don't produce the strategies and habits necessary for organizational survival. Etec is accepting a new culture — a new set of assumptions and values — because it has discovered a pattern of management behavior that effectively solves its problems and accomplishes its work.

Summary

We have described Etec System's first steps toward becoming Change-ABLE. Their story illustrates:

1. There is an advantage in having top level management understand and commit to the process.
2. Understanding is not perfect at first; it grows with experience.
3. Commitment is not universal at the start; it, too, spreads as the renewed parts of the organization begin to exert new pressures for change on the others.
4. Each new practice delivers greater rewards as it links up with the other practices.
5. The process takes time — but not time "off-the-job."
6. The process is not easy — people experience transitional stress.

For Etec Systems, the process of becoming Change-ABLE is already valuable to customers, employees, and stockholders. It is a better way for people to govern themselves at work.

16

Warnings: What Happens
in the Early Stages

Overview

This chapter offers a list of things people should anticipate as they begin the process of making an organization Change-ABLE. We call them "warnings" because some of the things that happen along the way are stressful and are sometimes mistaken as signs of failure when in fact they are the signs of organizational healing. We separate these "warnings" into three categories:

1. Warnings regarding changes to expect in relationship to the organization's external, social, and economic environments;
2. Warnings regarding changes to expect in relationship to internal dynamics of the organization; and
3. Warnings regarding the change process in general.

Changes To Expect in Relationship to the External, Social, and Economic Environments

As your organization becomes Change-ABLE, several things will happen affecting its relationship to the external, economic, and social environments. They are not negative consequences, but they almost always feel that way in the early stages of development.

The Definition of Your Business Will Shift

As your Individual Contributors gain confidence in their perception of what their own performance is accomplishing, they will bring information to the rest of the management structure that was previously unavailable or ignored. Your organization's eyes, ears, and sense of touch will be reactivated, and your awareness of what is happening to your business and your customers will expand.

The first new perceptions usually focus on threats—unhappy and failing customers, delinquent suppliers, and tough competition. This is akin to being awakened by an alarm. For a while, there is disorientation and sometimes fear or anger. Then comes a deep sense of fatigue and a desire to go back to sleep. In this case, however, you won't be able to turn off the alarm. You will validate the threats and begin rethinking your strategy while making immediate adjustments to stand out of harm's way.

The early stages of rethinking the strategy will continue to be painful. A frank appraisal of your company's competencies activates the least desirable aspects of your current culture—hopeless passivity, desertion by key individuals, and interdepartmental finger pointing as scapegoats get thrown overboard. Basic Assumptions regarding the survival agenda that got your organization into its current troubles now generate another set of self-destructive solutions. Your leadership must keep a firm grasp on the practices of the Change-ABLE organization to keep the old assumptions from channeling energy into the familiar paths of failure. The struggle to stay focused becomes especially intense in the sixth month of the effort and remains a critical challenge for the following year.

All along the way, however, small breakthroughs in understanding and performance will take place. During the second year, these changes become a critical mass and a force field within the organization. More and more people turn around in the boat and begin paddling. What was previously seen as threatening now gets taken so seriously that the organization's responses start converting problems into opportunities. Angry customers become a source of insight into the real demands of the marketplace, and different facets of your organization turn their energies toward these demands instead of each other. Delinquent suppliers become the evidence of disjointed planning and broken processes that now must be improved. You swallow your pride and its defensiveness and let your tough competitors become models and tutors. Toward the end of the second year, your business will show signs of new life—even the bottom line metrics of volume and profitability will show the change.

A new, more unified strategy emerges from all this. It may seem to other organizations as though you have had a "vision," but you will know it is the eclectic combination of many small and continuing corrections. These corrections are possible because of the renewal of your organization's ability to gather reliable information, make intelligent decisions, and distribute those decisions for rapid implementation. Your organization's performance feedback systems and methods of governance are improving. From this, the organization is gaining a new self-understanding of both its weaknesses and its strengths. This self-understanding gives birth to your new strategy, which is unique yet fundamentally sound.

You Will Frighten Your Current Competition

The new environment is not one of peace and harmony. It is very dynamic—huge forces are in conflict as the information economy emerges everywhere on the globe. When your organization begins to exhibit the flexibility, speed, and intelligence of the Sea-Going Canoe, it will attract attention.

Your competitors will be the first to notice your Change-ABLEness. They are likely to become alarmed and jealous. Everything you've ever experienced as an assault or as a defensive tactic on the part of your competitors will escalate in intensity.

You must now be on the alert for new competitors. Become sensitive to your current customers and suppliers. They often want to lead the dance as per their previous roles—to determine a slower pace of performance. They may be threatened by your growing vigor and will seek ways to slow you down or even destroy you.

You will also discover many new allies. Some of them will be other Sea-Going Canoes eagerly seeking effective partnerships. Some of the new allies, however, will be the big old Galleys and Rafts now desperate for help and focusing on you as their solution. Be careful! These desperate cultures may grab you like a drowning victim and take you with them.

Changes To Expect in Relationship to Internal Dynamics of Your Organization

As you become Change-ABLE, many threatening and depressing things will come to light within your organization. It is humiliating to discover how insensitive, timid, or wasteful you have been. This initial humiliation will diminish in its intensity, but it never goes away completely. It becomes a permanent practice of self-evaluation.

You Will Be Shocked by Strategy Disconnects

As the executive Team becomes immersed in the disciplines of the Change-ABLE organization and grows convinced of the appropriateness of the culture's more balanced assumptions, values, and norms, they will be shocked and embarrassed to discover their previous isolation from the rest of the organization. This usually becomes obvious in their strategic discussions.

At first, there is the confrontation of the fact that members of the executive Team are promoting products and services unrelated to those of any other member. These distinctions are the basic arguments for the organization's departmentalization, so many of the executives will be slow to question their validity. Eventually, however, it will become clear there is no real strategy by which all the resources of the organization can be integrated and focused. Instead, there are only products and services sharing a technological affiliation. Most of these products will be produced in such small volume or at such low margins of return, they offset all the potential profitability of higher margin products and services. It may also be discovered that departments are very nearly (if not exactly) duplicating the products and services of other internal groups.

This old problem will be revisited as strategic thinking improves, and the line of products and services is narrowed and focused. It is a traumatic time—with each product, certain customers, suppliers, and competencies lost. Old and powerful domains of political control within the organization are broken up. But this "letting go" is necessary as the executive Team drops its need to dominate whole technologies and starts to seek a truly nourishing position in the market.

You Will Discover You Are Disorganized

As strategic focus begins to emerge, the current processes and structures of the organization become embarrassing burdens. They never made sense in the first place; they existed simply because some Manager was able to provide political protection for them.

The organization will focus on its strategic tasks and let processes and structures evolve as task performance improves. The organization will probably invest heavily in new information technology, reduce the number of Managers, and literally subject those who remain to their appropriate role of resourcing Individual Contributors.

This reorganization does not happen in the familiar get-it-right-once-and-for-all "restructuring" of the business. It is much more likely to emerge as a series of small changes—most of them at levels of authority below middle management. Some of the most common "small changes" include:

- The initiation of Task Forces to reduce cycle-times;
- The merging of functions as some Managers retire or drop out;
- The authorization of new Linked Teams; and
- The formalization of groups already meeting and accomplishing important coordination.

These are some of the ways organizations display and further develop competency for constant organizational redesign.

Some of Your Organization's Members Will not Like the New Dance

No Raft, Dory Regatta or Galley will become Change-ABLE without experiencing a major change in relationship to its environment. The marketplace — or zone of service — will stop looking like a threatening swamp or a world to conquer. Instead, the organization will build its strategy on the assumption that the environment is constantly changing and that it is possible to harmonize with that change, becoming a part of its creative potential. It will not settle for a role of abject dependence upon environmental forces; nor will it seek to dominate everything around it. Instead, interdependencies will be acknowledged, and roles will be learned—sometimes supporting others, sometimes taking the lead and demanding support. The organization will notice that its energy and resources are not completely self-contained and controlled, and it will enjoy the multiplier on its power that comes from the synergy of intelligent cooperation. It will get up on its toes for a dance with all the forces in its environment.

The warning is this: those accustomed to the Raft culture will consider this new relationship a terrible demand for accountability. They will feel unjustly required to produce results—to take initiative, behave proactively, and take the rewards — or punishment — for doing so. They will see the new relationship as unreasonably risky—a mandate to go where no survivor has ever gone before.

For the Dory Regatta and the Galley, this new role of interdependency will appear to be a lack of control. All the definitions of competence will be challenged. Their sense of dignity and self-confidence will be undermined. They will see it as an invitation to dance, believing, all the while, that dancing is for wimps.

Morale Will Dip

In the initial stages of the transition to being Change-ABLE, morale goes through a valley of shadows. Most of the behaviors of the Canoe can be learned quickly, as they are never entirely new to Managers or Individual Contributors. But the challenge presented to the old culture's Basic Assumptions, values, and norms is experienced as nameless confusion and irritation. For many, the challenge to their fundamental attitudes feels disrespectful and immoral. They are emotionally upset, but can't quite figure out why. Exhaustion and restlessness are common along with crankiness and insolence. Issues are invented, little issues exaggerated with emotional intensity, and real issues seem overwhelming and may cause explosive acts of punishment, depression, or resignation.

Some of this trauma can be diminished, but it cannot be avoided. It is important to anticipate the crisis in morale and especially to prepare and support upper level management as they go through this valley first. Do not to abandon or abuse positions of formal authority as upper level management personally wrestles with this emotional disorientation. Their leadership, more than ever, must encompass patience, perseverance, and sympathetic listening.

Upper level Managers should not be expected to ignore their emotions. Most executives are skilled in emotional self-control. This may not be equivalent to emotional sophistication and resilience. These Managers may need encouragement to pay attention to their emotions. (We strongly discourage making management Teams or any other groups within the organization the scene for such therapy — this is best done in privacy with family, friends, and counselors outside the organization.)

Remaining Change-ABLE does not mean everyone will work in a constant state of emotional confusion. The crisis passes. The renewed channels of communication, the rising quality of decision-making, and the confidence that comes from self-management in Breakthrough Systems make the issue resolution easier. Problems previously festering in the dark of organizational denial and ignorance are no longer so fearsome.

Don't Take Your Eye Off Productivity

Many Managers, Individual Contributors and Human Resource specialists in the organization will see the emotional intensity of this transition as an unavoidable cause of low productivity. This is not, however, a necessary or constructive sacrifice.

High morale and high productivity are almost coincidental in all research regarding this process. What is constantly clear from our consulting experience is that the causal relationship between the two starts with being productive and flows to experiencing high morale. To pass through the morale crisis accompanying the Change-ABLE transition, it is important to emphasize the measurement of organizational performance and the display of those results.

Individual Contributors should be moved rapidly into Breakthrough Systems to perform this task for themselves. (Remember the data generated in this way must remain informal and private.) Increasing the focus on productivity is the way to focus emotional energy on what can be done instead of helplessly feeling bad and wringing one's hands.

It is a mistake to begin moving toward being Change-ABLE by accepting excuses for defocusing the organization's purpose. In the Change-ABLE organization, the primary passion is for faster delivery of better products and services.

Change Will Become More Radical

As your organization becomes skilled in the use of the five practices and comfortable with the underlying assumptions, values, and norms, the nature of its changes will become more radical. In the early stages, the organization is only willing and able to make small adjustments. The leadership should not be discouraged by this nor should it push for more.

But as the new culture matures, "adjustments" become more significant. In particular, the capacity to engage in what Michael Hammer and James Champy call "Reengineering" becomes possible. Fundamental processes of the business will be redesigned to take advantage of information technology. These processes will underlie many existing departments and lead to large scale structural change, new metrics systems and new attitudes toward work and competency. Such radical change often kills Raft and Galley cultures—the medicine is more than the patient can stand.

Warnings Regarding the Change Process in General

You Will Need Time for Learning

Few individuals can make a cultural transition in less than six months. As a community, this process usually takes two to three years at a minimum—and that is considered fast!

You cannot accelerate learning by going off-line to training events and workshops. The fastest learning anyone ever does in the organization is on-the-job. This is especially true for Managers.

Use management's Regular Meetings as "classrooms" for learning to be Change-ABLE. Don't hold seminars in these meetings; do your work differently. Get your Performance Plans aligned, and do your Work Reviews in these meetings. The time currently spent by Managers in these meetings is enormous, and most of what they teach each other is, at least, a waste of time and often harmful. This time must be reallocated.

Coach Individual Contributors with informal feedback systems and weekly stand-up meetings designed as "classrooms" where they can learn their role in management. Stay focused on the immediate work, and start listening to complaints and suggestions.

You Will Need Outside Assistance

Remember, everyone in your current organization is a master and advocate of your current culture—everyone! Even those who are unhappy and talking about change do so according to the assumptions, norms, and values of the current culture. This work is not magic, but it is subtle and insidious. It is a good idea to work with someone thoroughly familiar with and conscious of the culture of Change-ABLE organizations. Don't hesitate to invest in this—it could be the last process consulting your organization will ever need.

Even the Way You Decide To Begin Matters

As we said in Chapter Fourteen, it is possible to begin the renewal process anywhere in the organization's hierarchy. It is not absolutely necessary to begin at the top with the executive Team. But when any Manager decides to start making his or her part of the organization Change-ABLE, it is important to put the model before one's subordinates and begin the process with a Team decision. A consensus or consultative process should be used. The concept of disagree *and* commit should be understood. The decision to begin is the first on-line lesson about being Change-ABLE. The Manager must begin with his or her own management Team.

Be sure your top management Team commits to embracing all five Key Management Practices. Each practice supports and depends upon all the others. If one is missing, the Change-ABLE culture won't emerge. Think in terms of initiating all five practices — the entire system — at once. (Remember that Etec, the subject of our case study chapter, is still completing this process.)

Expect to make the practices a way of doing business — permanently. Decide to make the first three years only the beginning.

Remember that becoming Change-ABLE is not a program. Becoming Change-ABLE means letting the practices take over and displace your current procedures of management. It is not something added to the plate; it is a new plate.

This decision to become Change-ABLE is a very personal one. It is a commitment involving the whole body right from the beginning—emotions, mind, and behavior. If people fail to take this decision personally, they do not yet understand the decision and haven't actually made their choice.

Don't Try To Replicate the Achievements of a Sea-Going Canoe with a Raft, Dory Regatta, or Galley

Finally, let us remind you that you cannot replicate the swift, intelligent, assertiveness of the Change-ABLE organization without being Change-ABLE. A contest is now occurring among the Rafts, Dory Regattas, Galleys, and Sea-Going Canoes. Battles are occasionally won by the others, but the war will be won by the Sea-Going Canoes.

Summary

Chapter Sixteen, the last chapter, has listed some warnings that may help anticipate the unavoidable stresses accompanying those on the way to making their organizations Change-ABLE. The warnings were organized into three categories as follows:

1. Warnings about changes to expect in relationship to the organization's external, social, and economic environment:

    *   The definition of your business will shift.
    *   You will frighten your current competition.

282 ♦ Change-ABLE Organization

2. Warnings about changes to expect in relationship to internal dynamics of the organization:

    • You will be shocked by strategy disconnects.
    • You will discover you are disorganized.
    • Some of your organization's members will not like the new dance.
    • Morale will dip.

3. Warnings about the change process in general.

    • You will need time for learning.
    • You will need outside assistance.
    • The way you decide to begin matters.
    • You can't replicate the achievements of a Sea-Going Canoe with a Raft, Dory Regatta, or Galley.

Endnotes

♦ ♦ ♦ ♦

Chapter One

Hampden-Turner, Charles. *Creating Corporate Culture: From Discord to Harmony.* The Economist Books, International Management Series. Menlo Park, Calif.: Addison-Wesley Publishing Company, Inc., 1990.

Miller, James Grier. *Living Systems.* New York: McGraw-Hill, 1978.

Schein, E.H. *Organizational Culture and Leadership: A Dynamic View.* San Francisco: Jossey-Bass, 1986.

Trompenaars, Alfons. *Riding the Waves of Culture: Understanding Cultural Diversity in Business.* (Revised edition in press, 1997) New York: Irwin Professional Publishers, 1993.

Chapter Two

Newsweek, February 27, 1995, pg. 37.

Chapter Three

Likert, Rensis. *The Human Organization: Its Management and Value.* New York: McGraw-Hill, 1967.

Chapter Five

Kanter, Donald L., and P. H. Mirvis. *The Cynical Americans: Living and Working in an Age of Discontent and Disillusion.* San Francisco: Jossey-Bass, Inc., 1989.

Chapter Eleven

Daniels, William R. *Group Power: A Manager's Guide To Conducting Task Forces.* San Diego: University Associates, 1986.

Daniels, William R. *Orchestrating Powerful Regular Meetings: a Manager's Complete Guide.* San Diego: Pfeiffer & Company, 1993.

Chapter Twelve

Allen, Thomas J. *Managing the Flow of Technology: Technology Transfer and the Dissemination of Technological Information within the R&D Organization.* Cambridge, MA: MIT Press, 1977.

Daniels, William R. *Breakthrough Performance: Managing for Speed and Flexibility.* Mill Valley: ACT Publishing, 1995.

Horsfal, A. B., and C. M. Arensber. "Team Work and Productivity in a Shoe Factory," *Human Organization.* (August, 1949).

Juran, J.M. *Juran On Planning for Quality.* New York: Free Press, Macmillan Inc., 1988.

_____*Managerial Breakthrough, The Classic Book On Improving Management Performance, Newly Revised.* New York: McGraw-Hill, 1995.

Kopelman, Richard E. "Improving Productivity through Objective Feedback: A Review of the Evidence," *National Productivity Review*, Winter 1982-83

Kraut, Robert, Carmen Egido, and Jolene Galegher, University of Arizona. "Patterns of Contact & Communication in Scientific Research Collaboration," *Computer Supported Work, Conference Proceedings.* New York: Association for Computing Machinery, 1988.

Miller, F. B., "Situational Interactions, a Worthwhile Concept," *Human Organization* (1958)

Chapter Thirteen

Kotter, John P. *The Leadership Factor.* New York: The Free Press, 1988.

Trompenaars, Alfons. *Riding the Waves of Culture: Understanding Cultural Diversity in Business.* (Revised edition in press, 1997) New York: Irwin Professional Publishers, 1993.

Chapter Fourteen

Beer, Michael, Russell A. Eisenstat, and Bert Spector. *The Critical Path to Corporate Renewal.* Boston: Harvard Business School Press, 1990.

Mohrman, Susan Albers, and Allan M. Mohrman, Jr. "Organizational Change and Learning," Chapter Four in Galbraith, Jay R. and Deward E. Lawler III, and Associates *Organizing for the Future: The New Logic for Managing Complex Organizations.* San Francisco: Jossey-Bass Publishers, 1993.

Chapter Fifteen

Etec Systems, Inc. *Company Backgrounder*, August 1996.

Chapter Sixteen

Hammer, Michael and James Champy, *Reengineering the Corporation: a Manifesto for Business Revolution.* New York: Harper Business, 1993.

Index

◆ ◆ ◆ ◆

C

G

I

J

K

Related Publications

Other ACT Books:

Breakthrough Performance: Managing for Speed and Flexibility   **$24.95**
How to create an atmosphere of self-management with employees
who are responsive, responsible, and eagerly working at maximum
productivity. (ACT Publishing: 1995.) ISBN: 1-882939-00-X

Group Power I: A Manager's Guide To Using Task-Force Meetings   **$24.95**
Shares the important role Task Forces play in problem solving, problem
analysis, and planning. Step-by-step procedures offered as well as
activities designed to practice using the procedures.
(Pfeifer & Company, An Imprint of Jossey-Bass Publishers,
Inc.: 1986.) ISBN: 0-88390-032-7

Group Power II: A Manager's Guide to Conducting Regular Meetings   **$24.95**
New findings about the "take action" function of Regular Meetings.
Step-by-step procedures offered as well as activities designed to
practice using them. (Pfeiffer & Company, An Imprint of
Jossey-Bass Publishers, Inc.: 1990.) ISBN: 0-88390-236-2

For information regarding the above publications, please
contact ACT Publishing:

655 Redwood Highway, Suite 395, Mill Valley, CA 94941

(800) 995-6651   (415) 388-6651   FAX: (415) 388-6672
E-mail: Lila@ACTcanoe.com